Marxist Models
of Literary Realism

Marxist Models
of Literary Realism

by George Bisztray

Columbia University Press / New York / 1978

The Andrew W. Mellon Foundation,
through a special grant, has
assisted the Press in
publishing this volume

Library of Congress Cataloging in Publication Data

Bisztray, George, 1938–
    Marxist models of literary realism.

    A revision of the author's thesis, University of
Minnesota, 1972.
    Bibliography: p.
    Includes index.
    1. Socialist realism in literature.   2. Realism in
literature.   3. Communism and literature.   I. Title.
PN56.S66B5   809'.91'2   77-23833
ISBN 0-231-04310-4

Columbia University Press
New York   Guildford, Surrey

RR 12-7-85

Acknowledgments

The basis of this book is my Ph.D. dissertation, defended in 1972 at the University of Minnesota. I owe gratitude to professor Peter Firchow, my advisor, for his supervision of my research and his aid in shaping the result.

The material was updated and revised since then. Ms. Carol Kasper and Ms. Linda Myers from The University of Chicago are to be credited for smoothing my style and helping me find the most appropriate English terms and idioms for esoteric, highly philosophical German and Russian ones. Invaluable further comments and true editorial expertise were later given to the manuscript by Mr. Leslie Bialler, Columbia University Press.

At the time the manuscript was given its final form, I was on a visiting appointment at The University of Alberta, Canada. I have much to thank to my supervisors and colleagues at the departments of Germanic Languages and Comparative Literature for genuine human and professional relationships which facilitated the complex process of revising a manuscript for publication.

The publication of the book was subsidized by a grant from the Mellon Foundation. I am most grateful for this generous support.

Emotionally, I have received the greatest encouragement and understanding from two very young ladies, Margit, 10, and Birgitta, 7. Although they still prefer pirate stories and fairy tales to literary theory, I hope that, when they grow up, they too will understand what two great children mean for a person involved in any kind of creative process.

Contents

Introduction

In his essay "Karl Marx und die Literatur" Hans Mayer specifically discusses Marxist literary theory and at the same time dismisses the relevance of the concept of realism as presented in Marxist aesthetics. He writes:

> A consequence of abandoning the original questions of Marxism is the more and more sterile discussion about the problems of literary realism. . . . Literature as a reflection of reality, realism as a criterion of literary evaluation—with these ambitions, Marxist literary scholarship seems to be condemned to fruitlessness. Progress and decadence, critical and socialist realism, the search for a solution—all these produced a mechanistic jigsaw-puzzle, and those meddling with the puzzle were proud of being supremely scientific. With the subject 'Karl Marx and literature,' it had hardly anything to do.[1]

Mayer also quotes, approvingly, his Czech colleague Karel Košik, who thinks it would be desirable to define the concept of "reality" more satisfactorily before further debates on literary and artistic "realism" are carried on and believes that such definition would give a truly Copernican turn to a stagnating and arid question.

Mayer and Košik are by no means exceptions in their sceptical attitude toward the concept of realism, especially as defined by Marxist literary critics. Ten years earlier, the Polish Catholic writer Stefan Kisielewski had already objected to the word "realism" (but not "socialist") in the phrase "socialist realism."[2] And if one digs deep into the semantics of Garaudy's concept of modern literature as a treasury of "shoreless realism," one finds that, in a sense, there is also a challenge to this concept: if realism has no bounds, one ought to regard it as a much too general and vague literary cliché.

The importance of these statements is not so much that they question the Marxist preoccupation with the concept of realism, but that they come primarily from admittedly Marxist theoreticians and reflect the scepticism of communist or communist-sympathizing intellectuals toward an issue they considered to be overworked. Furthermore, these doubters were sooner or later officially branded as revisionists: Mayer was put on the party's list of the "revisionists of the sixties" in 1963, Košik in 1968, Garaudy in 1970.

Ironically, while the cry for a radical revaluation of the term "realism" is getting ever louder in the socialist countries, in Western Europe a simultaneous interest has been arising in basically conventional Marxist interpretations of the concept. Lucien Goldmann joined the celebrities of structuralism with his theory of the "homology" of society and art in 1964; and Georg Lukács became world famous shortly before his death because Western European literary scholarship finally discovered the concept of realism he had developed some thirty-five years earlier. Generally speaking, the worldwide interest in Marxist literary theory is ultimately an interest in the concept of realism. Noteworthy contributions to the question have come not only from the great cultural centers of the West but also from Third World countries like Brazil and Mexico.

Scepticism toward the realism-oriented theory of literature in the East, along with the frequently orthodox cultivation of oftentimes old-fashioned Marxist views of art in the West—what are the sources of this paradoxical situation? Although they are perhaps not identical in the two parts of the world, more often than not, these sources were originally the results of interrelated historical, political, and philosophical developments which, in themselves, sometimes may seem to be fairly remote from the problems of literary realism.

By the later sixties, the younger intellectuals of the Soviet Union were separated by the greater part of a generation from World War II; by half a century from the October Revolution and the civil war; and by some seventy years from the social evils of Czarist Russia. At the same time, these intellectuals were still told to read, as supreme examples of *contemporary* realism (and, if they were writers, to follow), the narrative and characterization of Maxim Gorky's sixty-year-old novel *Mother*, Sholokhov's civil war tetralogy (1928–40), and Bek's, Kazakevich's, or Alexandr Fadeyer's World War II "pep-novels." A similar anachronistic situation was developing in the socialist countries: The epic sweep of the old tabloid literature was fading away, together with the bitter Aristotelian joy of recognition it had created in the previous generation which had witnessed the apocalyptic events of two world wars, as well as the revolutions of 1917 and the subsequent civil wars. Everywhere in the socialist countries, the need to look for new identifications and human experiences in art became unavoidable. There is good reason to believe that similar developments will soon take place in China; Mao has died, and the young generation is becoming increasingly removed by the passing time from the pathos of the civil wars.

The East had also to reckon with the necessity of intensified technological development and its unavoidable complexity. One of the reasons why Roger Garaudy was branded a revisionist was that he pointed out the social role of a powerful new group, the scientific-technological intelligentsia. Yet this group, given priority but also manipulated in the socialist countries as much as in the Western democracies, made it impossible, by virtue of its prestige, to shun the integration of the achievements and methods of the natural and applied sciences, even in such seemingly different fields of intellectual activity as literary terminology, theory, and analysis.

Historical changes are almost always inseparable from definitive political turnovers. De-Stalinization, interference with a new national policy in Hungary and Czechoslovakia, and armed conflicts between the Soviet Union and China are all matters of history now; one or two decades ago they were matters of politics. More recent events are still in some sense "political"—still in the process of fomentation, pregnant with unpredictable implications. One such event is the death of Mao Tse-tung; another is the informal establishment of a united Atlantic-Mediterranean party policy at the 1976 Berlin conference of the communist parties. This policy constitutes an open challenge from the West to the traditional Soviet party theses, as did the earlier Chinese ideological secession from the East.

Philosophically, the 1960s in the socialist countries could be characterized as an era in which relativism began penetrating the consciousness of convinced but intelligent Marxists. The pre-Copernican certainty of Stalinism was over, and man had to face those challenges of modern existence which had long been shoved under the rug. Marxists finally admitted that such areas as computers, statistical evidence, and entire fields of science (notably sociology and information theory) were acceptable channels or sources for gaining new knowledge. Georg Lukács himself illustrates this process: his writings from the sixties show a rapid opening up to the problems of his times. Ironically, Lukács died before he could reevaluate more radically and thoroughly the rigid theoretical system he had developed in his middle years. But, except for his earliest critical period, never was Lukács so much in touch with the cultural arteries of his time as during his last decade.

A process analogous to the one which took place in the people's democracies after Stalin's death also started in the

Western democratic world during the sixties. The Vietnam war—the major blunder of a country which, since World War II, had appeared to be an inexhaustible moral and economic resource of the free Occident—gradually began to weigh on the conscience of many honestly thinking men of letters. The panicky and often brutal reaction from the authorities of supposedly impeccably democratic countries even to quite peaceful, organized expressions of civil dissent had strong emotional significance for the new doubters. In addition to the much debated but short-lived "countercultural" movements, a serious—albeit not infrequently orthodox—preoccupation with Marxist ideology started to develop, slowly but steadily, from the turmoil.

Parallel with this sociocultural fomentation, the political structure of the Western world also went through certain changes. Through a series of negotiations and treaties, the West established at least an illusion of military security, and made economic and cultural agreements with the Soviet Union, China, and the other socialist states. The Soviet Union itself, challenged and threatened by China's unexpectedly aggressive policy during the sixties, accepted the necessity of closer cooperation with the West in political, scientific, and economic matters. Even before the treaties were concluded, the mass media reflected the changes of interest. Media research has demonstrated how the villains of American films and television programs during the 1960s were, in increasing number, mostly Chinese, North Koreans, Albanians, or East Germans rather than Russians.

The academic world reacted to this turn of the wheel in its usual manner—that is, slowly. Even so, in the later sixties books on Marxist views of literature and culture started appearing; by about 1970 courses about these kind of subjects were put on the curricula of several European universities; and during the present decade the same fascination reached the North American continent. Marxism became tame, scholarized, acceptable, or in certain scholarly circles highly fashionable.

The late sixties, a time in which the protective Chinese Wall of the Western spirit suddenly became simultaneously out of place and vulnerable, gave the final blow to that kind of hermeticism which the postwar idea of a supreme Atlantic Culture had solidified before. In literary criticism, cultural and political hermeticism had its parallel in the various text-centered, isolative trends (*explication de texte, Werkinterpretation,* New Criticism). By the mid-sixties, the time of aesthetic hermeneutics was over; the "intrinsic" could no longer be the only value of art—life came to the doorsteps of campus halls.

From all these "happenings," East and West concluded that they had not quite evaluated "reality" correctly, and especially not in a way which kept pace with the rapid changes. And what else could have been chosen as the kernel of the new theoretical debates if not realism, a term which claims to express the relation of man to his world and of literature to life? The registrable results seem to point toward a synthesis of extreme standpoints. In the East, the debates mellowed the old orthodox aesthetic theses; in the West, they did away with the artificial isolation of literature from its vast sociohistorical and material context; in both hemispheres, they led to significant literary and philosophical recognitions.

Although the intention of this survey is to clarify the literary background against which the new interest in realism has developed, my aim is not at all to put an exalted emphasis on recent developments. Instead, I am convinced of the necessity of objectively retracing the history and reexamining the definitions of the concept of realism in the entire Marxist critical tradition. It is my contention that, in the heat of various debates, it is precisely the demand for solid and systematic knowledge, historical insight, and the sophistication needed to make fair evaluations that has been neglected. Although I share the opinion that, by necessity, one main criterion of any kind of scholarship is evaluation, it seems to me that in recent times the zeal for evaluation at the expense of information has taken on a disproportionate dimension in literary theory and criticism, especially in the Anglo-American world. The task of systematic clarification which precedes evaluation is indispensable for literary scholarship in general, and in particular for the controversial, not yet sufficiently surveyed fields of this scholarship. In the Western hemisphere, the tenets and history of Marxist literary theory form one of these fields. The quantity of articles and books more or less relevant to the subject may easily persuade one to forget the extreme scarcity of objective, synthetic, widescope survey works.

In order to compress the vast amount of critical material to a manageable size, I chose to apply two delimitative criteria. First, all the critics whose ideas are discussed in depth had to be committed party critics, not self-assigned Marxists. Consequently, interesting quasi-Marxist critical groups and leading socialist intellectuals (notably Walter Benjamin, Ernst Bloch, the Frankfurt school of social philosophers, several radical Anglo-American critics of the 1930s, and the French structuralists of the 1960s) will *not* occur in the book as primary examples. Second, an exclusion of the history of literary realism as such appeared to be a necessary prerequisite for keeping the material relevant and under control. Therefore, the reader will find only a sketchy survey of the pre-Hegelian views of realism, and is advised to turn to existing standard literary handbooks for further information.[3]

Any discussion of the Marxist concept of realism should start with Hegel, to whom all socialist aesthetic theories are indebted, though sometimes indirectly. Next, we ought to consider references in the leading theoreticians of Marxism to literary realism, followed by an analysis of the differences between "critical" and "socialist" realism. This study will first deal with these issues. Next, the concept of realism will be compared with naturalism on the one hand, and "modernism" or "formalism" on the other. Finally, all four basic views will be discussed as possible models of the Marxist definitions of literary realism.

I. The Classics and the Bureaucrats

1. Pre-Hegelian Views: A Summary

In the nineteenth century, realism became a dominating tendency in the great prose of Stendhal and Balzac, Thackeray and Dickens, Turgenev and Tolstoy. Previously, the "realistic" representation of life had been regarded primarily as an outcome of the Aristotelian idea of imitation (mimesis). The view that art imitates nature reappeared in the aesthetics of Alberti and Leonardo, after the discovery of Greek antiquity during the age of Humanism. In seventeenth-century classicism, however, Aristotelian aesthetics took a turn which we may see as highly questionable for realistic mimesis. This classicist interpretation of mimesis was accompanied by more abstracting and stereotyping of individual features of literary and dramatic characters, and fewer attempts at describing the complexity of truly human situations. By the second half of the eighteenth century, classicism was a dying movement in Europe, and evoked the disapproval of some brilliant new luminaries like Diderot and Lessing. While Diderot demanded a more sophisticated representation of situations from the playwright, Lessing asked for the individualization of literary heroes, even allowing the presentation of psychic deviations.

The unclassifiable and gigantic figures of Goethe and Schiller grew above the pettier debates of their age between classicists and romanticists, and marked the way to Hegel's aesthetics and nineteenth-century realism. While it was Schiller who first used the term "realists" for opponents of different idealistic trends in literature, Goethe, as Lessing had earlier, stated that the dramatic representation of the relationship between art and reality should be fully dynamic. For Goethe, art was a reflection of life, but through the filter of the poet's mind. General and specific phenomena appear in a balanced form in the ideal work of art. Goethe seemed to have been much closer to accepting the possibility of such synthesis of extremes in art than Schiller, who believed that a synthesis of the authenticity of naive poetry with the powerful idealism of sentimental poetry, though desirable, would still be fairly improbable.

It is interesting to notice that throughout history an element of didacticism appears closely linked to the concept of realism. Aristotle claimed that the classical Greek tragedy evokes catharsis in the spectators, which is, in the last analysis, a personality-changing process through an individual emotional experience. Moral, philosophical, or even "factual" teaching was an artistic goal not at all alien to the Renaissance man, and the seventeenth- and eighteenth-century classicists, including Shaftesbury and even Diderot, were outright teachers. Goethe and the romantic generation, but also Hegel, constantly emphasized that one always learns something from literature and art. It is not the factual aspect of learning, but the quality and human relevance of the knowledge gained, which divides literary movements until the late nineteenth century.

Because of this division on the issue, the concrete problems of didacticism should be examined at different levels. Do particular artists or critics emphasize the value of their art for the moral education of the individual, or do they seek a general, explorative enrichment of human knowledge? Classicism and romanticism are equally moralistic movements, while some eighteenth-century and most nineteenth-century literature tends to depict life in order to inform. We should observe these two trends in their interaction, although, as we shall see, knowledge and consciousness have frequently and unjustly been contrasted with each other in the various attempts to define realism, both in a Marxist and in a non-Marxist sense.

2. The Hegelian Heritage

What probably most attracted Marx, Engels, and their disciples to Hegel is the synthetic, monistic, universal character of his philosophy. Engels, for instance, regarded Hegel as the high point and the conclusion of a period of human thought which had started with Kant; and Georg Lukács called him one of the synthesizers of classicism and romanticism, and a leading exponent of bourgeois aesthetics.

Aside from numerous references to the problems of art which one finds in almost all of Hegel's writings, his main contribution to literary and artistic theory is his *Vorlesungen über die Ästhetik*. This work is a compilation based on notes of students who attended Hegel's lectures at the universities of Heidelberg (1817–19) and Berlin (1820–29). It was one of Hegel's pupils, Heinrich Gustav Hotho, who later published the *Ästhetik*, probably with radical revisions. Many leading Marxists came under the spell of this remarkable work. Engels called it "amazing," and Lukács adopted its general theses to form the methodological basis of his own Marxist aesthetic theory.

Hegel himself never used the word "realism" in an aesthetic sense. But the terms "unity," "totality," "objectivity," "fidelity," "truth," "authenticity," appear frequently to denote characteristics of some ideal art which Marxists, and especially Lukács, later called realism.[1] Although generally classicism seemed to impress Hegel most favorably, his "ideal art," with its concept of the integrated hero, came equally close to romanticism (*Sämtliche Werke* 13:192). Below, we shall summarize those basic theses of Hegelian aesthetics which helped to shape Marxist views on literary realism. As Hegel is not even a pre-Marxian socialist, however, his theory functions here only as an introduction to the subject proper. There is no space, consequently, even to cite samples of the extensive number of concrete literary examples Hegel provided in his works, and the following summary must unavoidably have a strictly theoretical character.

It would be hard to single out the most striking characteristic of the Hegelian aesthetic system. Anthropocentrism is certainly a central thesis. A work of art is as much of a human product as is the idea of beauty, which does not exist independently of human consciousness (12:50–54). Since Hegel emphasizes beauty created by man, natural beauty receives little attention (pp. 20–21).

Art being a human product, it also has a human content (12:77). Hegel's appreciation of romanticism is also a result of the fact that this movement reinstated the prestige of human feelings and passions (pp. 111ff), and the totality of man as a rational and sensuous, observing and acting individual at the same time. Since it is the hero who stands for the totality of existence, characterization has a central place in the Hegelian critical tradition. What is more, the hero as he stands in the focus of events, with a specific attitude to life, can even define the genre of the work (pp. 318ff). The epic hero, for instance, fits into the particular mold of the distant heroic age; therefore the epic as a genre irrevocably belongs to the past (p. 265ff).

Hegelian aesthetics states that there is an unavoidable conflict between the hero and his conditions, but it takes different shapes, depending on the concrete historical circumstances (12:244–45). Analyses of epic heroes such as Odysseus, Hercules, or el Cid, are justly renowned examples of speculative Hegelian historicism. The "real integrity" of these characters, in Hegel's view, could not exist in a society with tight authoritarian ties and well-defined concepts of the State and civil responsibility (pp. 247ff).

Though Hegel's taxonomy of literary characters in the "romantic" age (to which he classifies also Shakespeare) is somewhat simplified, it is still an important part of his aesthetics. Hegel speaks about finished and developing characters. Heroes like Othello, Macbeth, or Richard III are "finished." They choose and follow their own way of life; their consistency determines their greatness; they cannot be measured by conventional moral standards. Fate as an abstract necessity crushes them. Juliet, on the other hand, is an example of a developing character. Shakespeare's drama traces the course of her inner life. Only a few signs reveal her sensitive soul at first. The calmness of the developing hero like Juliet is, however, like "that of the endless depth of the sea" (13:196–205). When such heroes awake to consciousness, a turning point comes in their life: their share will be either happiness or death. Juliet grows from an unconscious, dependent child to a strong, passionate woman before the eyes of the spectators. According to Hegel, "finished" characters illustrate problematic aspects of human consciousness at its different stages, while the developing ones show the process of the ascending human consciousness in its transition from a lower to a higher stage.

Hegel believes that characterizing a hero through his acting and his own words is a method superior to descriptive characterization. Through his actions, the protagonist becomes the embodiment of an age. Also, hero and plot are inseparable (12:295–96).

Hegel places art itself between the spiritual and the natural spheres of existence. The intrinsic world of art is intellectualized and immediate, abstract and sensuous at the same time (12:27–67). He sees no dichotomy between art and science—both are legitimate approaches to truth and knowledge. He believes, however, that science differs from art in that it dissects reality and makes it abstract. Owing to the constant presence of the observing and acting individual, art represents life in its sensuous, vivid totality (pp. 24–25, 67).[2]

The "content" of the work approaches concrete existence through its "form" (12:40, 43, 107–8, 140–42). Hegel implicitly defines form as the ways in which the artist organizes and utilizes the mediating "material" of his art (language, shapes, colors, etc.) in order to effectively convey his "idea." The underlying rationalism of Hegelian aesthetics becomes evident in the fact that Hegel never identifies "idea" with "vision": the origin of the artistic inspiration derives from a rational process of observation and representation. Whether form determines content, or vice versa, remains a question to which the Ästhetik offers only highly ambiguous answers. The basic Hegelian system, and particular references in Hegel's works, should suggest that the content determines the form. In other instances, however, the emphasis is on the unity of content and form, even in the genesis of the work. In Vorlesungen über die Philosophie der Geschichte, Hegel writes (11:109): "There is not only a classical form but also a classical content. Besides, form and content are so closely tied together in a work of art that one of them can be classical only if the other is classical too." The relationship of form and content later became an overworn, speculative issue in Marxist criticism.

As to the function of art, Hegel emphasizes its mimetic and didactic aspects. Though he does not identify the Aristotelian idea of mimesis by name, he rejects the concept of mimesis as a reproduction of real life, for two reasons. In the first place, he does not believe that the imitation of nature expands human knowledge or sensibility, since it only reproduces well-known, easily accessible episodes from everyday life. Instead of exploration, art turns to recognition. Secondly, the concept of imitation reduces the prerequisites of artistic talent to technical skill and formal devices which do not leave room for genuine creative activity of the mind (12:72–76). Craftsmanship alone never satisfied Hegel, or the Hegelian Marxists.

Real objectivity, in Hegel's opinion, lies between banality (a reality evident and too easily accessible to everyone) and extreme subjectivity (a "reality" accessible only to the writer—12:388–90). The double function of art is to reflect the human sphere of existence in sensuous images, and to realize the idea of beauty. But Hegel ultimately equates the two functions: beauty and reality are identical (p. 132). This is why he calls beauty definable, knowable, and desirable (pp. 135–36). Though he also attributes a certain value to "abstract beauty" (sound quality, structural qualities like symmetry, etc.—pp. 188–99), the true source of beauty in his aesthetics is still the tangible human reality. In the Hegelian system, however, art is only the first stage of existence for the absolute spirit in its process of gaining self-consciousness. Lukács later challenged Hegel's placement of art (or the "aesthetic attitude to life," as Kierkegaard called it) on the lowest level of consciousness. He asked how art could reflect deeper connections of reality if it is but the lowest level of cognition, thereby pointing out a basic paradox of the Hegelian aesthetic system.[3]

Besides indirectly attacking Aristotle's assumed identification of art with a mirror ("things as they were or are"), Hegel also wanted to do away with the classical tendency to moralize ("things as they ought to be"). Abstract moralizing, in his view, has nothing to do with poetry (12:85). Macbeth and Richard III may be villains by socioethical standards, but they are integral, total individuals from the point of view of Hegelian aesthetics (13:197–200). If there is any moral message in literary works, it must be implicit in the work and must grow organically out of its context (p. 85). Similarly, Hegel defines the function of literature as only indirectly didactic: to introduce changes by elevating the readers' consciousness (pp. 81–82).

Hegel did not give as much consideration to how realism appears in the different genres. Lukács seemed to regard as correct Hegel's characterization of prose as the typical medium of realism;[4] his own commitment to the novel may explain why. The lyric is the most neglected genre in the *Ästhetik*. Hegel (and later Lukács) regarded any attempts to revive primitive arts and medieval literature as retrogressive escapes to lower, supposedly not man-centered forms of culture. Hegel appreciated romanticism in theory rather than in its actuality—again, a paradoxical attitude not quite unfamiliar to scholars dealing with the Marxist classical heritage.

Marxist criticism inherited at least two basic ideas from Hegelian aesthetics. The first is the thesis that great literature represents reality as a process. At the center of this process is man in all three stages of artistic communication: as creator, hero, and reader. This concept raises such questions as what is reality; does it exist outside of man, or is it created by man? Hegel's answer is that reality is *human* reality—man's social environment elevated to the level of consciousness, where it also becomes a rational and beautiful (i.e. aesthetic) object. In this process, man gets acquainted with things and interprets them for himself until they become conceivable and familiar (12:58). This organic, constantly changing, complex character of realism and its reflection in human consciousness is already a radical departure in the pre-Hegelian romantic tradition from the Aristotelian classical, static, mechanistic mirror-theory. In early-nineteenth-century German aesthetics, the reflection process is conceived as interaction between man and man, instead of between man and things.

The second trace of the Hegelian heritage in Marxist aesthetics concerns the view of artistic form. As Hegel's aesthetic system is fairly hostile to a purely formal, stylistic approach to the literary work, he seldom discusses technique in itself as detached from the impact of the "spirit." The reference to reality in the work gets concrete shape in the plot, hero, or general characteristics of the genre. But the structure of the work, its symbol systems, or even its language are almost irrelevant in Hegel's view. He categorizes language as "abstract beauty," and places symbols at the lowest level of artistic expression: both, in his view, are of merely secondary importance. This Hegelian antiformalistic tendency has long characterized the Marxist tradition also, leaving the question still open whether realism can be defined in technical or stylistic terms at all.

3. The Contribution of Marx and Engels

There is only one clear-cut definition of literary realism in all the writings of Marx and Engels. In April 1888, Engels expressed his gratitude to the British writer Margaret Harkness (the pseudonym of Joan Law) for sending him her novel *A City Girl* (published in 1887). In this letter, we find the following definition of realism, extensively quoted by works on Marxist literary theory: "Realism, to my mind, implies, besides truth of detail, the truthful reproduction of typical characters under typical circumstances."[5]

Further definitions, like those of "typical," "character," and "circumstances," are missing in the letter. Nevertheless, scattered and casual references in Marx's and Engels' writings, and two or three of their more detailed essays or letters on certain literary works, throw some light on the sense in which the two authors used these terms. The clause "to my mind," is also significant in itself. It shows that Engels was expressing his personal opinion, not claiming any universal relevance.

Hans Mayer reminds us that Marxist literary theory is inseparable from the total context of Marxist philosophy.[6] That the question of realism is not independent of general philosophical problems is one of the numerous traces of the Hegelian heritage in Marxism. The view of literature as a specific reflection of reality, and as such a complicated cognitive process, has a distinguished place in both Hegelian and Marxist aesthetics.

The Marxist standpoint says that matter creates consciousness, existence gives birth to essence: "It is not the consciousness of men that determines their being, but, on the contrary, [it is their] social being that determines their consciousness."[7] The active, productive man gradually creates an increasingly sophisticated relationship to his material world and to his fellow men. The sum total of production-factors is called the "economic basis" of human existence, "on which rises a legal and political superstructure and to which correspond definite forms of social consciousness. . . . With the change of the economic foundations the entire immense superstructure is more or less rapidly transformed."[8] In short, there is nothing in human consciousness, or in its products (to which literature and art also belong), that does not originate in the economic conditions of a given age. Or, taking a hypothetical definition of realism by Marx, realism would mean the "reflection" of the modes of production in art.

Since 1859, when Marx gave this outline of his view of basis and superstructure, the usual reaction has been either to accept this thesis unconditionally or to reject it indignantly as a "mechanistic" outlook on the products of the human mind. Those who make either choice, however, tend to forget that the theoretical heritage of Marx and Engels is highly controversial, and could also yield to other, equally "Marxist," interpretations of the interaction between society and literature. Besides the above statements by Marx and Engels, which restrict the function of literature to the reflection of the economic basis of society, you find a series of other utterances, expressing a fairly different view of the sphere of consciousness.

In 1867, in *Das Kapital*, Marx defined labor as a mutually interactive process. While natural and social conditions shape man, he himself shapes the very same conditions.[9] Marx also defined the realm of life outside the relations of production as the realm of freedom where man can execute his free will.[10] In 1890, Engels described his and Marx's attitude to this issue as follows: "According to the materialistic view of history, production and reproduction of real life are *ultimately* the determining element of history. [Neither Marx nor I said more than this much.] But now if someone twists that around to mean that the economic element is the *only* determining one, then he transforms that proposition into a meaningless, abstract, absurd phrase."[11]

It is precisely this nondeterministic relationship between basis and superstructure from which Marx derived the thesis of the *unequal development* of the different spheres of human activity. In 1857, Marx wrote: "It is well known that certain periods of highest development of art stand in no direct connection with the general development of society, nor with the material basis and the skeleton structure of its organization."[12] If this were not true, why could not poets of the modern technological society write an epic superior to the Homeric one? "Since in mechanics and other fields we are [further along than] the classic Greeks, why shouldn't we also be able to write an epic? So we get the *Henriad* for the *Iliad!*"[13]

To illustrate his point, Marx asks why the Greek myths had not vanished with the old economic basis: why are they still influencing the consciousness of the modern machine age—if not because of the *relative freedom of the "superstructure"* from socioeconomic determinants?[14] Though the genesis of the work of art is coordinated with the sociohis-

torical conditions, the existence of the work is relatively independent of these conditions. This is what makes the trans-
mission and appreciation of realistic reflections of the past
possible for later ages.

Both Marx and Engels relied extensively on literary evidences in their various writings. Engels regarded the Bible
and the *Edda* as documents respectively of the old Semitic
and Germanic religions and of tribal traditions.[15] In *The Origin
of the Family, Private Property, and the State* (1884), he used
the *Iliad* to demonstrate how tribal structures turned into
state structures.[16] The *Iliad* and the *Odyssey* also became illustrative of the position of women in the decaying age of
tribalism,[17] and the Greek tradition of tragedy manifested the
change from matriarchalism and promiscuity to patriarchalism
and a fixed family system.[18]

These examples also reveal Engels' attempt to define
myth from a materialistic platform, as a loosely organized
form of social consciousness, ultimately derivable from a certain mode of production. In other instances, Engels discussed
ethical standards through literary parallels and related them to
social conditions and practices. He mentioned Provençal poetry to prove that monogamy is but a social convention, and
not a part of man's physical makeup. He even traced back,
though superficially, the "immorality" of the French and the
"dullness" of the German novelistic traditions to differences
in family structure and moral values.[19]

Marx, too, referred to a score of writers, poets, and artists in his principal work, *Das Kapital*. Most notable are his
characterization of Robinson Crusoe as an industrious seventeenth-century British gentleman;[20] the demonstration
through Shakespeare's *Timon of Athens* of how the introduction of the capitalist *laissez faire* financial economy parallels
the bourgeois concept of political freedom;[21] and how Balzac's *Les Paysans* reflects the relationship between small
farmers and usurers.[22]

Such literary references in Marx's and Engels' works prove that the two "Founding Fathers" of Marxism regarded literature as a reflection not merely of the social and material "realities" of a certain age but also of the consciousness of the age, appealing at the same time to the readers' consciousness. Most of Marx's and Engels' literary examples consist of books which had immense impact on the cultures that produced them. The Bible and the *Edda* had ritual functions; *Robinson Crusoe* instigated a whole cult of the modern, inventive, civilizing Western man; and both Shakespeare and Balzac were active public figures whose works had never served as merely a source of pleasure for their spectators and readers.

Given these facts, the widespread idea of a deterministic Marxist view of literature seems to need a revaluation. The heritage of the intellectual cold war is the conception of a deterministic, dehumanizing Marxist subordination of the creative genius to the rigid laws of economic necessity. This idea appears in Sartre, Demetz, Barilli, Barthes, Steiner,[23] and innumerable other critics of Marxism, but would become untenable when confronted with *another* set of Marxian quotations than those it conventionally relies on—like the set of literary remarks about the impact of consciousness on literature.

Marxist criticism has especially exploited two of Marx's and Engels' few exhaustive writings on literature. One of these is the opening chapter of *The Holy Family*, the first of their joint works, which they wrote in 1844 and published in 1845. The other material, the correspondence of Marx and Engels with Ferdinand Lassalle about his historical drama on Franz von Sickingen, was first published in 1922. Both the so-called "Sue-critique" and the "Sickingen-debate" provide some insight into what Engels might have meant by "typical character" and "typical circumstances" as criteria of realism.

As a whole, *The Holy Family* is a sarcastic critique of the

Jung-Hegelian gurus to whom the young Marx and Engels had once belonged. Its opening chapter deals with an essay on Eugène Sue's extremely popular bestseller, *Les Mystères de Paris*. The author of this essay was a scion of Prussian Junkers, Franz Zychlin von Zychlinski, who published his review under the pseudonym Szeliga. Marx and Engels especially criticized Szeliga (or "Szeliga-Vishnu," as they called him). To a lesser extent they criticized Hegel, and Sue only marginally. Nevertheless, their objections to Szeliga's pamphlet, which was more philosophical than literary, contain valuable references to a prototypical realistic literature as well.

In Szeliga, Marx and Engels objected mostly to his tendency to mystify reality. The title of Sue's work determined his basic attitude to the novel, and compelled him to reveal "mysteries" hiding behind everyday phenomena. Szeliga interprets Sue's descriptions of the daily life and conditions of Parisian criminals as revelations of "the secret of the driving forces of Evil." In contrast to this belated Kantian and early surrealistic attempt to find the essence behind the phenomena, Marx and Engels contend that "the dens and jargon of the criminal reflect his character, they are parts of the criminal's existence, their description belongs to his description, just as much as the description of a secret meeting-place belongs to the character of a *demi-monde*."[24] In other words: the writer describes no inferior materialized projections of a Platonic moral sphere, but a tangible reality, where characters are inseparable from their environment. Any "mysteries"—if they exist—are revealed by the description of the internal and external reality. In addition to the setting, the language of the characters complements their totality, so that individual usage of language and a vividly depicted environment help the author to shape a well-rounded character.

The critique of the tendency of Hegel's disciples to build abstract, speculative, idealistic systems is apparent in the frequently quoted paragraph from *The Holy Family* in which

Marx and Engels ridicule the idealistic, typically Hegelian, attempt to regard the concept (the "substance") of fruit as something higher than the particular fruits (like "the pear, the apple, the almond.")[25] More applicable to art seems to be a similar remark on the dance: you cannot philosophize about the Dance unless you single out and describe a particular dance.[26] In other words, to look only for the general means to neglect the specific, the material concreteness of existence. Paradoxically, this requirement corresponds to Hegel's thesis that real art reflects objectified, specific existence. Marx and Engels were supposedly not rejecting this particular idea of Hegel but his speculative system, which was about the only aspect of his philosophy that the Jung-Hegelians appreciated.

Finally, Marx and Engels analyzed Sue's novel from the point of view of characterization, by choosing three fairly central characters to illustrate their point.[27] The first one is *Le Chourineur* (The Knife), a criminal whose career Sue depicted in *The Holy Family* with vivid realism—until his meeting with the main hero, a certain Rodolphe, Prince of Gerolstein and a knight of middle-class morals, who continues a heroic struggle for the moral conversion of the entire Parisian underworld. The title of this chapter is "The Transformation of a Butcher into a Dog." The analysis shows how Rodolphe teaches *Le Chourineur,* by sheer power and hypocritical logic (which Sue, in the view of Marx and Engels, idealizes), how to betray his buddies, how to lose his human identity and become a "moral being"—that is, a bourgeois—not only in his hypocrisy but also in the way he walks. Rodolphe's next victim is a prostitute called Fleur de Marie. Though day after day she solicits in a tavern, in the words of Marx and Engels, "even in this humiliated position, she preserves a certain human dignity of soul, openness of mind, and human beauty." Again, thanks to Rodolphe, she goes through a "purifying" process and comes out a nun. The third example is another criminal, "The Schoolmaster," whom Rodolphe blinds in order to confront him with his criminal past and force him to repent.

What Marx and Engels were opposing in Sue was the dualism of plot and message, of authenticity and moralization. In their view, as Georg Lukács paraphrases it, Sue disintegrated the initial realistic description of his characters and the milieu by imposing his banal philanthropic ideas, his "sentimental half-truths" on them, thereby creating some modern "morality play" in prose rather than reflecting the organic and authentic dynamism of life.[28] The theory that a writer cannot completely dominate his work but must recognize the inner necessities, laws, and potentials of the world re-created in the work was later crystallized in an important contribution of Lukácsian-Marxist criticism to the theory of literature: in the idea that the writer's revealed sociopolitical sympathies should better be absent from his literary writings. Also, a few comments on Sue's shallow *deus ex machina* devices show Marx and Engels' agreement with Aristotle in his rejection of the "improbable possible."

The other contribution of Marx and Engels to literary theory, the so-called "Sickingen-debate" with Lassalle, proves the relative constancy of their aesthetic ideas through the fourteen years that separated the two documents. The basic problems of the author's relationship to the inherent inner life of his work—moralism versus objectivity—and the question of authenticity also turn up in this debate. Furthermore, the whole discussion can be regarded as the first Marxist attempt to define some principal laws of the dramatic genre. The definition of the tragic, the specific function of the hero on the stage, and the dialogue are a few of those particular problems on which the participants of the debate reflected.

A few words about the background of the controversy: Ferdinand Lassalle, a prominent figure of the German working-class movement, wrote a historical drama about Franz von

Sickingen in 1858–59. As he himself admitted, he wanted to show how the revolutions of 1848–49 had failed owing to the "eternal conflict of all revolutions," the conflict between diplomacy and *Realpolitik*—the "means" on the one hand, and the noble "aim" on the other.[29] He asked Marx and Engels for their opinion about the drama, but their critical remarks irritated him. Therefore, Lasalle attempted to explain his point of view in a lengthy letter, to which Marx and Engels did not respond.

According to Lukács, Marx and Engels did not initially coordinate their criticism of Lassalle's tragedy.[30] Independently, they wrote to Lassalle that they regretted the "Schillerian" character of his drama.[31] Marx wrote, "You would have to Shakespearize more, while at present I consider Schillerism, making individuals the mere mouthpieces of the spirit of the time, your main fault." Engels' point of view was very similar. In short Marx and Engels believed that the characters must not be abstractions, mouthpieces for ideas, idealized "great personalities," but flesh-and-blood individuals. Besides, as they thought, to write *the* tragedy of *the* revolution is an abstract pursuit and, as such, an undesirable one for literature. These ideas are familiar from the Szeliga-critique. Also, both Marx and Engels doubted that Lassalle had made the right choice in picking Sickingen to embody allegorically the typical revolutionary hero of the nineteenth century.

Marx and Engels were by no means the first nineteenth-century critics to have established the Shakespeare versus Schiller contrast. Georg Büchner, the short-lived genius of the German drama of the 1830s, for instance, characterized Schiller's heroes as "marionettes with sky-blue nose and affected pathos," and Shakespeare's heroes as "characters of flesh and blood."[32] Among the contemporaries of Marx and Engels, Otto Ludwig had been working on his *Shakespeare-Studien* since 1851. In these essays, Ludwig used critical arguments in favor of Shakespeare and against Schiller which correspond to the ones we find in the letters of Marx and Engels to Lassalle. Ludwig also thought that Shakespeare, unlike Schiller, did not fill his characters with strange ideas in order to make them appear more interesting, but rather developed their inner, organic personality traits until they attracted the interest of the spectators. Also, Ludwig preferred action to rhetoric as much as Marx and Engels did, and regarded "robust, life-like color" and distinct individualization of character as the main attributes of realistic drama.[33] However, Ludwig's essays on Shakespeare were not published at the time Marx and Engels responded to Lassalle's letter. Consequently, we cannot speak of causal, but only of parallel developments.

Lassalle's answer to the two critical letters was as consistent and appropriate as it could be. He simply held a completely divergent view on the essence of tragedy. In the debate, the rhetoric of the classical tradition was opposed to the psychological and action-oriented Shakespearean drama, and stylized verbal expression to colloquial communication. The basic controversy repeated itself in a modified form some seventy-five years later, in the debate between Brecht and Lukács.

It would be fallacious to deprive Marx and Engels of the right to redefine tragedy, but it seems evident that their definition is insufficiently developed. Did the same Shakespeare whose characters they considered as ideal also represent the new concept of the tragic hero? Actually, this interpretation is not wholly unlikely. Soviet attempts to represent Romeo and Juliet as symbols of a new generation born to reconcile the warring Italian urban republics seem challenging in their sociohistorical orientation. The interpretation of Hamlet as an early existentialist hero is well-known from Western European criticism too. But, again, does the Shakespearian tradition automatically discard the relevance of reviving the classical one? Marx and Engels left this theoretical question unanswered.

In the light of nineteenth-century literary debates about realism,[34] Marx and Engels' views appear hardly original. Rather, they might strike one as results of a skillful, if not far-reaching, compiling activity, somewhere in between outright eclecticism and integrating synthetism. Aside from the influence of Hegel's *Ästhetik*, the two main sources for Marx and Engels seem to have been the later-nineteenth-century French and German critical views on realism. Observation, truthfulness, and the absence of the author's personality (and values) are spelled out by Balzac, Desnoyers, and Flaubert. Otto Ludwig attached as great significance to the typification of themes and characters as did Engels. Objectivity, type, nonmoralization, as well as the term realism itself were, most probably, commonplaces of polemic literary criticism in the entire second half of the nineteenth century. But it appears that, above all, Otto Ludwig, with his synthesizing of the then-fashionable French scientifism with German speculative philosophy, can be regarded as a veritable "missing link" between the Hegelian and the Marxist theories of realism.

At the same time, the very introduction of new ideas into the consciousness of socialist intellectuals gives significance to Marx and Engels' statements on literature and art. On the general plane of literary theory their aesthetic ideas may not be particularly striking; yet the extremely status-conscious international socialist movement became acquainted with the concepts of personal detachment, type, and so on, from Marx and Engels' writings on literature—when they were finally published, less than half a century ago.

The trend which becomes apparent in Marx and Engels' numerous, though dispersed, casual yet relatively consistent literary remarks is neither explicit nor safely deducible. A dislike of separating perceived reality from the sphere of human consciousness seems to be one attribute of this trend. Another is a preference for a complex, overall image of life, to which characters, scenes, and motives should be subordinated. At the same time, this complexity should, as Marx and Engels constantly remind us, remain specific instead of turning general and abstract. They also spell out the desirability of a dynamic development of plot and character, claiming that there should be some implicit reference in the literary work to the origin and outcome of this development. There is an autonomous inner kernel in the plot and the characters which the represented dynamism of events should not antagonize: the work should not serve any *telos,* any prefabricated moral idea, program, or bias of the writer.

Considering this heritage as a whole, the normative feature of Marx's and Engels' critical writings is striking. Instead of taking literary works as they are, Marx and Engels constantly emphasized what they should be like, by measuring these works against norms derived from certain masterpieces of world literature. Some recent critics, like Demetz or Konder, who have written about Marx's and Engels' literary views, disapprove of this practice which, on the other hand, impressed Lukács so much that he built his whole aesthetic system on it.

If inclined, one might reduce the problem to the conventional gap between aesthetics and literary criticism. Whereas aesthetics measures the work according to external principles, literary criticism discusses it on its own terms, by accepting the writer's intentions, choice of characters, etc., and only verifies whether or not the materialization of the individual creative project is successful. Marx and Engels are closer to the aesthetic practice. In itself, this is neither a merit nor a defect. Unfortunately, the whole official cultivation of "socialist realism" later adopted exclusively a normative (but hardly any longer "aesthetic") view of literature. The practice of literary criticism suffered so much from this view in the socialist countries that a series of debates during the last fifteen years has brought only a cathartic recognition of the problem but little working solution.

4. The Later Engels: A New Concept of Realism?

After Marx's death in 1883, Engels seemed to be more concerned with the publication of older manuscripts and the clarification of various controversial issues than with the practical problems of the international working class movement. His personal correspondence between 1883 and 1895 deserves our special attention.

Before the letter to Margaret Harkness, in which Engels mentioned his idea of literary realism in one sentence, he sent another letter to Minna Kautsky, mother of the leading Social Democrat Karl Kautsky. The letter (dated November 26, 1885) contains his personal opinion of Mrs. Kautsky's politically radical novel *Die Alten und die Neuen*. Engels' view of tendentiousness in literature can be paraphrased from these two letters in the following way:

Tendency is nothing else than the wish of the writer to communicate his ideas. This tendency must, however, be "hidden"—that is, integrated in the plot and characterization. This makes the work more authentic and more effective, since good tendentious literature ought to shake the bourgeois reader to the very roots of his world view, instead of openly reproaching him for social evil. Though the critique of the bourgeois world is an inherent characteristic of all tendentious literature, the author need not suggest any solution to the problems he is discussing.[35]

In addition to these primarily literary letters, there are documents from the same period showing that Engels was growing increasingly discontented with the interpretation of the original Marxist theory by late-nineteenth-century socialists. His greatest concern seemed to be a deterministic simplification of the role of economic production in the sphere of consciousness. On September 21, 1890, he complained to Joseph Bloch that the "younger generation" of socialist ideologists were attaching far greater importance to the economic factor in social existence than he or Marx had ever intended.[36] In a letter to W. Borgius (January 25, 1894), Engels emphasized the significance of the reactive, feedback function of the superstructure to the structure.[37] He even granted so much independence to the sphere and products of consciousness as to admit that in different parts of the superstructure (especially in the history of ideas) there might be invariable factors working. He felt that economic changes did not necessarily result in total change of the consciousness, but only modified inherited constants.[38] Engels did not regard Marx's and his own theory as a final word in the perpetual process of disclosing natural and social laws. Therefore, he warned the younger generation of socialists against epigonism, advising them to restudy the entire course of human history if they ever wanted to point out traces of any interaction between economic conditions and individual consciousness.[39]

Engels' letter to Paul Ernst (June 5, 1890), touches on a concrete literary question: the interpretation of Ibsen. Engels criticized Ernst for simplifying the Norwegian social conditions which partly explain Ibsen's dramas. He reminded Ernst that "the materialist method" is badly misused if employed as some ultimate wisdom, as a "ready-made pattern" and not as a guideline in historical investigation. It was a gross mistake of Ernst, Engels explained, to mix up the "philistine" German petty-bourgeois with the Norwegian, as the former was a spiritual and intellectual cripple, while the latter still possessed some positive features of the classical bourgeoisie of the eighteenth century, such as initiative and independence.[40]

This letter is the more important as it brings up the possibility that the bourgeoisie, owing to the laws of unequal social development and sociocultural peculiarities, is still able to function positively in certain circumstances. As we shall see, the possibility of such interpretation later became a major impetus for the controversies between Lukács and advocates of socialist realism, as well as between Garaudy and Fischer on the one hand and the Soviet literary ideologists on the other.

In a hypothesis based on these late letters of Engels, Peter Demetz presents a gentle Engels who, having gotten rid of the tyrannic charisma of the economic genius of Marx, started on a radically independent course which his death tragically cut short.[41] Demetz is not the only scholar who believes he has found some striking differences between Marx—the classicist free-thinker allied to the Enlightenment—and Engels—brought up in a more deeply German tradition, and interested in myth, general linguistics, and cultural anthropology. Also, these differences may generate a view of Marx and Engels as basically opposite personalities.

If one puts these letters in the proper historical context, however, a hypothesis like Demetz's appears highly vulnerable. Actually, the only new idea in the late letters is the statement about the constancy-factor in the (European?) cultural heritage. Otherwise, everything else—the necessity for the "hidden message," the demand for concreteness and fullness of characterization, the relative independence of the literary work of the economic-historical conditions, contempt for abstract clichés—are ideas which, as we have seen, already appeared in the Szeliga critique and in the Sickingen debate. Instead of attempting to find in these letters what is not at all new, one should try to interpret them with regard to the historical circumstances.

Only a few day after Marx's death, Engels wrote gloomily to a friend: "The local experts and the little talents, if not the swindlers, will get a free hand."[42] He was referring to certain functionaries of the Second International. Several ideological leaders of the labor cause around the turn of the century (Lafargue, Labriola, Mehring) were educated men who regarded the popularization of Marxism among the working classes as their main intellectual task. Popularization of sophisticated ideas is, however, an enterprise which may easily end up in a simplification of the original ideas. And the more politically oriented leadership of the International (Bebel, Bernstein, Kautsky) welcomed this popularized version of Marxism which served political rhetorics better and provided more effective slogans than the original works of Marx and Engels. Socialists around the world had to see even Engels' authority challenged when he became involved in an irreconcilable conflict with Bernstein's reformist fraction.

Engels died at a time when the doctrine of an unconditional socioeconomic determinism and the practice of hiding a lack of knowledge behind socialist slogans was gradually becoming a credo of the working-class bureaucracy. The real importance of Engels' late letters is not that he wanted to revise Marxism but that he foresaw those uninspired, ruthless simplifications which have become so fatal, especially for the aesthetic applicability of this theory.

5. Lenin's View on Partisanship and the Reflection of Reality

What Hegel (and Feuerbach) was for Marx and Engels, the encounter with the Russian "revolutionary democrats" was for Vladimir Ilyich Lenin. What separate Marx and Engels from Lenin are the decades of the Second International. There was not much to learn from its leaders, whose short-sighted diligence was prophetically caricatured by Zola in the figure of Pluchart (*Germinal*). In the writings of Bernstein, Kautsky, Bebel, Labriola, and others, we look in vain both for the complexity of theoretical problems and for the diversity of literary references that we find in Marx and Engels. The only two significant socialist literary critics of the decades before World War I are Franz Mehring and G. V. Plekhanov: we shall discuss them later.

The peculiar ideology of the revolutionary democrats attracted Lenin more than the post-Marxian Western development of socialist theory. This ideology, which he integrated in his philosophy, is relevant for us from the point of view of defining realism and looking at the tendency of social development.

In Russia, the period 1840–60 was the era of the revolutionary democrats. The best known figures of this movement were Herzen, Belinsky, Chernishevsky, Dobrolyubov, and the extreme utilitarian Pisarev. They shared a radical idealism with the Jung-Hegelians but, as a result of the peculiar social situation in Russia, they stayed in closer touch with the social realities. Their ideology had a critical and strictly social orientation, was eclectic and nonsystematic, emphasized the value of active social participation and adopted a practical attitude of life. (At a subjective level, Belinsky summarized the program of the revolutionary democrats in this rhetorical question: "What care I for the existence of the universal when individuals are suffering?"[43] Besides their essentially Hegelian and social-radical foundations, which also characterized their aesthetic views, a peculiar populism separated them from the West. In the advanced capitalist countries, nineteenth-century reformism either took the shape of philanthropic moral criticism (as in Dickens or Sue) or ended in romantic radicalism (as in Hugo, Freiligrath, or Daumier). The belated social development of Russia, however, secured a greater homogeneity for the urban and rural masses, which probably made revolutionary democrats believe that the programs of pro-rural Slavophiles and pro-urban Westernizers were ultimately reconcilable.

Marx and Engels knew and appreciated Herzen, Chernishevsky, and Dobroloyubov,[44] and the revolutionary democrats in turn were eager to absorb the theory of socialism. Their approach to literature was basically sociological. Chernishevsky, for instance, defined beauty as a relative concept which people from different social classes interpret differently.[45] This group of Russian intellectuals regarded literature as an active factor of the social practice, inseparable from the writer's own ideology. According to Dobrolyubov, the characteristics of the writer of the people (that is, a good writer and a realist) were these: ". . . in order to really become a poet of the people, [one must] integrate the spirit of the people, live its life, . . . reject all feudal superstitions, book knowledge, etc., feel everything with the simple feelings of the people. . . ."[46]

This demand for the identification of the individual with common people implies the idea of artistic leadership in the political sphere. Besides, one may conceive also an undifferentiated view of reality as something individually *and* collectively experienced, understood, expressed, and changed at the same time. Such views seem to have long disappeared from Western European consciousness. Although this is not the place to analyze the cultural historical roots of these phenomena, it must be noted that, within the East-Central European cultural community, the philosophy of revolutionary democracy does have parallels. In Poland Edward Dembowski, in Hungary Sándor Petöfi and Mihály Táncsics, in Serbia Svetozar Marković, in Bulgaria Dimitâr Blagoev and Hristo Botev, in Rumania Dobrogeanu-Gherea represented the same spirit of radical social populism.[47] After Stalin rose to power in the Soviet Union, and later his protégés in the people's democracies, party bureaucrats grossly overestimated and unscrupulously exploited the heritage of the revolutionary democrats. Stalin, Zhdanov, and Khrushchev equally liked to quote opinions of this generation completely out of context, without even referring to the work quoted.

Knowing the importance of the revolutionary democrats for Lenin's intellectual development gives us an insight into, though no certain solution for, his article "On Party Organization and Party Literature" (1905). This short essay is one of Lenin's most remarkable writings, as well as a most significant contribution to a Marxist theory of realism.[48] Although only about six printed pages in length, it is the epitome of stylistic ambiguity. The essential questions are to what extent must "reality" (the objective external world) penetrate the writer's consciousness? and, is the direct, participated experience superior to the indirect, observed one?

As two equally possible, equally relevant, and yet diametrically opposite interpretations should be considered simultaneously, let us establish a formal comparison:

	Interpretation I.	Interpretation II.
1. Definition of "literature":	Any kind of written communication (not belonging to the sphere of natural sciences?), also fiction and poetry.	Only popularizing (polemic?) literature written by party theoreticians on social, philosophical, economic, political questions, etc.
2. Function of literature:	Not private matter but part of party machinery.	Private matter and also part of a larger social context.
3. Place and freedom of writers:	Must belong to some party organization; their work must be party work.	Complete freedom of press and speech; the only requirement for authors with party membership is to be loyal to the basic policy of their party.
4. Cultural policy:	Publishers, bookstores, libraries must be subordinated to the party.	The literature of the future will be free from profit considerations of publishers and need not serve a shallow bourgeois taste.

Understandably, the two different interpretations also support two completely different definitions of literature as such. Aesthetically uneducated party ideologists from Zhdanov to Khrushchev, and subservient literary "experts" with party membership, always emphasized Interpretation I. At least one of the party decisions Lenin initiated seems to support this interpretation: the making of the ultra-leftist Prolet-kult movement an auxiliary body of the People's Commissar-iat of Education in 1920.

On the other hand, Lenin's wife, Nadezhda Krupskaya, herself explained in a posthumously published letter that Lenin's only intention was to remind party theoreticians of their obligations.[49] Also, Lenin's view of Tolstoy and his toler-ance of experimental art support the second interpretation of his newspaper article. Certainly, they do not support the first. As for realism, the first interpretation is fundamentally a nega-tion of literary freedom and objectivity, the second the recog-nition of these. This dilemma, as we shall see, has become one of the central problems in the Marxist definition of real-ism.

In practice, Lenin tended more toward critical under-standing than uncritical condemnation. As a politician and later as leader of a newly formed, turbulent state, his cultural activ-ity was mostly concentrated on the practical, social aspects of literary life. Education, journalism, rhetoric, mass media, and communication research are the fields which could profit by his analysis.[50] His direct contribution to literary criticism or aesthetic problems remained even more marginal than that of Marx and Engels. Though he frequently referred to writers and poets, he used them only as rhetorical examples.

As we have seen in Marx's and Engels' case, however, in-direct contributions to the theory of realism may include ma-terial that is aesthetically highly relevant. Scholars investigat-ing Marx's and Engels' literary views are concerned primarily with an analysis of the economic basis and ideological super-structure. Similarly, critics interested in the Leninist aesthetic heritage are concerned mainly with Lenin's writings in epis-temology. True, the specific problems of literary-artistic re-flection do not occur in Lenin's main epistemological study, *Materialism and Empiriocriticism* (1909), yet this book touches on a process that is central in both the philosophical and the aesthetic theory of realism—namely, the process of perceiving and re-creating sensuous reality in human consciousness.

Lukács reminds us of the difference between the Aristotelian and the Marxist-Leninist concept of "mimesis" (or "reflection"). Both classical and modern materialism call sense impressions caused by the objective world "copies" or "photographs" (*Abbilder*) of reality. But Lukács maintains that classical ("mechanistic," as the Marxists call it) materialism did not admit that there was any difference between natural and conscious reflection.[51] In the aesthetic theory of classicism, strict rules limited the process and potentials of reflection. Specific laws prescribed for the various genres made the author simplify his topic and follow a formula, which was quite frequently a stereotyped one already. The rules of craftsmanship deprived the topic of any "deviating" specific existence of its own. This created the illusion that the author was in perfect command of his work, although it would be more accurate to say that strict prefabricated rules were controlling the author.

Again, it was Hegel who, supposedly, brought the revolution in artistic epistemology. In the Aristotelian tradition, the emphasis is on exactitude, on "minute fidelity," the symbol of which is the lifeless mirror. The synthetic Hegelian aesthetics, on the other hand, already bore elements of Lenin's reflection theory in its thesis of the object-subject relationship. The observer, the receptive "subject," was no longer a passive mirror-like element of reflection.

Materialism and Empiriocriticism is a controversial work. Primarily, it was written as a ruthless polemic against two influential leaders of German positivism, Mach and Avenarius. Their attempt to rejuvenate Berkeley's and Hume's subjective empiricism found a warm reception among socialists around the turn of the century. Lenin, however, was unhappy about the mechanistic and deterministic implications of this neopositivistic tendency, and tried to clarify his own view of the relationship between matter and consciousness.

In the epistemological process, Lenin argues, the basic factor is matter—elementary, inextinguishable, varied yet homogeneous, historically preceding consciousness. Consciousness, in its turn, is complex, versatile, differentiated and unique, but also extremely fragile and easily degradable into matter. Yet functionally it is qualitatively different from other combinations of matter. Matter is a determining factor, insofar as the material world is the source of images "copied" in the consciousness. That is, the human mind receives and stores not symbols and hieroglyphs but imprints of concrete existence. These imprints of reality reach the human consciousness basically intact, but with slight modifications. The modifications are the result of the sensual process, of the complex transmitting activity of the nervous system. More specifically, they are caused by the unique structure of matter in the sense organs, and by the peculiarities of these organs, which of course differ from individual to individual.

This emphasis on reflection as a process is characteristic of twentieth-century science. Instead of the idea of an undifferentiated monism, matter and consciousness, object and subject, are still distinct in Leninist epistemology as well as in modern neurology, theory of learning, or communication theory. However, the interaction between perceiving subject and perceived object, the feedback factor, creates a united, mobile structure.

It belongs to the historians of science to determine whether Lenin was as much of a pioneer of modern epistemology and model theory as the party ideologists maintain. Within the theoretical framework of the international socialist movement, Lenin's views have a special importance. Together with Lenin's weight of authority, they became a major weapon against the Stalinist-Maoist corruptions of the idea of socialist realism. The way in which the Hungarian critic Dénes Zoltai exploited the Leninist epistemological heritage is the leading example of several such achievements. As Zoltai put it, cautiously but clearly, a more consciousness-oriented concept of reality would correct the untenable thesis of a "misunderstood epistemological aesthetic" that art must reflect an external world in the way it would if it had been completely detached from human consciousness.[52]

6. Realism—As It Ought To Be

The basic Marxist assumption that literature reflects social reality is also applicable to the history of Soviet literary theory since the October revolution. How the concept of realism has been defined and redefined during the twenties and since then is a development paralleling the history of the changing interests and conflicts of the party leadership. At this point, we shall concentrate on the details of a process in which a valid literary concept was turned into an empty extraliterary cliché.[53]

After the revolution, the problem of realism did not immediately become a central critical issue, though it turned up in the programs of certain literary groups. Revolutionization of the forms of literary expression and the spontaneously "proletarian" or "communist" character of the new art were popular demands. Lenin, and later Stalin, were preoccupied with the survival of Soviet Russia and did not attempt to control the literary scene rigorously. The result of free experimentation was the debut of several truly talented writers and poets, but also increasing political demagoguery on the part of certain literary cliques. Some form of centralization was certainly in the interest of party strategists; however, moderate aestheticians like Vorovsky or Lezhnev also welcomed it.

The first steps to control literature were taken on June 18, 1925, when the Central Committee of the Bolshevik Party issued its resolution "On Party Politics Concerning Imaginative Literature." This resolution emphasized the necessity of creating a new "socialist" literature. By the late twenties, one of the many literary groups, the doctrinaire and demagogic Russian Association of Proletarian Writers (whose acronym was RAPP), became a mouthpiece of officially supported aesthetic views. As such, the RAPP's literary monopoly reflected the progressive consolidation of Stalin's power. It exterminated virtually all other groups, prepared the ground for a centralized, controlled cultural life, and created a cultural sterility comparable only to the two decades between 1935 and 1955. Ultimately, its autocracy came into conflict with the party itself. The movement was officially dissolved in 1932 and the party placed all the blame for the impoverished cultural conditions on the RAPP.

By 1932, the party had the following heritage to build on: the single, centralized cultural leadership; the demand for a new, socialist character from contemporary Soviet literature; the "Five-Year Plan novels" (mostly documentary accounts of everyday industrial work—a subgenre which the RAPP encouraged); and finally, a claim for an "optimistic" outlook on life.

In two further respects, the RAPP did not fulfill the expectations of the party. There was a growing official demand to reinterpret the concept of socialist culture and incorporate earlier traditions, both Russian and Western. In addition, the "fellow-travellers" (noncommunist writers and artists of middle-class background who were willing to continue their activity in the Soviet system) received increasing social and official respect, yet the RAPPists failed to appreciate their contribution. Both trends were results of political and social consolidation and necessitated the acceptance of a more traditional view of literature.

The codification of a reinterpreted realism came at the First Soviet Writers' Congress in Moscow, in August 1934. This congress accepted and theorized about (though it never truly *defined*) the term "socialist realism," which had already been in use since 1932.[54] (An analogous term, "social realism," had appeared throughout the twenties.) The concept and its basic interpretation were later dutifully credited to Stalin.

At the congress of 1934, the two main proponents of socialist realism were Andrey Alexandrovich Zhdanov and Maxim Gorky. Gorky was a man of literature and should be regarded as such, in spite of his highly confused theoretical mind. In the following chapter, we shall compare him to Georg Lukács, a person worthier of comparison than Zhdanov. The latter was a career bureaucrat, a party functionary whose narrow-mindedness made him versatile enough to fulfill any position. His biographies indicate that he held a series of "odd jobs."

Zhdanov's contribution to the congress is significant, since his speech marked the beginning of an era when people without even the most elementary literary education could make decisions about literature and art. His congressional speech bore a modest title—"Soviet Literature: The Richest in Ideas, the Most Advanced Literature."[55] His ideas were full of ethnocentric clichés: the Soviet social system and Russian culture were superior to all the others, and socialist realism was the only correct view of life and literature. Since "realities" were decaying in the capitalist countries, the literature of these countries also appeared to Zhdanov as manifestation of this decay (p. 19). On the other hand, as a result of the enthusiasm, heroism, and optimism of the builders of socialism, the same characteristics appeared in socialist literature (p. 20). The utterly simplified nature of the Zhdanovist concept of literature is obvious. In his view literature reflects economic conditions and everyday life directly, without any transformation of the material, without any stylistic specificities whatsoever. Though Zhdanov emphasized the need for "high quality of artistic production," he thought that literary techniques may be borrowed from "previous epochs," that is, no new technique is necessary for socialist literature (p. 22). Zhdanov's list of the new heroes of literature is equally characteristic: workers, peasants, party cadres (p. 20).

What is socialist realism, then? Zhdanov characterizes it as a literature which describes the present but also points out the trends of the future, which provides objectivity as well as commitment, which is historical and actualizing at the same time. Above all, socialist realist literature is consciously tendentious (p. 21).

Besides Zhdanov, the man of the future, two vanishing stars of the party hierarchy, Bukharin and Radek, spoke at the congress. These two men, along with Trotsky, have usually been treated favorably by Western European scholars.[56] This is apparently because they were Stalin's rivals and victims. The truth is, however, that Bukharin's and Radek's contributions to the congress show nothing but a servile support of Zhdanovism. Radek made sympathy with the Soviet Union a prerequisite for classifying European writers as acceptable or nonacceptable (pp. 91–93). He called T. S. Eliot a fascist (p. 115), and labelled Joyce's *Ulysses* "a heap of dung, crawling with worms" (p. 153). Finally, he prophesized that socialist realism would create a greater culture than the Renaissance, as the latter "derived its models from slave-owning Greece and slave-owning Rome" (p. 161). Bukharin, for his part, retrospectively debunked the only influential, scholarly postrevolutionary critical movement which concentrated on stylistic aspects of the literary works, the Russian formalist critics (pp. 199ff). But this movement had been long dead in the Soviet Union by 1934.

The First Soviet Writer's Congress did not put an immediate end to genuine, individual artistic approaches to reality. At the congress itself, a renowned writer, Yury Olesha, warned the party delegates that demanding standard themes, such as workers or industrial construction, only forced writers to lie.

"It is difficult," he said, "for me to conceive the type of a worker, a revolutionary hero. Because I cannot be him. It is beyond my strength, beyond my understanding. And this is why I do not write about him."[57] As a whole, Olesha's apology for literary sincerity resembles Zola's passionate attack on Proudhon's short-sighted socialist-utilitarian view of art some fifty-five years earlier.[58]

Socialist realism as an ideology turned from "recommended" to "required" for Soviet writers after the Moscow trials of 1936–37, and the situation only worsened after World War II. The warning that the horrible wartime sacrifices of the Russian people would not make Stalinism forego its "vigilance" was delivered by Zhdanov in Leningrad at two meetings in 1946. By this time, Zhdanov was the chief literary expert of the Soviet Union; Stalin himself did not make any remarks whatsoever on concrete literary questions. In Leningrad, the two principal targets were Zoshchenko, a satirical writer who had once been quite popular, and Anna Akhmatova, a fine prerevolutionary lyricist. After a long period of silence, some of their works were again being published in Leningrad, and Zhdanov swooped down on these.[59]

Zhdanov's "critique" of these two writers does not deserve much discussion. His basic message was a series of further restrictions of the concept of socialist realism. Individual perception and reflection were to be excluded, as was satirical description of anything within the borders of the USSR. Literature was to become an organic part of the production process; consequently the writers were responsible for the quality of their "production" just as much as engineers or factory managers. Literature was no longer even a corrupted reflection of reality, but a didactic political tool. Its "great mission" was to bring up Soviet youth "in the spirit of cheerfulness, of confidence in their own powers," not in a defeatist pessimism. Chastity and modesty were desirable, since vulgar topics or language would have perverted the masses. The two reports, both full of chauvinistic clichés and personal accusations against Zoshchenko and Akhmatova, marked the low point of cultural decay under Zhdanov and Stalin.

After Zhdanov's death (almost certainly an unnatural one) in 1948, the literary situation did not change until Stalin published his article "Marxism and Linguistics" (1950), in which he declared that language was not a part of "superstructure" since it did not depend on economic changes.[60] This recognition is a commonplace one, yet it is also a correction of a mechanistic, insensitive view of language derived from Marx and Engels, who regarded language as a part of consciousness, hence part of the superstructure.[61]

However, Marx and Engels lived before Saussure and the modern linguistic revolution. One could hardly find such an excuse for Nikolay Marr, a Soviet linguist, who clung to the outdated Marxian definition of language and whose view Stalin rejected in his article. The idea that language does not "reflect" socioeconomic reality made some literary critics believe that if the medium is not a part of a mechanically predetermined superstructure, then neither is the message, the literary work. This view was heresy, of course, and even Georg Lukács participated in the witch hunt against it. In 1951, he separated language from message, and called the former only a resource, in the same sense that wood and marble are only raw materials for the artist. What the sculptor makes of wood or marble, and the poet of language, is socially determined.[62] This is not the place to analyze the (mostly personal) reasons for Lukács' surprisingly deterministic, insensitive, simplified view of poetic language. It is enough here to observe that, as his critique shows, any stylistic problems connected with the language were subsequently also excluded from a party-endorsed theory of realism.

After Stalin's death, artistic-literary practice and competent literary theory changed significantly, but during the Khrushchev era the party view of realism did not change. Khrushchev's statements about literature, collected in the volume *The Great Mission of Literature and Art,* show not only that he practiced aesthetic dilettantism but also that he used Marxism to justify his personal prejudices.[63] He believed that the Soviet reading public had a largely coherent literary taste; that this taste was unsophisticated and favored a socialist realist representatition of life; and that his own views happened to be identical with the views of the masses (p. 67). In addition to this, he seriously believed that this (i.e., *his*) view of literature would be adopted by the whole world (p. 135). For him, it was natural that ready comprehensibility was an aesthetic merit, just as much as didacticism (glorification of physical labor, p. 33), populism (p. 20), and biographical evidence of the author's support of the Soviet system (in wars, manual labor, etc.). Though he emphasized that "the method of socialist realism provides unlimited opportunities" (p. 33), he also carried unprincipled subjective ciriticism to an absurd limit. Precisely because there were no criteria set for a socialist realist creative *method,* theoretically any work of art could be excluded or included. And another paradox: though Khrushchev (unlike Zhdanov) emphasized that he was "neither a writer nor a literary critic" (p. 122), he too passed judgments freely about anything related to literature.

It would be a vain effort to summarize the most recent developments in the cultural policy of the different communist parties of the socialist countries. There are simply too many. However, the most significant change seems to be the disappearance of the party resolutions on different problems of literature and culture which once tried to clarify concepts like socialist realism or bourgeois decadence. Until Khrushchev was ousted, such resolutions were issued, sometimes considerably more often than once a year, in the USSR, the German Democratic Republic, and Hungary. This practice is fading away now.

The traditional view of Western European and American literary criticism, that the "official" party definition of socialist realism is a farce, is not far from the truth. Its characteristics (as Zhdanov, Bukharin, Radek, Khrushchev and the party decisions of the 1930–60 period state them) are banalities: identity of art and life, a "true" description of life in the spirit of party ideology with a foolproof optimistic outcome, personal "knowledge" of the phenomena described, "vivid imagery," active propagandistic function of the literary work, avoidance of vulgar language as well as esoteric subjectivism and primitivism, etc. While the "classics" of Marxism, as well as recent significant literary theoreticians, still use the term "realism" with qualifications and often sparingly, the "official" literature today still abounds with it.

The importance of the term for the political leadership rests precisely in its intentionally vague definition. Socialist realism has hardly ever been used officially for the benefit of literary scholarship and terminology. During the 1930s, party bureaucrats were already exploiting this concept to justify a planned economy, to reeducate the young, and to defend the ethnocentric cultural separation of the Soviet Union from the rest of contemporary Europe. Zhdanov's performance in Leningrad was not primarily directed against Zoshchenko and Akhmatova (they survived the attack, though their writings were no longer published) but against the cultural and party leadership of Leningrad, the number one target of Stalinism at the time. Also, Khrushchev's literary utterances were simply means to fight Stalinism on the one hand, and the increasing demand for liberalization on the other.

Yet the complete denunciation of the term and theory of socialist realism itself may be as fallacious a simplification of a significant literary concept as that of the party bureaucrats. The theory of a predictive, "curative,"historically oriented realistic tradition, as compared to a descriptive, "diagnostic," positivistic one, is a central problem of the European literary, artistic, and cultural tradition, but this problem has apparently not yet been analyzed on its merits. The habit of identifying socialist realism with the party definition only clearly demonstrates the survival of the spirit of cold war among Western literary scholars. Subsequent analyses of some sophisticated problems of literary realism are intended to do justice to a perverted, but potentially quite relevant and useful, literary term.

7. The Coherence of The Tradition

As we have seen, the term realism in classical Marxist-Leninist theory is as much an aesthetic projection of the theory of dialectical and historical materialism as naturalism was an extension of positivism into the artistic realm. The most general assumptions we can discover both in Marxist philosophical materialism and in the definition of realism are these:

—there is some order in the world;
—this order is in the main reliably manifested in the phenomena of the world;
—phenomena, for their part, are relatively completely, though indirectly, reflected in human consciousness in an orderly way;
—the whole process of knowing and reacting to reality is a dynamic one.

The question is: can this satisfy scholars of literature? Can one build a literary system, method, or terminology on a relatively few direct remarks on literature combined with a much more explicit but still very general outlook on life? In short, is there any homogeneity in the original Marxist literary theory (which, as we have pointed out, was not precisely "original," either)?

The answers differ. According to Ludz, Ljungdal, Steiner, Mayer, and Žmegač, the answer is no.[64] On the other hand, the Soviet scholar Mikhail Lifshits, whose views otherwise are often strikingly similar with those of Lukács, seems to affirm the homogeneity of the Marxist tradition quite unreservedly.[65] There are hesitant opinions too: Demetz's conclusion in the original German edition of his work on Marx's and Engels' literary views is a fairly definite no, while in the revised English edition he comes closer to a "yes" answer.[66] Finally, there is a set of cautious, balanced, dialectical views, the essence of which is that though the classics of Marxism-Leninism hardly established any homogeneous aesthetic tradition, their scattered remarks on literature form an adequate basis from which a Marxist aesthetic theory can develop. Among others, Lukács, Bente Hansen, and Leandro Konder share this view.[67]

Though the heritage of Marx and Engels does not yield to any definite aesthetic interpretation, the dialectical "golden middle way" of the third group of critics makes good sense. There is not much doubt that Marx's, Engels', and especially Lenin's literary views are unsatisfactory as the solid basis for a theory of art and literature. On the other hand, we should keep in mind that none of the major literary-artistic movements can be analyzed without reference to its connections with society and history. Neither classicism nor the baroque, nor romanticism, nor any other movement was ever simply literary. The relevance of applying Marx's and Engels' theses to literature is deniable only from one solid basis: if one consistently excludes anything "extrinsic" of the relevant approaches to literature.

If Marx's and Engels' literary views appear unsatisfactorily elaborated in their writings, could it have been otherwise? Would they have been capable of producing a coherent literary theory? Again, there are divergent answers. According to Demetz, they were not capable of this, since an economic theory is too narrow a basis on which to explain the complexity of life. As evidence Demetz cites the fragmentary *Einleitung zur Kritik der politischen Ökonomie* (1859), which ends exactly at the paragraph where Marx attempts to apply his political-economic ideas to literature.[68] On the other hand, Lafargue mentions in his memoirs that Marx had been planning to write a whole study about Balzac's *La Comédie humaine* and was prevented from realizing this project only by lack of time.[69] Among the contemporary scholars, Garaudy also hints that time, rather than ability, did not allow Marx and Engels to discuss literature more thoroughly.[70]

Others, like Fromm, remind us that even economic theory can indirectly serve the cause of art. According to Fromm, economic determinism as revealed by *Das Kapital* was the rigid force of a certain historical age against which Marx and Engels were fighting in order to reestablish the creative freedom of human spirit in its various spheres, among which were literature and the arts.[71]

As a conclusion, we might say that original Marxist theory is neither more nor less "ambiguous" than any other set of theories which generated large historical and cultural movements. Precisely because this theory is general and has very few direct references to literature, its interpretation may take different shapes. Neither the party theoreticians nor any particular literary critic or group can claim that theirs is the only true interpretation of Marx's, Engels', and Lenin's works. Though it has happened at times that certain cliques claimed this right of ultimate authority, the variety of socialist interpretations of literary realism shows that the constant, flexible reconsideration of theses and definitions is unavoidable.

II. Critical and Socialist Realism: Terminology and Models

1. Description, Prediction, Prescription

Though the criterion of literature as a description of what *is* and a prescription of what *ought to be* comes from as early a critic as Aristotle, the paradoxical character of this definition has ever since fascinated theorists of literature. True enough, the two functions are, at first sight, as different as they can be. "Is" means an analytical description of heroes and social circumstances which, though detached as they might be from a larger sociohistorical context, nevertheless exist in the persuasive immediacy of here and now. A definition of realism which adopts this "is"-perspective appears as relatively "objective," and consequently "free" from programs, utopias, or personal biases. "Ought to be," on the other hand, supposedly means an historical approach to things (not in the sense of Taine's positivistic historicism, but in that of the romantics and of Hegel), extending into all three dimensions of time, and not simply the present. Also, moralism, program (if not a vision of future), and subjectivity are inseparable from this criterion.

The dichotomy of a predominantly present-oriented and a basically future-oriented view of realism has produced an endless flow of speculative critical writings in both the East and the West. In the West, those scholars who did not throw out the concept of "realism" entirely, have traditionally preferred the descriptive, classical (or by Marxist terminology, "critical") realism to the more future-oriented ("socialist") variant of realism. Peter Demetz, for instance, discusses the prescriptive, "prophetic" tendency in European literature with considerable disapproval, implying that this tendency is due to romantic frenzy.[1] René Wellek, for his part, believes that "in theory, completely truthful representation of reality would exclude any kind of social purpose or propaganda. Obviously, the theoretical difficulty of realism, its contradictoriness, lies in this very point. . . . There is a tension between description and prescription, truth and instruction, which cannot be resolved logically." Of course, "socialist realism" is a term in which "the contradiction is confessed quite openly."[2] Also, at the 1968 congress of the International Comparative Literature Association in Belgrade, Harry Levin called "critical realism" a tautology and "social [sic] realism" a compound, an intellectual Bombay Duck (i.e., neither fish nor fowl) which, "in the long run, cannot prove acceptable to objective historians of literature."[3]

The rigid opposition of twentieth-century "socialist" realism to nineteenth-century "critical" realism has been a matter of politics, power struggle, and cultural biases. Consequently, it has been discussed neither on its merits nor in its complexity. Therefore, socialist realism appears as the ultimate method for convinced communists for whom a socialist world system is not a dream but a scientific premise. On the other hand, it appears as a contradiction to those who apply Cartesianism to the dimensions of time and find that, if you observe present conditions, you cannot describe a fancied future and call your description realistic.

Concerning the cultural roots of a future-oriented form of realism, we can distinguish between two theories. According to the first one, predictive socialist realism is a completely new phenomenon which came after the victory of the October revolution. Besides Zhdanov, Gorky, Radek, and Bukharin,[4] Wellek, and Levin also—though with disapproval—regarded socialist realism as something radically new. Their arguments are basically the same, no matter whether they support or deeply dislike the new, tendentious form of realism: without a communist system, no socialist realism would be possible, for better or worse.

Critics belonging to the other group maintain that socialist realism is an organic offshoot of an all-European intellectual development. Among these few critics are Georg Lukács, Demetz, Arvid Hansen, and Gunnar Gunnarson.[5] Also, recent studies and anthologies published in the socialist world try to break away from the earlier ethnocentric Gorkian-Stalinist definition of socialist realism and find precedents in the Western tradition.

Anybody who wishes to pass any judgment on the genesis of socialist realism faces two initial questions: Are there any traces of a prescriptive, propagandistic, social-activistic literary trend in the nineteenth- and twentieth-century Western European tradition? Are, as Wellek believes, description and prescription logically contradictory and practically exclusive of each other? The first question probes the novelty, the second the relevance, of a future-oriented, committed form of literary realism.

When discussing the first of these questions, it seems to be in order to recall Gorky's multifold definition of socialist realism. At the First Soviet Writers' Congress, Gorky summarized the features of socialist realism by the following four points:

Socialist realism is *programmatic* literature: unlike the earlier critical realism, it affirms something.

Collectivism appears in this literature as the main factor in shaping man: "socialist individuality can develop only in conditions of collective labour."

An *optimistic* outlook on life is provided: "Life is action, creativity," with "the great happiness of living on earth," as an ultimate aim.

The *educative* function, the developing of "socialist individuality," is a central aim of this literature.[6]

When considering the European literary heritage from these (according to Gorky, "qualitatively new") four points of view, any reader who is reasonably well acquainted with nineteenth- and twentieth-century literature might easily get the feeling of *déjà vu*. There is a set of reading experience which seems to challenge Gorky's (or for that matter also Wellek's) dichotomic theory of the "two realisms." After a second, more systematic, consideration, we find that each and every criterion of Gorky's "new" realism suffers from the social deterministic assumption that without a socialist order (in particular, without a party dictatorship, as Wellek puts it) a socialist representation of reality is incomprehensible in art.

On the other hand, the reader may object that long before Gorky wrote his *Mother* (acclaimed as the first socialist realist novel, published in 1906), several writers had already professed a committed, programmatic method of writing. An example of a writer on the border between romanticism and realism is George Sand, who wished she could witness the birth of a poetry of high artistic value depicting the life, hardships, and active self-assertion of the working people.[7] In the second half of the century, positivism and the scientific spirit did not put an end to this literary attitude, as the spontaneously socialistic sentiments expressed in Whitman's and Anatole France's numerous writings prove. The collectivistic program, Gorky's second assumption, also stems from prerevolutionary times. These years produced such ultra-committed poetry as Herwegh's renowned "Die Partei" (1842), and such mass-conscious critical ideas as those of the Chartist Ernest Jones. However, even nonsocialist poets like Baudelaire occasionally expressed their commitment to the oppressed classes in literary essays.[8]

The other two characteristics of the "new" realism also appear in one form or another in nineteenth-century poetry. The optimistic, creative, and reformistic function of literature was by no means a view alien to Sand, Whitman or France. Again, a figure almost incongruous with any political conception of reality, Charles Baudelaire, believed that poetry should not only describe but also improve the world.[9] Finally, the didactic function of literature, its role in the process of educating a new type of man, was echoed by William Morris: "It is the province of art," he writes, "to set the true ideal of a full and reasonable life before [the worker], a life to which the perception and creation of beauty . . . shall be felt to be as necessary as his daily bread. . . ."[10] We find essentially the same confession in Lev Tolstoy's *What Is Art?*

These are only a few examples drawn from different nineteenth-century writers to show that the ideas of commitment, education, and program were not entirely new in Western European and North American literature in pre-Bolshevik times. Furthermore, one could refer to writers with a more consistent social commitment, like the representatives of utopian socialism (Saint-Simon), the Eastern European revolutionary democrats, and, of course, the theoreticians of the Second International. The only aim of this short survey is to illustrate that a programmatic-predictive undercurrent is, indeed, as little alien to the Western tradition as is the idea of socialism itself.

Where does the demand of some "impassionate" attitude as a prerequisite of realism come from? Two famous documents of modern realistic literature, Balzac's introduction to *La Comédie humaine* (1842) and Zola's "La Roman expérimental" (1879), provide some clue. Even though both essays emphasize analogies between the creative process and scientific investigation, they indirectly point out something else, too: that no science can exist without interpretation and application. Georg Lukács might well have overestimated Balzac's realistic vein, but at the same time he certainly misinterpreted Zola, whom he accused of positivism, forgetting about Zola's programmatic statement: "we reveal the determinism working in human and social phenomena, *so that it be possible for us some time to dominate and control these phenomena.*"[11] In other words, literature only describing present conditions, and without connection to the future, does not exist. Today's knowledge will—indeed must—serve as a weapon to change tomorrow's world.

As long as no dimensions of time but the present serve as the basis for defining realism, even the thought of introducing any future perspective automatically raises two problems:

1. If it is true that realism means description of verifiably existing things, can one call any programmatic or predictive literature realistic?

2. If it proves true that there are no literary works without implications of, or references to, the future, can one accept the definition of realism as a description of verifiably existing things?

Which, then, is to be discarded: the future perspective or the concept of realism?

It is impossible to resolve the dichotomy of present and future within a metaphysical framework. Would it perhaps count as a biased Marxist suggestion if one were to turn to dialectical logic? Curiously enough, one could just as well turn to modern scientific theories and the philosophy of science. Both reflect the same dialectical solution that Hegelian-Marxist philosophy would advise.

Let us remain "at home" and review the opinion of two American "bourgeois" philosophers of science on this issue. A survivor of the logico-positivistic Vienna Circle between the two world wars, Herbert Feigl, states that prediction is as much an integral and inseparable part of pure science as retrodiction. According to Feigl, prediction is closely related to description and explanation, and as such belongs both to the function and to the definition of science.[12] A leading mathematician with a great interest in philosophy, John G. Kemeny, is another example. In *A Philosopher Looks At Science*, he dismisses the difference between seemingly "detached" explanation and openly committed prediction as a pseudoconflict. In either case, he says, "we have facts which we can start with, and from the theories and facts known to us, we deduce a certain new fact." Therefore, Kemeny speaks about a "logical identity of the process of prediction with the process of explanation."[13]

Aside from being the philosophical reflections of modern scientific discoveries and theories, these statements show the increasing awareness among scholars of science and letters that the present perspective can be (and must be) extended to the future and, in the social sphere, cannot be detached from a certain healing, corrective function. Neither Marx's economic nor Freud's psychoanalytical theory are results of some pure scientific curiosity alone; although *Das Kapital* and Freud's case descriptions are persuasively "scientific" in their objective and analytical character, both were devised to induce changes at the social and individual level. Also, in the interpretation of Wallace, Ward, and other humanistic scientists, Darwinism served as a weapon for a planned, socialized society. During the past hundred years, science seems to have had many fewer pretensions with regard to its future social function than certain theoreticians of literature.

As we have seen, in the late nineteenth and the twentieth century the Aristotelian "prophetic artist" got support from the sciences and occasionally tended to turn into a scientist himself. Therefore, predictions of writers and philosophers should appear in a light different from the one Anglo-American academic criticism, particularly, has thrown on them. At the same time, however, it is also true that the dichotomization mentioned by Wellek of description and prescription, without the consideration of the connecting link—prediction—was a major, undialectical blunder of Zhdanovist literary practice. Uncontrollable processes can be predicted but not prescribed. Processes in which human consciousness plays an active part, on the other hand, can be predicted and (theoretically) also controlled, that is, prescribed.

To illustrate the difference, we may quote the reminiscences of Marx's son-in-law, Paul Lafargue. He writes that Marx appreciated Balzac especially for creating "character types which still existed only in embryo form during the reign of Louis Philippe, and which only reached full development under Napoleon III, after Balzac's death."[14] It is fairly clear that Balzac did not *prescribe* these types—he did not say that their appearance was desirable or a result of any controlled process, but only that their coming could be *predicted* with some certainty. (Whether Balzac was conscious himself of being predictive, however, reaches beyond the problem his example illustrates.) But whereas Balzac was unable to prescribe the existence or nonexistence of a whole upcoming social *class* (namely, the monopolist bourgeoisie), it is hard to say what several other realists (like Dickens, Ibsen, or Tolstoy) were doing if not consciously prescribing certain social norms and attitudes to the *individual* in a persuasive number of their works.

The idea of the immediacy of global communism comes from a one-sided interpretation of the original Marxist heritage. This naive ideology, the source of a down-to-earth concept of socialist realism, deserves objective criticism—but not without reference to sophisticated interrelated issues.

The comparison of two leading theorists of the "two realisms," Lukács and Gorky, should serve well the purpose of illustrating the complexity of the concepts of both critical and socialist realism.

2. Two Models of Realism: The Theories of Lukács and Gorky

During recent decades, when communication theory has made revolutionary progress, it has become increasingly fashionable even among Marxists to talk about "models." *Das Kapital* has been interpreted as a model of production under capitalist conditions. Brecht used the concept of a model in his theater. Recently, Roger Garaudy applied the word "model" to designate the literary image as something neither merely reflecting a static external world, nor projecting the inner life of the soul onto blank paper, but as a plastic, operational copy of the interaction between these two (inner and outer) worlds.

The sense in which Brecht, Garaudy, and other artists or men of letters referred to the term is a "humanized" and somewhat obscured interpretation of model theory as used in communication. The following summary was compiled from a larger sample of works containing definitions or applications of the model. The intention was to explore the possibility of attaining a more accurate and more comprehensive definition of the term than the ones which have been utilized in the humanities and, more particularly, in literary theory. Also, I hope that the following description of the characteristics of the model will open up new channels of interaction between literary investigations and general communication theory.

1. Quantitatively ("structurally") defined, the model is a reproduction of a system in corresponding proportions.

2. Qualitatively ("functionally") defined, the model is a reproduced system which reacts to certain inputs (such as signals, information, or stimuli) in approximately the same way as the actual system would.

3. Models may have an experimental character, in which case they serve a research hypothesis.

4. There are no unique models, as the same reality can

be modeled in different ways, depending mostly on the research goals which the particular models serve, but also on the perception of their builders.

One may notice that general literary theory, as well as (more particularly) Hegelian aesthetics, shows numerous correspondences to the concept of the model. Object-subject balance, copying, reflection, and symbolizing are some of the functions which the model shares with aesthetics, as theorists of communication have already observed. Such concepts as type, parable, and allegory could also remind literary critics of other functions of the model.

In the conclusion of this book, we shall return to model theory for summing up the general Marxist views on literary realism. In this chapter, we shall analyze two theories which can be regarded as primary models of a Marxist concept of literary realism.

The first model is Georg Lukács' work, which may serve as the archetype of different definitions of critical realism. Lukács' theory of realism has increasingly interested scholars all over the world. Though in the USSR and the German Democratic Republic especially he is still considered a revisionist, he received a state funeral in his native Hungary in 1971, and his collected works are in the process of being published there.

The second model is Maxim Gorky's prominent view on socialist realism. Gorky's role in making socialist realism an ideal outlook and method for writers during the thirties has already been mentioned. Though less well known as a literary theorist outside the socialist countries, his credentials there are at least as good as Lukács'. Lenin patronized him and corresponded with him from the beginning of the century; and Lunacharsky, the first commissar of education and culture, said that in Gorky's writings the working class recognized itself for the first time in literature, as it had recognized itself earlier in the philosophical writings of Marx and Engels.[15] Soviet critics and writers still mention him with reverence, and Lukács himself wrote about Gorky with appreciation. Besides Lukács, other Central and Western European Marxist critics and writers, for example Brecht and Aragon, have also hailed Gorky.

Both the ideas of Lukács and those of Gorky are clear-cut enough to illustrate the similarities as well as the essential differences between the two definitions of realism. Moreover, whatever other attempts to reinterpret realism have emerged subsequently, they all are related either to Lukács' or to Gorky's model of realism.

Originally, Lukács had been under Kant's influence, or rather that of the Neo-Kantian philosophers he had learned from in Germany (Simmel in Berlin; Windelband, Rickert, and Weber in Heidelberg). He had already switched to Hegel before World War I, and became a Marxist during the conflict. After fairly extreme leftist activity during the twenties, Lukács seems to have arrived at a Hegelian synthesis of his dichotomic earlier periods, the "bourgeois" and the "ultra-Marxist," in the 1930s. In this decade, his attention turned more and more toward literature.

Beside this "synthesis" of two previous stages of his intellectual development, his significant critical and theoretical activity during the thirties also bears the marks of a continued strong Hegelian influence, which at times turns into ingenious epigonism. If one were to start applying Hegel's views liberally in evaluating Lukács' critical activity, one could credit him with little original work. Where Lukács does offer something truly new is, first of all, in his combination of Hegelian aestheticism with a historical materialist outlook; secondly, in his application of the Hegelian theses and method to modern literary phenomena. Besides, Lukács provides concrete analytical examples much more generously than Hegel. Finally, it was he who gave a permanent name to the balanced, complex literary-artistic Hegelian ideal by calling it *realism*.

Like Hegel, Lukács is anthropocentric in his definition of literature. Realism is, in the widest definition of the term we find in the German collection of Lukács' writings (*Werke*), the reflection of active humanism in art.[16] Also, realism is never a matter of technique; it is not one kind of style opposed to other kinds, but the expression of a certain personal world view. As such, it expresses a high degree of consciousness and a set of human experience on behalf of the writer (4:152–53). Also, literature generates consciousness, not only originates in it. (5:310).

The writer's experience takes shape in his work (4:156; 10:220). In Lukács' work, scores of examples underline the significance of the Hegelian idea of the "concrete universal." Should we summarize the characteristics of realism as defined by Lukács, we could list the re-creation of a concrete, vivid, tangible human situation in the first place. Lukács contrasts Tolstoy's death scenes with those of Maeterlinck in order to demonstrate how the immediate situations and reactions, the sociohistorical and moral interpretations of these scenes in the former, supersede the abstract, metaphysical, animal fear of perishing in the latter (4:283). Elsewhere, Lukács praises Romain Roland's *Jean Christophe* for its specific criticism of the imperialist-bourgeois way of life, and not life per se (4:440). For the same reason, Lukács disapproves of Ibsen's discussing marriage as such, instead of bourgeois marriage as Tolstoy did. In Maeterlinck, Ibsen, and others, Lukács believes he has discovered, instead of concrete realism, an abstracting tendency which ends up in fatalism, "dissolved in psychologism based on moods, never getting human" (4:76).

Lukács uses the idea of concreteness also for reconsidering literary history. For instance, Lukács refutes what he calls the Nazi interpretation of Büchner, namely that he was a writer of revolution, and consequently also the writer of the national socialist "revolution." Lukács argues that Büchner was the writer of one particular revolution: the French Revolution (7:249–72).

Next to concreteness, a second characteristic of realism is the "total" view of life. Totality is not a quantitative term (4:218); Lukács accuses the naturalists specifically for seeking the illusion of totality through endless details. The totality of "great realism" is "a polyphony of many components" (5:197). In other words, details are not self-justifying, but must contribute significantly to the overall picture. Lukács does not at all oppose an attractive, evenly flowing plot; on the contrary, a good plot is a prerequisite of realism, as it reflects life in its complex dynamism. The predominant descriptive style of naturalism and documentarism, on the other hand, suggests a static world, and as such is anti-realistic (see esp. "Erzählen oder Beschreiben?" 4:197–242). As a whole, the great writer should not concern himself with things and people, but with their development and interaction, since these are the real subject matters of literature (4:224,253; 5:205).

A third characteristic of realism is the concept of the typical. Everyday life is chaotic, and full of coincidences (4:199). It is up to the writer to distinguish the representative and significant experiences from the accidental ones and to reorganize their sequence (5:200). During the 1950s Lukács established the aesthetic category of the "specific" in order to give a theoretical justification to his already widely used, more practical (critical) concepts of the "type" and the "typical." The specific is neither a collection of incoherent empirical details from everyday life, nor a conceptual abstraction, but rather the reflection of the essential dynamism of a society in concrete persons, situations, and images. Put another way, the specific is a category observing both the particularity of an event, person, or thing, and whatever connects it to the general context of existence.[17] The specific also brings the national and historical peculiarities to the surface. For example, the milieu one finds in eighteenth-century English novels may be more bourgeois than that found in Tolstoy's works, yet the latter show more clearly the complex effects of capitalism on the individual (5:202).

The underlying logic of Lukács' whole literary theory is the Hegelian-Marxist dialectical logic. A dialectical synthesis of social existence and the individual's specific microcosm is Lukács' fourth characteristic of literary realism. Motivating this dynamic interaction is, as those familiar with Hegelian logic know, the abundance of conflicts implicit in and between persons and things (4:324). The character of conflicts and the tendency of their inner dynamism are knowable, and one of the realistic writer's main tasks is to reveal these, consciously or unconsciously, Lukács repeatedly criticized modern literature for betraying this task by substituting the reflection of irrational "moods" for the rational analytical process (4:76–77, 80; 5:359).

We shall discuss below the honest objectivity of the realist writer, which may antagonize his subjective, and eventually erroneous, political views. Here, we shall mention only the problem of commitment as a fifth characteristic of realism in Lukács' definition. The writer is committed only to himself, to his objective judgment of perceived reality, his humanism, and his capacity to reflect his experiences in a dialectical way. The great modern artist is one "swimming against the current" of bourgeois reality (5:209). Lukács detects signs of the protest against tedious, impotent bourgeois reality as early as Defoe's *Robinson Crusoe*, in which the writer makes his hero develop his human capacities far from the capitalist realities of his time (5:210). One may ask, however, whether Lukács is choosing here an example too far removed in still fairly prebourgeois times to be relevant. Later instances, such as his analysis of late-nineteenth-century literature and writers, or his essays on Thomas Mann (4:441–42; 7:499–617), support his argument more convincingly.

Realism, then, is neither a matter of technique or style nor a feeling of life; it is a specific, and the best, way of organizing and reflecting material as well as subjective-psychological reality. As Lukács puts it, "realism is not style, but the collective basis of any great literature" (5:27). This is ultimately a subjective value judgment: it leaves the door open for any writer the critic likes, and closed for those who, for one reason or another, do not win his sympathy. Indeed, Lukács is willing to go quite far in rationalizing his approval of some of his favorite writers as realists. In his idol, Balzac, he willingly accepts the irrational element of *La Peau de chagrin* by providing the argument that "Balzac used the romantic element . . . only in order to point out essential human and social relationships" (6:519; see also 10:222–23). In Balzac and other favorites, naturally, the "romantic ingredients" of the "somber, gruesome and fantastic" indirectly serve the realistic depiction of life (6:485, 502). Among the German writers, he exonerates Eichendorff by calling his writings examples of a fairy-tale-like, idyllic realism (7:232–48).

Furthermore, Lukács attempted to prove the applicability of realism, seemingly best fitted to the description of directly experienced contemporary events, to history (*Der historische Roman*, 1955). He also studied the theory of satire and allowed realistic writers employing this style more freedom to use fantasy, to rearrange events, or to employ other technical devices (4:83–107).

In other instances, however, Lukács treats realism as a literary period. As in his definition of realism as ideology, Lukács makes amazing concessions to his conception of realism as a literary period. For instance, he draws a clear dividing line between, on the one hand, romanticism and, on the other, realism. Lukács defines romanticism as the artistic reflection of the Holy Alliance, and as such a thoroughly reactionary movement. It is classicism, not romanticism, that paved the way for the French Revolution and those of 1848–49 (6:24–26). He deprives preromanticism of its distinct characteristics; Rousseau's ideas on human feelings and civilization signify a new stage of the Enlightenment, not a new movement (7:53–56). Also, historicism is a product of the Enlightenment and appears only in an abortive, reactionary form during romanticism (7:49).

In order to claim for realism the greatest poets and writers of the late eighteenth and early nineteenth centuries, Lukács establishes an intermediary link between the Enlightenment and realism by borrowing the term *Kunstperiode* (in somewhat free translation "aesthetic period") from Heine. This special form of postclassicism, or if you wish prerealism, makes it possible for Lukács to regard Goethe and Hölderlin, Walter Scott, Byron, Shelley, and Keats, Pushkin, and even E. T. A. Hoffman as early realists.

There is only one statement in Lukács' work which says that directly or indirectly, all great writers were exposed to some extent to romantic influence after the French Revolution (6:492–93).[18] It is true, however, that there, too, Lukács proved to be a convinced follower of Marx; he showed a considerable degree of dislike for romanticism and eventually regarded only Chateaubriand and Vigny as typical representatives of this movement. The only way to look at this extremely insensitive view of romanticism is by interpreting it as a desperate reaction to the party-endorsed Soviet artistic optimism, sometimes also called "revolutionary romanticism," which was obligatory for socialist writers and critics during the 1930s and 1940s.

Who represented realism at its best in Lukács' view? In his essay "On Socialist Realism," he provides the following list of his ideals: "Homer and Sophocles, Dante and Rabelais, Cervantes and Shakespeare, Goethe and E. T. A. Hoffmann, Pushkin and Balzac, Tolstoy and Gorky." Elsewhere, he adds the names of Swift, Defoe, Fielding, Voltaire, Diderot, Sterne, Stendhal, Keller, Scott, Thackeray, and Gogol. He does not sympathize, however, with Schiller, Victor Hugo, the Goncourts, Flaubert, Zola, Maupassant, and Mark Twain. While in the 1930s he radically changed his earlier positive view of the great Scandinavian realists (Ibsen, Strindberg, Jacobsen) to a much less favorable one, he constantly mentioned some other, potentially "realistic," writers (like Hemingway) with indifference.

The interpretation of modern realism is a problem which deserves particular attention in Lukács. For Hegel, art and literature were a means for the absolute spirit to attain a higher degree of self-consciousness. Within Hegel's system, however, their time was over with Goethe and his *Kunstperiode*. Heine later challenged this view by saying that Goethe did not mark the end of an old period but the beginning of a new one. Similarly, Belinsky thought that an old period of Russian literature ended with Pushkin and a new one started with Gogol (5:107; 10:129–32). Marx and Engels apparently extended the idea of some "great old literature" to Balzac.

Lukács establishes the link between the old "great realism" and "new realism" especially in two works, "Erzählen oder beschreiben?" (1936), and "Die Gegenwartsbedeutung des kritischen Realismus" (1957). The period of "great realism" in Western Europe comprises the six decades between the French Revolution and the revolution of June 1848 (4:165). Though the belated appearance of the bourgeoisie in Russia and Scandinavia made it possible for Tolstoy, Ibsen, and other writers there to create great realistic works in the second half of the nineteenth century (5:180–90), as a whole realism suffered a setback with the dawn of imperialism, and disintegrated either into subjectivism ("avant-gardism") or objectivism (positivism). (*Ibid.;* also 4:429).

During the 1930s, Lukács tended to represent realism as something which had passed away forever by the turn of the century. There are several other writings, however, in which Lukács does not bury realism but revives it. His essays on Thomas Mann are one example. Then, after Stalin's death, he started consistently referring to the revivals of realism in the twentieth century. In his "Die Gegenwartsbedeutung des kritischen Realismus," he says that during World War I and after, great realism returned in the writings of Thomas and Heinrich Mann, Stefan Zweig, Romain Rolland, DuGard, Galsworthy, Shaw, the late writings of Anatole France, and of course, Gorky and Sholokhov (4:465–66; indications of the theory occur in earlier works (e.g. 5:273). It was Tolstoy who preserved the tradition of the great realists and passed it on to the new generation (5:180, 259–60).

Realism is alive and well, says Lukács. But the question is, which kind of realism? This is the issue which made him, against his will, an antagonist of the dominating Zhdanovist trend in the party view of literature.

Of the four characteristics of socialist realism as defined by Gorky (program, collectivism, optimism, and didacticism), the first two, on which Lukács held an opinion adverse to Gorky's, will be discussed later. Lukács' view on optimism and didacticism as assumed characteristics of (socialist) realism should be discussed here.

In the thirties and forties, Lukács reluctantly yielded to the idea that communism puts an end to deep personal conflicts, or a tragic sense of life. In 1951, exposed to constant party attacks, he distinguished between the world-embellishing "happy end" of bourgeois bestsellers and socialist optimism, which is based on "the correct reflection of a great process of world significance" (5:494–96). But five years later, he was expressing a completely different view: "Happy ending is an optimistic ending which has no strength of persuasion and no evidence which would organically grow out of the nature and character of the situation" (4:654). Moreover, he added that this had been a regrettable characteristic of recent socialist realist practice. In spite of his unique apology for at least one kind of optimism, a series of veiled sceptical remarks on this issue dominates his writings even before Stalin's death. By 1940 he had already criticized the conflictless, ahistorical, metaphysical outlook of "bureaucratic aesthetics" (4:453).

The protest against didacticism particularly is not explicit in Lukács' works. On the other hand, if one considers his numerous scattered comments on socialist realism, he appears to be quite an outspoken critic of the literary dogmas of the party. In addition to his protest against the minimal importance granted to the hero and human consciousness in the so-called socialist realist literature, he criticized the tendency to simplify and stereotype the plot, and to change "the theme for fable" (4:236). Lukács' view of tendency in literature is more evidence of his dislike of using literature to advocate some "ultimate truths."

Lukács' observations on the future perspective in literature show a deep insight into the problem of prediction. He accepts the possibility of prediction, but protests against its being confused with prescription (10:222–26), as this latter deprives the work of the impact of consciousness and changes the scientific perspective to a utopian or fatalistic one (4:651). Besides, socialist realism is not a literature of prophecy, and cannot prescribe holy norms (5:385). Lukács warns against complacency and the loss of aesthetic values in favor of political and other merits. He cannot find excuses for bad socialist literature (4:13–18, 20), and he never accepts the Gorkian-Zhdanovist interpretation of socialist realism as something superior to realism (4:462). For him, socialist realism is primarily realism.[19] Future perspective is not a distinct characteristic of socialist realism, since any realism shows "the existing but still hidden tendencies of objective reality" (4:332). In Les Illusions perdues, argues Lukács, Balzac predictively depicted a type of poet still rare in his period, but char-

acteristic of the decades from Verlaine to Rilke (6:477). Therefore, any attempt to separate old and new Russian literature
(and this is precisely what Gorky tried to do) is only a manipulation of "reactionary criticism"—whatever this term means
(5:9).

It is true that in 1951 Lukács was compelled to withdraw
his view of 1946 that the works of Gorky and Sholokhov are
but continuations of the great Tolstoyean realistic tradition
(5:10–12, 17–19). Still, his extremely noncommittal attitude to
socialist realism (for which all his party critics reproached him)
shows his general disbelief in any truly qualitative difference
between critical and socialist realism. At the same time,
though he regarded socialist realism only as a new phase of
realism, he never discarded it or denied the aesthetic value of
its best products (5:552).

If, for whatever reason, one insists on taking a critical attitude toward Lukács, one would find it difficult to single out all
of the major inconsistencies in Lukács' controversial work.
For us, the contradiction between his aesthetic and historical
definitions of realism is probably the most immediate one.
Realism is, as we quoted, "the basis of any great literature."
In other instances, however, Lukács defines realism as a
bourgeois movement, whose typical genre is prose (10:137).
He thereby should automatically exclude, for instance, Homer
or Dante (who were poets) and Gorky (who was not a
bourgeois) from his own list of great realists. Thus, he never
really answers the question of whether realism is an aesthetic
value category or an historical concept.

Even so, Lukács' work is one which, despite inconsistencies, fallacies, and occasionally formidable misinterpretations,
evinces some form of respect in most of its readers. One
main reason for this respect is the admirable scope and size
of this work, and the variety of particular observations and
statements which make the somewhat repetitive general aesthetic theory enjoyable.

Maxim Gorky's artistic view constitutes only a fraction of Lukács' and is much less varied. Still, his ideas on realism are almost polemic answers to Lukács.

In their lives and in the general development of their ideas, we find a peculiar parallel of contrasts between these two men. Lukács developed from a rich bourgeois milieu to committed Marxism, while Gorky's life is an emergence from semi-rural Russian poverty to world-wide literary and political fame. Lukács' works move from Kantian idealism to Hegelianism and Marxism, while Gorky arrives at his theory of socialist realism from spontaneously romantic early writings and from an anarchistic view of realism as such. In 1900, he wrote to Chekhov (the letter was later reprinted in *On Literature*): "so I say that you will [do] away with realism. I'm teribly pleased, for it's time that it went. To hell with it! . . . Indeed, the time has arrived when the heroic is needed. . . ."[20] Later apologists may find this a burial of *bourgeois* realism and not realism as such, but certainly Gorky made no such distinction at the time.

Lukács studied in Germany under the most celebrated thinkers of the early twentieth century; Gorky was a self-educated man. In his reminiscence "How I Studied?" (1918: pp. 9–22), Gorky gives a moving and impressive account of how he, as a poor apprentice, borrowed books or bought them for a few kopeks, and read them in the most incongruous places in his scant free time. In this manner, he accumulated a large amount of reading experience which remained, however, uninterpreted, subjective, and impressionistic. In his youth, and also later in his life, Gorky looked at books through the eyes of a self-made, self-educated reader and writer. Unlike Lukács, he was not a scholar with a systematic education.

A realistic portrayal of life in its concreteness is just as much a matter of active humanism for Gorky as it is for Lukács. Owing to their backgrounds, however, they define the term humanism differently. In Gorky's case, physical work was a prerequisite for satisfying his thirst for culture, partly because he earned money to buy books, partly because, as he believed, he learned a great deal about the world by interacting with a great number of people. Gorky defines the learning process as an experience one gains from both intellectual *and* physical activity, since both activities are parts of a general cognitive human interaction with the world and with society. Hence, the great importance he attached to the dignity of human work as such, and to manual labor in particular.

His didactic zeal not infrequently took Gorky to extremes. He appreciated work so much that he did not want to acknowledge great qualitative differences—not to mention the finer nuances—between different modes of human activity. This is why he wanted to prove that great artists and scientists were also only "ordinary working men." Shakespeare and Molière, for instance, were "ordinary actors" (pp. 46–47, 265–66). This populistic idea, which maintains that crafts or skills and artistic or scientific genius are basically the same, is not unfamiliar to nineteenth-century socialist thought. In Western Europe, however, it gradually disappeared during the twentieth century and influenced only leftist writers affiliated with the extremist postrevolutionary Proletkult ideology. Gorky's view of the writer-worker is certainly in sharp contrast to Lukács' view, which conceives of writing as a complicated, unique, creative act ending in a heightened awareness of writer and reader. In Gorky's work ethic, on the other hand, there is no place for any distinction between production and creation (p. 254). He himself gave a series of speeches on what he called literary *craftsmanship* (1930–31; pp. 138–213). To summarize this issue, we may say that Gorky thought literary skill could be learned as readily as any manual one, and that apprenticeship and a "school of life" was as much of a necessity for the shoemaker as for the writer.

The second characteristic of Lukács' realism-concept, its

representation of life as a dynamic totality, is, in Gorky's theory, a characteristic of socialist realism alone. He finds it convenient to refer to Engels' statement that "life is consistent and continuous movement and change" as a basic definition of socialist realism (pp. 394–95). However, in the letter to A. S. Shcherbakov, where he makes this reference, he forgets to mention Engels' critical view of the revealed, direct, sheer tendentiousness in literature. As a whole, Gorky regarded the totality of the literary reflection as an issue far less significant than Lukács thought. He called heroes, but not human situations, "typical." Furthermore, Gorky conceived of conflict only as class struggle, never as an inner structural tension with aesthetic or psychological value. The lack of these categories does not so much show the irrelevance of comparing Lukács and Gorky as the great difference between their original terminologies of critical and socialist realism.

A central element of realism, according to Gorky, is commitment, which Lukács considered the least important one. Learning, achieved through work as well as through books, can only result in a growing emotional response. Literature, in addition to developing a social commitment, should generate moral commitment in people. Literature should free man not only from false ideology or superstition, but also from moral vices such as "greed, envy, sloth and aversion for labour" (p. 28).

In Gorky, there is no end to the sentimental-pathetic preachings on the values and beauties of labor, and the willingness to work is also a basic criterion of categorizing the hero. The "good guys" of the socialist realist fiction work, the "bad guys" don't. In the Western world, it is customary to talk about the Protestant work ethic. Gorky offered something similar to the Soviet people, especially in his later years. The comments of the refugee Trotsky on Gorky reflect a sarcastic understanding of this ambition of the ailing writer: "[In] the last period of his life . . . his tendency to didacticism received . . . its great opportunity. He became the tireless teacher of young writers, even schoolboys. He did not always teach the right thing to do but he did it with sincere insistence and open generosity that more than made up for his too inclusive friendship with the bureaucracy."[21]

Clearly, Gorky here followed in the footsteps of the Russian revolutionary democrats, with their didactic zeal so remote from any path Lukács took. Owing to his Western European orientation, Lukács no longer considered any prophet-role possible for the modern writer. Not so Gorky, who, like Belinsky and his generation, did his best to preserve the traditional high status of the literati in Russian society (On Literature, pp. 252–53).

Lukács and Gorky are equally far apart in their view of two further issues: the questions of tradition and of romanticism. Gorky's views on literature of the past show a remarkable development. Until about 1930, a sensitivity to talent characterizes his literary statements. Like the early Lukács, he is not preoccupied with evaluative pigeonholing. He likes Flaubert for expressing the tragedy of human existence, and Hamsun who "amazes me in the same way as the Odyssey does" (p. 25). But Edmond Goncourt and Victor Hugo, these "true children of France," also win his appreciation.[22]

During this period, however, a deterministic view of modern European culture began to appear in Gorky's works, and this view in an extreme form dominates his statements during the 1930s. As early as 1909, he tried to establish a connection between the decay of the bourgeoisie owing to historical necessity, and the physical degeneration of its members owing to natural necessity (pp. 90, 98). His novel The Artamonovs (1925) is a product of the same social Darwinist determinism as Thomas Mann's Buddenbrooks; both novels depict the physical and historical degeneration of a merchant family. Finally, the 1930s were the time of Gorky's complete negation of Western culture (pp. 200ff., 395–96). In his congressional speech, he plainly declared that the role of the bourgeoisie in the process of cultural development had been "greatly exaggerated," and that the only culture this class had ever established was a material one (pp. 233, 251). This is a blatantly anti-Marxist notion. Both Marx and Engels made scores of appreciative comments on different periods and representatives of post-Renaissance bourgeois art and literature. To demonstrate what he felt was a decline in literature of ideas and characters in favor of verbal ornaments and details, Gorky contrasted Shakespeare, Pushkin, Tolstoy, and Flaubert with Proust, Joyce, Dos Passos, and Hemingway.[23] What Shakespeare and Flaubert were, however, if not bourgeois, is hard to tell. At any rate, for Gorky (unlike Lukács), *their* view of the world ceased to exist in the twentieth century. For a truly modern artist, the only way to look at life is through the eyes of Gorky's socialist realism.

We have already quoted the four characteristics of socialist realism that Gorky enumerated. Comparing him with Lukács, we may say that while Lukács' whole critical activity shows a constant struggle against what he considered different forms of irrationalism or antirealism, Gorky gradually switched from denouncing modern literature to criticizing earlier realism. While for Lukács socialist realism is primarily *realism,* for Gorky it is primarily *socialist,* in contrast to earlier "critical realism" (which corresponds to Lukács' "great" or "bourgeois" realism). In Gorky's view, "the realism of bourgeois literature is critical but only inasmuch as criticism is needed for class 'strategy,' to show up the bourgeoisie's errors in the struggle to render their rule stable. Socialist realism is directed towards a struggle against survivals of the 'old world' and its pernicious influences and towards eradication of these influences" (*On Literature,* p. 395; see also p. 264). That is, critical realism is apologetic and reformist, while socialist realism is revelatory and radical realism with reference to the bourgeois world.

Gorky apparently took this theory so seriously that he became an apologist himself for the low artistic quality of whatever might have been called "new" or "socialist" literature in his time, and according to his definition. In 1930, he found as an excuse for the lack of socialist masterpieces the fact that Soviet literature was still a young literature.[24] This kind of apology for the absence of aesthetic qualities, with constant emphasis on the presence of the ideological "correctness" of the work, fits well into a major trend of Soviet literary criticism, which had originated before the thirties. Alexey Tolstoy, for instance, stated in 1924 that the new realist need not be afraid of providing "clumsy, lengthy descriptions and tiresome characterizations"; his work still may become a superb one by virtue of its socialistic ideological content.[25] As late as in 1956, Khrushchev boasted about the anemia of Soviet literature. After all, he said, Soviet reality was "immeasurably richer than its reflection in art and literature" could ever be.[26]

Gorky's theory of socialist realism supplied one element for which there was no room in Lukács' pretentiously rationalistic system. This element is his attempt to synthesize the previous romantic and realistic tendencies of world literature in socialist realism.[27] In 1928, Gorky made a distinction between a "passive" and an "active" trend in romanticism. The passive trend wanted "to reconcile man with his life by embellishing that life," or to distract him from life by "barren introspection into his inner world." The active trend, on the other hand, "strives to strengthen man's will to live and raise him up against the life around him, against any yoke it would impose" (pp. 32–33). Later, Gorky wove these characteristics of constructive romantic literature into his theory of socialist realism. Not only the thesis of the freedom of the new man and his art, or the appreciation of activism and passions, but also trends like a new regionalism (pp. 258–60)[28] and a pronounced cultural nationalism (pp. 264–65) betray the romantic undercurrent in Gorky's realism-theory. Romanticism and realism, however, did not become synonymous, as Harry Levin believes.[29] Gorky did not even use the term "revolutionary romanticism" (which later became a fairly empty aesthetic slogan) in his congressional speech. He regarded the romantic element not as a synonym, but as a characteristic of socialist realism.

Georg Lukács, however, proudly stated in 1957 that he had never in his life accepted the false idea of romanticism mixed with realism, and had never used the term "revolutionary romanticism" (*Werke* 4:459; 5:553). In fact, his rigid separation of the two concepts is a result of his somewhat naive acceptance of Marx's personal dislike of romanticism. However, in his book *Der entfremdete Mensch*, Heinrich Popitz points out several similarities between the romantic and the Marxist view of man.[30] Also, in his renowned "What Is To Be Done?" (1901–1902), V. I. Lenin, quoting Pisarev on dreams that predict the future "natural march of events" rather than escaping from reality, exclaimed: "We should dream!"[31]

In the same way that Gorky divided realism as a method and movement into bourgeois and socialist realism, he distinguished between bourgeois and socialist romanticism. While the former gradually lost the logic of prediction and took an escapistic turn all the way from Novalis to Céline, the latter is destined to enrich socialist realism. "Myth is an innovation," Gorky wrote. "But if to the idea extracted from the given reality we add—completing the idea, by the logic of hypothesis— the desired, the possible, . . . we obtain the romanticism which is at the basis of the myth and is highly beneficial in that it tends to provoke a revolutionary attitude to reality, an attitude that changes the world in a practical way" (*On Literature*, pp. 244–45).

However great the element of propaganda is in Gorky's arguments for romanticism, his flexible view of this issue is closer to a desirably differentiated way of looking at literary movements than is Lukács' dualism. Instead of claiming all great writers for classicism and realism, as Lukács did in a questionable manner, Gorky recognized that

> it is hard to say with sufficient precision whether such classics as Balzac, Turgenev, Tolstoi, Gogol, Leskov, or Chekhov were romanticists or realists, for in great artists realism and romanticism seem to have blended. Balzac was a realist, but he also wrote novels such as *La Peau de chagrin,* a story that is far removed from realism. Turgenev also wrote in a romantic vein. . . . This fusion of romanticism and realism is highly characteristic of our great writers, imbuing their works with an originality and a forcefulness that has exerted an ever mounting and telling influence on the literature of the entire world. (p. 33)

3. The Hero: Unique Being, Demi-God, or Tool of Production?

We have already mentioned the distinguished place of the hero in Hegelian-Marxist aesthetics. It is the hero who embodies the idea the author wants to represent.

There are sporadic references to problems of characterization in Marx's and Engels' works. We may recall how much emphasis they put on the vivid, multidimensioned character of the hero when contrasting Shakespeare with the Schillerian dramatic tradition. Their remarks about the embellished, "ideal" hero (as opposed to the typical hero in other instances) were hardly flattering. While Engels, in particular, ridiculed the self-satisfied Tell-cult of the Swiss,[32] neither he nor Marx approved the idealized depiction of radical and socialist leaders. They were expecting not idealizing and glorifying but "harsh Rembrandtian" literary representations of the outstanding progressive heroes of history.[33] The distinctly characterized and independent hero plays a much more important part in Marx's and Engels' literary view than in their theory of history. Historical materialism states that great historical changes were brought forth not by great men, but by economic necessities and mass movements. However, mythological and literary heroes (for example, Prometheus, Don Quixote, or Faust) were extremely important for Marx and Engels. They regarded real historical heroes as but executors of historical necessities, while they appreciated fictive heroes for their revolt against those very necessities.

Some of Lenin's remarks on literature show the importance that he also attached to characterization. In his critique of the Ukrainian Vinnichenko's novel, *Paternal Testaments*, he disapprovingly mentions the extreme features of the characters the writer created.[34] In 1919 he repeatedly praised Barbusse's *Clarté*, and even more so his *Le Feu*, in which the author describes "with extraordinary power, talent and truthfulness . . . the transformation of an absolutely ignorant rank-and-filer, utterly crusted by philistine ideas and prejudices, into a revolutionary under the influence of the war."[35] Although this particular literary statement strikes one as both casual and dilettantish, it is obvious that Lenin appreciated the "developing heroes" (to use a Hegelian terminology) in literature, perhaps because they lent corroboration to his attempt to convert hundreds of millions to his own ideology.

It is striking how well one can apply most of the criteria of realism, as established by Lukács and Gorky, to characterization. Both critics argue that the realistic feature of any literary work is made up by two interrelated sets of criteria: structural-aesthetic and character-shaping. Taking first the concrete, active feature of realism, we find that Lukács regards this vivid concreteness as much a characteristic of the outstanding realistic hero as of the whole work. From Plato through Diderot to Balzac, literary heroes can be classified according to their reactions to other persons, to concrete situations, or to more abstract problems of life (*Werke*, 4:151–53). In the concrete human response to abstract problems, the former always dominates over the latter in the realistic tradition. In "Die intellektuelle Physiognomie des künstleris-chen Gestaltens" (1936), Lukács criticizes Gide for seeing a general and eternal conflict in the struggle of father and son in Racine's *Mithridate*. He contrasts this "purely rhetorical achievement" of Racine to what he calls the "intellectual physiognomy," the re-created complex psyche of Shake-speare's and Goethe's heroes (4:153–54).

Thus, the representation of the hero has several dimen-sions in realism. It also has a totality which reaches beyond the individual and constitutes the social spectrum of his times (6:479–80). The hero functions as a Hegelian microcosm, or more precisely as a focus, mediating in his concreteness the real conflicts of his age, revealing these beyond the merely phenomenal material values ("fetishism") and pseudo-conflicts ("mystification") of class-societies (4:275).

To illustrate how supposedly "eternal" human feelings appear in concrete form in great literature and how they refer to sociohistorical conditions, Lukács repeatedly analyzed various aspects of love in the realist tradition. In Gogol's *Taras Bulba*, the Cossack Andry's love for the Polish aristocratic girl is not merely a matter of passion, nor even of betrayed na-tional solidarity, but an indication of the vulnerability, the decadence of the hermetic Cossack society which cannot withstand the attraction of a higher and larger culture (5:73). Similarly, the passionate love of Grigory and Axinya, the main heroes of Sholokhov's "Don Tetralogy" is but a projection of the disintegrating self-sufficiency of the Cossack village sys-tem. This peculiarly decadent form of human emotions is con-trasted by another, supraregional and constructive love: that of Bunchuk and Anna (5:390). Lukács' argument is obviously based on Bunchuk's being a communist worker of Cossack origin, and Anna a Jewish socialist college student. Unlike Grigory and Axinya, therefore, both have broken out of their own enclosed social and family background.

These instances of characterization, these focal points at

which coincidental and/or individual human tendencies cross historical and social necessities, make "types" of the heroes. We may recall that Engels defined realism as the representation of typical heroes among typical circumstances. One encounters this emphasis on the "typical" in Marxist criticism so often that one tends to forget the rich "prehistory" (pre-Marxist history, that is) of the concept. Bernhard Küppers, a German scholar, traces this history all the way back to the Greeks in his published doctoral dissertation. He also provides a semantic survey of the development of the term. For us, it is probably significant that in the Platonic tradition, as Küppers points out, the word *typus* had the connotation of "idea"— *eidos*, meaning "model" as well as "copy."[36]

Georg Lukács uses Engels' somewhat commonplace definition of realism as the basis for his concept of the "typical" character, but, as usual, he specifies and extensively develops his initial remarks. "In the representation of the type, in typical art, the concrete and the necessary, the eternal human and the historically determined, the individual and the social, general elements mingle together" (10:221). "Type" is, therefore, a central category of artistic synthesis, and corresponds to the structural and aesthetic category of the "specific" in the sphere of characterization. It should become neither an abstraction (as in the Greek tragedies), nor an idealization (as in Schiller), nor an embodiment of "the average" (as in Zola), but a dynamic, dialectical synthesis of the major social, moral and intellectual-spiritual conflicts of an age (*ibid.*). The essence of this latter argument is probably that typification should not come "from above," deductively from a preconceived idea of the artist, but from the creative process. Moreover, creating types is possible only by constantly relating the hero to other heroes. Hamlet becomes "typical" only if one contrasts his relationship to Laertes, Horatio, or Fortinbras. He could never achieve this general significance alone, detached from human realities and relations (4:161).

Lukács constantly emphasized, openly or in disguised

form, that the literary hero must not necessarily be a vehicle of direct political or social ideas (e.g., 4:276ff.). As for
a moral commitment, this is something which Lukács demands not from the hero but rather from the author. Creative
consciousness does not necessarily give birth to figures of
whom it completely approves or disapproves. The author
usually has a critical yet understanding attitude toward his
heroes. In this relationship between author and created hero,
the proportions of criticism and understanding vary from
writer to writer, and from work to work. Pushkin, for instance, was more critical toward his blasé heroes (Aleko, Onegin) than was Byron (5:55).

The creative artistic consciousness thus has the leading
role in shaping literary characters. Characterization is not a
matter of skill ("technique"), but of a creative attitude toward
life. This does not mean, however, that Lukács did not provide any systematic typology of characters. In an essay on
Sholokhov, he discusses patterns of characterization in the
Homeric epic, in the critical realist tradition, and in the socialist realist novels of Sholokhov and Fadeyev. The basis of this
typology is the hero's relationship with society—that is, individual consciousness compared with social consciousness.

Lukács finds a static distance between the hero and the
"others" in the heroic epic. In the bourgeois novel, the fate
of the hero coincides with the problems and development of
society. In Sholokhov's "Don Tetralogy," Grigory Melikhov
starts out as a rebel, and his character is more interesting than that of the others. After the revolution, however, his
inability to make choices slowly disintegrates him, while the
consciousness of the Cossack community moves upward in a
slow, progressive development. Finally, in Fadeyev's *Nine-
teen*, the consciousness of the communist hero attracts and
gradually elevates the consciousness of other members of the
partisan group. Lukács calls this latter pattern the "novel of
example" and emphasizes that this is but one of the many

methods of characterization for socialist realism (5:384–87). Later this didactic method became the only officially acceptable way of characterization, for which Lukács himself criticized socialist realism in 1964 (5:553–54).

Though the creative consciousness of the realist writer is of cardinal significance, the level of consciousness of the created heroes is likewise important. Hamlet and King Lear are not major heroes simply because Shakespeare has named his plays after them; the degree of their awareness of their situation is also important. This high awareness becomes apparent when one compares them with Laertes or Gloucester. Lukács notes, in discussing the hero's consciousness, that "the essence of his personality is his capacity to fight back, by force of his experiences and with all his inner energies, against the bare, given reality; and his wish to take his individual fate in its general character" (4:158).

Lukács also puts Hegel's definition of "static" and "dynamic" characters into an (artificial) historical frame. The "static" hero is that of the Homeric epic, and the "dynamic" hero is that of the new bourgeois epic (5:388–89). The dynamic hero sometimes functions against the background of a perfectly "reified," "finished" world (for example, in Tolstoy's late prose), thereby providing the only organic, living element for the total picture (5:214–21, 236–38). Lukács finds this transition from the classical rhetorical character to the realist dynamic character occurring not so much in the eighteenth-century English novel as in early-nineteenth-century historicism. In Scott, he emphasizes the significance of choosing heroes among more common people, instead of among historically authentic and leading individuals, as the fate of commoners reflects the deep social problems of an age more clearly than that of kings and dukes (6:46).

The worship of communist super-heroes during a certain period and by a certain trend of the socialist realist tradition is one of the reasons why Lukács blatantly criticized socialist re-

alism even more for its methods of characterization than for
its aesthetics. In more veiled forms of criticism, he used the
"bourgeois" cult of the great man as his target (e.g., 6:519).
What he says about this phenomenon could just as well be
applied to Gorky's Pavel Vlasov, N. A. Ostrovsky's Pavel Kor-
chagin, or any other immaculate hero of Zhdanovism. Indeed,
it is hard to conceive of any Ivanhoe-cult or Bezukhov-cult
whatsoever, to say nothing of the dimensions of the semi-
religious adoration received by young communist heroes of
fiction, such as the two mentioned above, during the thirties,
or the so-called "young-guardists" (a group of teen-age
Ukrainian guerrillas in World War II, hailed in a novel by
A. A. Fadeyev) during the late forties and early fifties.

What primarily made Lukács an opponent of the Soviet
trend of socialist realism was the subordination of man to
"things." Lukács saw the survival of "reification," the representation of man as part of a mechanized existence, which he
criticized in modern bourgeois literature, reappear in the Soviet "Five-Year Plan novels" of the thirties. In his essay "Erzählen oder Beschreiben?" (1936; 4:197–242), he first demonstrates how story-telling and plot give way to description in
modern bourgeois literature, and how details, no longer serving the totality of the work, gain independent existence. Following this, he expresses his concern that socialist realism too
may become but a new form of worship, not of productive
human qualities, but of the product itself; and that consequently literature will again turn into a "biography of
things." He is also afraid that the description of the work-
place might become more important than the characterization
of heroes, and that the representation of the "dynamism of
life," the élan of socialism, will deprive literature of its concrete human essence. This essay is Lukács' most sincere and
sharpest critical attack on the perverted cult of socialist realism before 1956. Furthermore, as we shall see, nothing sepa-

rates him more from Gorky than the status he assigned to the hero as opposed to the status he assigned to "things."

Lukács is a humanist; so is Gorky, but in a different sense. For Gorky, man's talent, power, and will create miracles which then supersede the greatness of their creator. "The history of human labour and creativity is far more interesting and significant than the history of man; man dies before reaching the age of one hundred, whilst his works live through the centuries" (*On Literature*, p. 28). According to Gorky, this creative dynamism of the hero has disappeared in modern Western literature, together with man's awareness that his material and spiritual world are products of a collective creative process. In his essay "The disintegration of personality" (1909; pp. 71–137), Gorky traces this process through the ages. His belief that man's consciousness develops from a collective consciousness ("we") toward an individual consciousness ("I," in opposition to "they"), is a point of view essentially corresponding to those of Marx and Engels. As a result of the disintegration of personality, the bourgeois artist "is no longer a mirror of the world, but a small splinter thereof . . . [which] cannot reflect the majesty of life in the world . . ." (p. 123). Gorky thinks that the attempt to re-create "we" (in the form of the proletariat) is an effort stemming from socialist thought (p. 85).

In this essay Gorky also comments on the disappearance of heroic woman figures in modern Russian literature. Implicitly, he seems to attribute this phenomenon to an increasing distribution of labor and social roles. Consequently, the vanishing heroine might be an aspect of the impoverishment of characterization in modern literature. Alas, what Gorky would like to find in literature are characters like Marfa Boretskaya, a fifteenth-century ruler of Novgorod, or the boyardess Morozova, a "martyr" of the orthodox seventeenth-century "*ras-*

kolnik" movement. Gorky's characteristically archaic taste neutralizes his interesting critical point.

Contradictions occasionally appear in Lukács, whereas in Gorky they are more frequent and often startling and utterly confusing. For example, subordination of the individual to "things" coexists in Gorky's critical writings with the romantic idea of typification. Küppers points out that this constantly recurring fantastic-pathetic inclination to create gods (*bogostroitelstvo*) is one of the principal phenomena that Lenin repeatedly criticized in Gorky.[37] The alternating glorification of the hero and of his work receives a synthetic but extremely confused representation in this remark: "We must make labour the principal hero of our books, i.e. man as organized by labour processes . . ." (p. 254). Did Gorky mean that the hero and his work are interchangeable? In any case, he obviously could not avoid the extremes whose avoidance was, in Lukács' opinion, the greatness of Walter Scott and the later-nineteenth-century realists: showing heroes either as superhuman giants by stylization, or as minuscule everymen by naturalistic devices (6:56–57).

The method of creating "types" that Gorky suggested is not particularly challenging. In his definition, a "type" is the common denominator of a class, whom the writer creates by first detaching characteristic features of a society from different individuals, and then embodying them in one figure (pp. 29–32).

Concerning characterization, Gorky finds nothing to praise in the past tradition. As private property is theft, the most typical figures of bourgeois society are the rogue, the thief, and later the detective. He then generously goes back to ancient Egypt and to Greco-Roman literature to demonstrate early occurrences of the picaresque rogue. His statement that Sancho Panza, Till Eulenspiegel, Simplicissimus, Gil Blas, the heroes of Smollett and Fielding, and Maupassant's *Bel Ami* equally show the cynical bourgeois robber-ethic in its nakedness, "with its lavish garnishing of all kinds of vulgarity, including the platitude of philistine 'common sense' " (pp. 237ff), is a completely ahistoric, absurd anti-Marxist mélange. However, it also contradicts his own earlier opinion (1923) that Till Eulenspiegel, Alarcón's heroes, etc., are representatives of a refreshing, straightforward, plebeian view of life (pp. 372–73). The recurring appreciation of naive popular realism in Gorky's critical works (e.g., pp. 80, 235–36) is a fascinating contrast to Lukács' somewhat aristocratic taste, which never allowed him to consider folk literature as an example and source of "belles lettres." Nevertheless, the constant contradictions make it difficult to understand exactly why Gorky wanted to use the example of folk literature.

Inconsistencies do not indicate unconcern. Characterization is a serious matter for Gorky—so serious that he virtually takes fictive heroes as living ones, and becomes personally involved in them. Gogol's figures in *Dead Souls* do not satisfy him since they are not more completely "bloodsuckers of the peasantry." Because of this lack, they are "not very characteristic" (pp. 249–50). Dostoevsky is more successful in his characterization, but he is an "evil genius," representing extreme attitudes of Russian reality: those of the sadist and of the masochist. Gorky calls the pathological symptoms of the violent anarchist-heroes "Karamazovitis" (*Karamazovshchina*, from Fyodor Karamazov.) The opposite attitude, a holy, meditating, passive fatalism, the choice of Alyosha Karamazov, is what he calls "Karataevitis" (*Karatayevshchina*, from Tolstoy's Platon Karataev, the pious peasant soldier in *War and Peace*, of whom Gorky violently disapproved.) In Gorky's opinion, both extremes create a kind of diseased atmosphere. What Russia needs is not to worship the geniuses of the past, but to create new literary ideals. Gorky is probably attributing the role of the new prophet to himself.[38] Lukács' idea that there may be a distance between the writer and the hero obviously never occurred to him.

4. Sincerity of Perception
and Sincerity of Consciousness

During the 1930s, two factions dominated Soviet critical life. One called itself *voprekhisty*. An approximate literary translation would be something like "against-ists," or perhaps "antagonists." Their basic thesis was that the writer's world view does not necessarily determine the overall quality of his works. That is, antagonism between what the artist sees and what he believes is conceivable. The *voprekhisty* usually made reference to Lenin's view of Tolstoy as a reactionary thinker, but a great realistic writer. They made reference as well to Engels' similar judgment of Balzac. Both of these views will be discussed subsequently.

The other group's popular name was *blagodaristy* ("forists" or "protagonists.") They maintained that ideology does influence the writer in his reflection of the world. Thus, the most advanced world view (Marxism) should create the most correct presentation of reality in literature. Perception and consciousness are inseparable. Again, the authority the *blagodaristy* often referred to was Lenin. They took as their slogan one interpretation of his article on party literature—the one which subordinated all artistic creativity to party discipline.

Lukács and Gorky reflect the basic difference between *voprekhisty* and *blagodaristy* quite clearly. The issue they discuss is the relationship between perceptual and ideological consciousness in the writer's mind. Lukács analyzes this relationship from the point of view of a literary critic, while Gorky's analysis is from the point of view of a committed writer.

As usual, Lukács is eager to find impressive historical precedents. He discovers them in the remarks of Engels on Balzac, and those of Lenin on Tolstoy. We have already discussed Engels' letter to Minna Kautsky (November 26, 1885) in which he separates two tendencies. One is the tendency found in all masterpieces: a nondidactic, nonmoralizing view of the world—the commitment of the writer to the faithful reflection of his experience. The other is the expressed, didactic tendency, which also offers solutions. In this case, the writer superimposes his social or political program on the integrated world of the work.[39] We have also mentioned the same critical attitude toward open tendentiousness in Engels' letter to Miss Harkness (April 1888). In this letter, he expresses his great admiration for Balzac. From Balzac's *Comédie humaine*, says Engels, "even in economic details . . . I have learned more than from all the professional historians, economists and statisticians of the period together." He then continues with the following comment, which has so often been quoted in Marxist literary theory:

> Well, Balzac was politically a legitimist; his great work is a constant elegy on the irreparable decay of good society; his sympathies are with the class that is doomed to extinction. But for all that, his satire is never keener, his irony never more bitter, than when he sets in motion the very men and women with whom he sympathizes most deeply— the nobles. And the only men of whom he speaks with undisguised admiration are his bitterest political antagonists, the republican heroes of the Cloître Saint Méry, the men who at that time (1830–36) were indeed representatives of the popular masses. That Balzac was thus compelled to go against his own class sympathies and political prejudices, that he *saw* the necessity of the downfall of his favorite nobles and described them as people deserving no better fate; that he *saw* the real men of future where, for the time being, they alone were to be found—that I consider one of the greatest triumphs of realism, and one of the greatest features in old Balzac.[40]

Besides this frequently quoted statement, we may also refer to both the Szeliga-critique and the Sickingen-debate. Though Marx and Engels could not withhold their disgust for Sue's moralizing *solution*, they appreciated his *initial* realistic characterizations and exposition of the vices of the big city. As well, in the Sickingen debate, they explicitly criticized Lassalle's didactic, programmatic, subjective way of characterizing his heroes and approaching sociohistorical issues. (On the other hand, Lassalle's view was that the writer could indeed attribute to his hero the most progressive consciousness and the most developed sharp-sightedness possible in *his* age.) Historical anarchronism was thus permissible in Lassalle's, but not in Marx's and Engels', view. Owing to this scepticism of any kind of political immediacy of the literary work, Engels doubted that any revolutionary poetry (except for "La Marseillaise") could constitute a lasting contribution to world literature.[41]

Lenin's view of Tolstoy is an exact copy of Engels' interpretation of Balzac.[42] He regards Tolstoy as a mouthpiece of the Russian peasantry. As far as description of rural life, sympathy for humble people, and indignation at their social status and problems are concerned, Tolstoy is a great realist and gives a truly reliable account of these issues. However, the sharp-sightedness of the peasantry which he adopted is combined in him with the shortcomings of the same class. After the liberation of the serfs, the Russian peasant was confronted with a new enemy: the industrial or financial capitalist. Disappointed and frustrated, Tolstoy as well as his peasants turned to "the eternal," that is, to abstract moralizing, mysticism, resigned nonviolent protest, and naive pseudosolutions such as vegetarianism.

It is not Lenin's total interpretation of Tolstoy which concerns us here, but the fact that he spells out clearly the same divergence between an objective (and probably correct) and a subjective (and often false) reflection of the world that Engels did. Actually, Lenin seemed to apply this idea more frequently than did Marx and Engels, though in Lukács and in Eastern European handbooks on aesthetics it is almost exclusively his view of Tolstoy that is quoted. For example, he repeatedly criticized Turgenev the man for his subservience to the emperor, yet praised Turgenev the writer for his "great and marvellous language," and for the humanistic realism of his writings.[43] Also, Lenin noticed fairly early the gap between literary greatness and a considerable theoretical inconsistency in Gorky, and wanted to keep him out of political life or cultural debates unless Gorky's particular idea was "correct." "There can be no doubt that Gorky's is an enormous artistic talent which has been, and will be, of great benefit to the world proletarian movement. But why should Gorky meddle in politics?" a puzzled Lenin asked in 1917.[44]

Lenin went so far as to write favorably about a "white" Russian emigrant writer, Arkady Avarchenko, whose book *A Dozen Knives in the Back of the Revolution* had, in his opinion, definite weaknesses, but also certain merits. Lenin considered the revolution and its leaders subjects that Avarchenko was unfamiliar with, and in this respect, his stories appeared "inartistic." On the other hand, Avarchenko depicted "with amazing skill the impressions and moods of the representative of the old, rich, gorging and guzzling Russia of the landowners and capitalists. This is exactly what the revolution must look like to the representatives of the ruling classes." Moreover, Lenin ended his short review with the recommendation that some of Avarchenko's stories be reprinted in Bolshevik Russia.[45]

In reading this, one can no longer wonder how Lenin's commissar of cultural affairs, Anatoly Vasilyevich Lunacharsky, could dare make a statement in 1924 which would sound subversive in the Soviet Union today. Lunacharsky wrote that if anybody were to write a work of true literary value, apologizing for the *kulaks* (the supposedly parasitic and reactionary big landholding peasants), the author could be criticized for his ideological views, yet he would still deserve the title of being a great writer.[46] Just ten years later, Zh-danov, Gorky, and the First Soviet Writers' Congress put an end to this kind of Leninist heresy.

Turning again to Lukács, we find that he organically in-tegrated the Marxist-Leninist idea of "consciousness lagging behind perception" in his aesthetic view. Lukács borrows Engels' expression and calls the outcome of the divergence of observation and opinion the "triumph of realism" (*Sieg des Realismus*; in *Werke* 4:268–71, 434; 10:227–28). On the other hand, rather than distinguishing two different meanings of the word "tendency," as Engels did, he instead uses two dif-ferent words. He applies the original word "tendency" (or "tendentiousness") for the illustrative, consciously propagan-distic trend, which he condemns as much as Engels did. He regards tendency as a concept important only for the "socio-logical" critics among Marxists, who, in his opinion, manipu-lated Marxism to fit their narrow social deterministic views (4:23, 34; 10:225). The other attitude is "partisanship" (*Par-teilichkeit*): the objective, dialectical representation of con-flicts and tendencies in the total social process, of which both he and Engels approve (4:23–34). Considering world litera-ture, Lukács finds that all masterpieces are "partisan," as the really objective writer reveals not only the state of things, but also the tendency of their development; therefore he must be committed to the authenticity of his social experience (4:32–34, 432; 10:225). Most great works of world literature (like *Onegin, Anna Karenina,* and Kleist's, Balzac's, and Chek-hov's writings) reveal no programmatic answer to the prob-lems they discuss, but only reflect implicit social tendencies (5:161–66). No "correct" political idea can ensure an auto-matic rise to literary greatness (4:270).

Following World War II, Lukács wrote two articles in which he seemed to maintain that any great realist writer should by necessity be a "partisan" himself in any society—

even in a socialist one.[47] Lukács' rejection of party control and strict socialist realism as a political norm soon provoked the most violent attacks against him by party ideologists.

It is true that Lukács made some concessions to "committed" realism in scattered remarks. He went fairly far in this direction with his essay on Chernishevsky's *What Is To Be Done?* (5:126–60). In reading this essay, one can sense how hard Lukács was trying to find aesthetic excuses for one of the artistically least significant, but politically most significant novels of world literature. He attempted to point out the aesthetic value of "trying to provide alternatives for man," and, on the whole, to contribute at least nominally to the unprincipled Chernishevsky-cult in the Soviet Union (which flourished particularly under Stalin). However, as all Lukács' arguments go against his own, theoretically solidly based, idea of the difference between tendency and partisanship, his attempt appears to have been unsuccessful.

Satire is one genre in which Lukács regards sincerity and political tendency as compatible. As he explains in his essay "Zur Frage der Satire" (1932; 4:83–107), the basis of the good satire is never formal, but exclusively ideological. Consequently, it is only the writer's point of view, the target and effect of his satire, which can determine the success of the work. Lukács mentions Goethe's example. Goethe's two satirical plays related to the French revolution (*Die Aufgeregten* and *Der Bürgergeneral*) are so inferior that not even the most conservative bourgeois critic would dare praise them. On the other hand, his opposition to the ideals of the revolution appears in highly artistic shape in the nonsatirical *Hermann und Dorothea* and *Die natürliche Tochter*.

Whether or not Lukács placed this Engelsian idea of the "triumph of realism" in any historical frame would be hard to tell. After 1938 and especially during the 1940s, he repeatedly mentioned that in the age of imperialism this "triumph" was becoming more difficult to achieve for the writer, and finally completely impossible. The bourgeois artist had three choices: to become an apologist for imperialism; to express only his own inner life (4:269); or to cling to some absurd, illusionary ideals (this Lukács illustrated with his analysis of Ibsen's *The Wild Duck*, 4:290ff). In his writings after 1956, Lukács did not make it sufficiently clear whether or not his idea that great realism had survived the age of imperialism also meant that the "triumph of realism" would, again, become possible for writers today.

In the interpretation of the writer's conscious relation to his world, Gorky began with Marx, Engels and Lenin, just as Lukács did. In fact, he even referred to Engels' view of Balzac as late as 1928. In the thirties, however, he modified this attitude, and he changed his view of European culture as well. Gorky converted from Engels' view of Balzac to the most polemic writings of Marx and Engels on class struggle. From the Lenin who interpreted Tolstoy in Engels' spirit, he converted to the "other" Lenin, who supposedly subordinated literature to party control in his "On Party Literature." In his congressional speech, Gorky openly demanded the greatest degree of party control over literature (*On Literature*, p. 263).

As Gorky is a far less systematic, far more impressionistic critic than Lukács, it is not possible to find any particular theory of the divergence of perception and consciousness in his writings. Nevertheless, we can compare his statements about particular writers to those made by Lukács.

Lukács' view of Balzac corresponds to that of Engels to the extent that he repeatedly paraphrases Engels (*Werke* 6: 464, 473, 503–4). Of his essays on Balzac's two novels, *Les Paysans* and *Les Illusions perdues*, the first one especially follows Engels' footsteps. Lukács, however, develops Engels' view of Balzac in a constructive and original way in his comparison of Balzac and Stendhal. He compares these two authors in order to illustrate the differences between a nonconscious but still great realism and a conscious but less sophisticated one in the early-nineteenth-century French novel (6:490–509). Of the two writers, Stendhal held the clearer and more progressive ideas, only they no longer grew out of the social reality of his age. Stendhal is a belated "enlightener" who follows the prerevolutionary realistic tradition of Diderot and Lessing, and as such he is a more progressive writer than Balzac. Balzac was under the influence of the reactionary ideas of the French Restoration, and to a lesser degree of those of romanticism. However, it was precisely his contradictory personality that made it possible for him to reflect his controversial age in a more complex, but still realistic, way than Stendhal was able to do. They both share, however, a keen sense of selectiveness, totality, and social concern which enabled them both to show the transformation of the bourgeoisie from a heroic to a parasitic class.

Among the Russian writers whom Lukács commented on, Dostoevsky and Tolstoy were primarily the two whom he regarded from Engels' and Lenin's point of view. It was precisely this point of view which enabled Lukács to assign Tolstoy a determining role in the history of modern realism. Since by Tolstoy's time capitalism had already stopped up the "pores of society," paralyzing human freedom and ambitions, he therefore presented the nightmare of capitalism, a "hideous 'finished' world of increasing horror" in his novels (5:219). Though this "finished" world is unprecedented in European literature, its appearance in Tolstoy's prose makes him one of the greatest realist writers, and one who saved and enriched the tradition of nineteenth-century Western "great realism" by transmitting it to the twentieth century (5:259–60). Likewise, Dostoevsky's greatness can be comprehended only if one focuses on the problems he states rather than on the solutions he offers. Unlike the Western naturalists, Dostoevsky shows the brutality of the big industrial city in its impact on the human psyche. His prophetic, exalted, mystical answers to the questions he raises do not diminish the masterful representation of the questions themselves (5:161–76).

Lukács' premises might be criticized, but the system he builds from them is nevertheless well-designed. This is by no means true for Gorky, however. We already indicated three differences between him and Lukács: he was a writer, a less educated individual, and something of an idealistic prophet. The style and method of Lukács and Gorky could not be further apart. Gorky, too, read Balzac. He maintains that at twenty he had already finished the whole Comédie humaine, and that it had been a "heavy blow on my still undeveloped romanticism."[48] Like Lukács, he recognizes that Balzac is a great writer of disillusionment. Yet, while Lukács measures the effect of capitalism on the literary hero, Gorky measures this on himself. Where Lukács is systematic and objective, Gorky is impressionistic and subjective. Lukács admits that, besides its social existence, the work of art also has an integrated individual existence—a point that is irrelevant for Gorky. He seems to develop his own argument that the center of literature is man, from substituting himself, with all his cultural biases, for "The Man."

It is the issue of theoretical-methodological clairvoyance, not the lack of reading experience, that separates Gorky from Lukács—provided that Gorky's statements concerning his reading were true. On May 16, 1928, he wrote Stefan Zweig that he had read all of Stendhal's books. In the same letter, however, he calls Stendhal a romantic writer and, as such, a sceptical one too, as "scepticism accompanies romanticism in general and inevitably" (On Literature, p. 380). Of course, this statement sharply contradicts his view of romanticism as a desirable complement to socialist realism, but never mind! In addition, it is in contrast to Lukács' view of Stendhal in two respects: Stendhal is, for Gorky, not a belated enlightener nor an idealist, but a romantic and a sceptic.

Concerning the Russian realists, for Lukács Dostoevsky's greatness in objective descriptions of life is more important than his false views, while for Gorky this is just the opposite. Only in Tolstoy's case did Gorky separate "instinct" from "intellect." In Tolstoy, "the creative power of the artist struggled during all his lifetime against the instincts of the preacher." Still, even in Tolstoy Gorky separates the works written "free of Christ," like *The Cossacks* and *Hadji Murat*, from those written "in Christ's name," like "the boring *Resurrection*" (pp. 380–81). We should note that Lukács admired *Resurrection* and never divided Balzac's or Tolstoy's oeuvre into objective and biased works. Finally, it is typical of Gorky that his personal reminiscences of Tolstoy (pp. 292–348) are far more interesting than his theoretical speculations about Tolstoy's art.

It is not the purpose of this study to enter into the details of Balzac- or Tolstoy-criticism. Lukács' analysis of the literary production of Balzac, Stendhal, Tolstoy, and others, may or may not cope with the challenge of particular biographical facts, or views of other literary critics. For what purpose and how he used his arguments is what concerns us most. By stating the idea that perception and consciousness do not necessarily correspond with each other, Lukács took issue with an ever-growing dehumanization and politicization of art in Zhdanovism. After 1933, he lived in the Soviet Union and witnessed both the reemerging spirit of the RAPP in the centralization of creative efforts under party control, and the subsequent impoverishment of Soviet literature. He needed arguments to fight this wave of laymanship and political manipulation, and he found them in the great humanist writers of the past. Leandro Konder attempts this perspective in his enthusiastic statement that the idea of the "triumph of realism" in its Engels-Lukácsian form is "one of the most brilliant theses of materialist aesthetics."[49]

After this exposition it would be easy, but unfair, to put down Gorky as Lukács' negative counterpart. Indeed, the uncritical praise of Gorky's views in the Soviet Union has tempted even objective Western critics to condemn him. This is but partially justifiable. Lukács' cold, objective model does not leave much room for sincere, devoted social idealists—and especially lyricists, even of great talent. Gorky's view of realism is a passionate, though theoretically vulnerable, confession of a committed socialist artist. As we shall see, Brecht himself took a standpoint similar to Gorky's on the issue of commitment versus observation.

It is not merely the idea of commitment, however, but also the Brechtian populistic vein, a true continuation of Villon's, Rabelais's, or de Coster's spirit, which we find in the Gorkian, but not in the Lukácsian, trend of criticism. After all, what Lukács appreciated most in literature was the agony of the bourgeois class, whereas Gorky leads us to the gypsy camp, the workers, or the sad lower levels of society (in his *Night Asylum*). What is more, Gorky urged other writers in his literary critical essays to take similar social excursions.

Also, as we continue to examine the possible applicability of a formally more flexible, inspirationally more subjective, romantic, and exalted Gorkian literary critical standpoint, we may win a few rounds over Lukács. D. H. Lawrence's sexual mysticism, for instance, could be appreciated from the point of view of an essentially Gorkian aesthetics, but not from that of a Lukácsian one. In spite of Gorky's dislike of Freudianism, some of his early writings, with their naturalistic representation of human passions, remind one conspicuously of Lawrence.

Similarly, a criticism which would follow the spirit, though perhaps not the letter, of Gorky's literary views, might appreciate irony, ambiguity, role-playing, or even formal experimentation in literature. Gorky himself wrote documentary works as well as prose poems in loose form, entirely based on metaphoric associations. Lukács was never able to make such concessions to "decadent avant-gardism."

In spite of evident merits in Gorky's literary views, Western critical tradition, which its preference for "systematic" presentation of ideas and "convincing" evidence, might reject him as merely a propagandist. Predictably, in the Eastern cultural sphere there is a completely biased overestimation of Gorky's critical qualities. But, to be fair to the conditions of criticism in the socialist countries, we must add that the literary scene is constantly changing there. Brecht seems to have almost more appeal now than Gorky in several socialist countries; and there is good reason to believe that Hungary's exceptionally high appreciation of Lukács will sooner or later force more dogmatic neighbor countries to reevaluate his image.

Let us conclude our comparison of Lukács' theory of critical realism and Gorky's theory of socialist realism, with a summary of their differences.

We have seen how the tradition which Lukács and Gorky built upon differs. Lukács emphasizes the greatness of eighteenth- and nineteenth-century bourgeois culture, and calls nineteenth-century European prose the manifestation of an ideal "great realism." According to Gorky, the bourgeoisie never really produced any great literature or art. They both rely on Marx and Engels, who believed that bourgeois culture had been great, but had fallen into decay by the mid-nineteenth century. Lukács faithfully follows this explanation, while Gorky projects the aversion of Marx and Engels toward the culture of their age into the past as well.

The interpretation of the romantic heritage also divides Lukács and Gorky. On the whole, Lukács rejects romanticism, but first carefully "saves" the great writers of the early nineteenth century through his intermediary category of prerealism or *Kunstperiode*. Like Marx and Engels, he equates romanticism with the reaction to the French revolution, and with an apology for the Holy Alliance. Gorky, however, takes a Leninist starting point and recognizes the potentially positive element of spontaneous revolt. He seems also to recognize intuitively the fact that romanticism functioned as a relevant antithesis of classicism, that it was a revolt against the French Restoration as well, and that it laid the foundation of utopian socialism and sympathy for the oppressed laboring masses.

Lukács, the critic, and Gorky, who was primarily a writer, differ on the issue of precisely what the criteria of realism are. In spite of his basic suspicion of science, Lukács attempts to find systematic, objective, "scientific" criteria which provide historical, social, moral and aesthetic arguments for or against movements, periods, particular writers or works, and so on. His moral criterion is the sincerity of writer and hero. Gorky, for his part, never provided anything but subjective criteria to justify his literary judgments. The only critical norm he consistently stressed was the moral message of the work. The issue was, however, not perceptive sincerity in Gorky's theory, but the attitude of the writer and his hero toward work and toward the working people. This arbitrary ethical (more exactly, "work-ethical") definition of literary values culminated in the admiration of labor, *per se*.

The criteria of realism in Lukács and Gorky define the system as well as the method they arrived at. Lukács' system is crystal-like, coherent, and relatively consistent; but metaphysical and exclusive at the same time. Realism is contrasted with different manifestations of nonrealism, with arguments which show an immense scholarly preparation. Gorky, on the other hand, never established any clear system. Great writers of the past and the present are claimed for realism without further ado—it is enough that they win the critic's sympathy. There are numerous good ideas and observations in Gorky's critical writings, but there are hardly any which he would not have contradicted, either before or after having stated them.

Lukács' approach to the literary hero is nonfunctionalistic. Man is interesting in himself; therefore, the literary hero might even be a usurer, criminal, or social dropout. What the individual produces and how his product serves society is an unimportant, if not an undesirable, element of literary and artistic characterization. Gorky, on the other hand, believes that only an active, working, creative individual can make a literary hero. He hails labor: you are what you do. Both Lukács and Gorky start off with Marx's challenging, but terminologically highly controversial, theory of "alienation." As certain interpretations suggest, Marx contrasted the "externalization" of human essence in material production or artistic creation with the "alienation" of the product in class societies. While Marx presumably regarded the former process as an innate human characteristic, he condemned the latter as an evil of class societies. Lukács seems to depreciate the relevance of any utilitarian criterion for evaluating the hero, while Gorky tends to forget the threat of alienation and glorifies production for its own sake. Gorky says that capitalism kills the literary hero, and Lukács agrees but is afraid that the same may happen to the socialist realist hero in Stalinist "socialism."

This last question, how they view socialist realism, puts a wide gulf between Lukács and Gorky. For Lukács, socialist realism is only a terminological variation of great nineteenth-century bourgeois realism, which was already predictive. For Gorky, socialist realism is a completely new phenomenon which appears with the dawn of the socialist order, and differs qualitatively from the "merely descriptive" bourgeois realism. In other words, Lukács emphasizes the element of preservation, and Gorky that of abolition, in the German category *Aufhebung*, which means both "preservation" and "abolition." Hegel used this term to illustrate the essence of dialectics: the synthesis of two opposite theses.

III. Problems of the Two Realisms: Variations and Developments

The analysis of two different models of realism seems to be necessary whenever the distinction between critical and socialist realism is made. Such a distinction forms a clearly demonstrable pattern in the history of socialist criticism. Consequently, comparisons in addition to that between Lukács and Gorky could be made to point out the essential differences. Comparing Lukács with Bertolt Brecht is an attractive alternative, but hardly original any longer.[1] It is also tempting to compare Ralph Fox with Brecht. Fox was a young English Marxist critic of considerable cultural background who died in the Spanish Civil War as the soldier of the International Brigade. His main contribution to Marxist aesthetics, *The Novel and the People*, shows a remarkable resemblance to Lukács' theory of realism and the novel, as applied to the English literary conditions. Furthermore, the comparison of Fox and Brecht might have shown approximately the same divergence in the concept of realism outside the borders of an established socialist system under strong party control as that between Lukács and Gorky.

Though Lukács' and Gorky's theories of realism are the most completely developed ones, they are not all-inclusive. Some further variations and developments deserve our attention. In this chapter is a selective survey of statements on realism by some dozen notable Marxist (mostly communist) literary critics; these statements should be considered as complementary to the Lukácsian and Gorkian models.

1. The Realistic Attitude

Most theories of the two kinds of realism, critical and socialist, are not especially penetrating. The "definitions" of socialist realism proclaimed at the two Soviet Writers' Congresses of 1934 and 1954 are full of commonplaces.[2] One interesting conclusion we can draw from them is that the general acceptance of the term "critical," or even "bourgeois," realism is a result of a fairly late campaign, though Lukács had already stated this concept in the thirties.

Throughout the thirties and part of the forties, the controversy between critical and socialist realism raised heated debates. The theory of critical realism facilitates a view of realism as a world outlook, and a more general one than socialist realism or any other subcategory. Actually, this view appears as a parallel to Lukács' conception that socialist realism is primarily realism. The main characteristic of realism is supposed to be that the "objective world," the social environment, is the source of the creative process in the author, as well as the generator of a series of experiences in the individual. Critical realism is realism on the level of perception, and is critical because of the conflict between objective conditions and the subjective consciousness of the hero and/or the author. Whereas the individual and critical interpretation of sociohistorical facts might be fallacious, the individual perception never is. Furthermore, the realist outlook is as much rooted in the classical heritage as in historicism and dialectical materialism.

The Lukácsian view of realism as a term more general and significant than its attribute of being "proletarian" or a "social mode of expression," appears in the writings of both Eastern (Lunacharsky) and Western (Halldór Kiljan Laxness) critics, and also in some of the many post-revolutionary Soviet artistic movements (e.g. "Pereval").

The other context in which the term realism appears prior to the mid-forties developed simultaneously with the one described. Realism is interpreted here as a matter of individual attitude to life. It is the active human consciousness that determines whether a literary work is realistic in a modern sense. The stress is on the differences rather than the similarities between old and new realism. As in Gorky, the old bourgeois realism of the nineteenth century appears as a photographic, metaphysical realism which creates not concrete but abstract heroes. Socialist (or new, or proletarian) realism, on the other hand, provides a larger scope as well as a greater depth for artistic representation. It is selective, humanistic, dynamic, and tendentious, urges participation and encourages collectivism, cultivates consciousness as well as fantasy and dreaming, uses a simple language, depicts working heroes, and can be pointed out in all genres.

Though most of these assumed qualities of modern realism are clichés, "borrowed" quite unscrupulously from the Lukácsian vocabulary by advocates of socialist realism, the fact is that, beside party ideologists, socialist writers all over the world have subscribed, either in part or wholly, to these kinds of generalities. The ex-aristocrat Alexey Tolstoy, who had just returned from the White emigration, was just as willing to accept these clichés during the twenties as were the earlier Red soldiers Sholokhov and Fadeyev, or the Czech pro-modernistic socialist critic Václavek. Obviously, national borderlines constituted no unsurmountable difficulty either. The German Brecht and the Haitian Alexis have several views in common on socialist realism.

Marxist critics at least tried to throw some light on the problem of the writer's attitude toward his social reality. The question of whether a work of art is a mouthpiece for the author's views or has its own aesthetic entity goes back to Hegel. We have followed its development through Marx and Engels to Lukács' separation of tendency and partisanship. If we substitute "consciousness" for "mouthpiece," however (as even Gorky's less sophisticated essays allow us to do) the attractive nonpropagandistic view of realism as a historical period in Lukács appears in a different light. A comparison of Lukács and Brecht brings up several instances of a still-unresolved contradiction.

It is precisely the impossibility of considering a "noncommitted" realism simultaneously with its opposite, a combatant and ideologically "correct" social awareness, which constitutes the Lukács-Brecht controversy. On the one hand, there are critics who maintain that political consciousness plays a role inferior to perception on the level of reflection. In their view, the impact of a socialist outlook, or of a party, or of a didactic method, are but secondary criteria by which to judge realism when compared to creative genius. Ervin Szabó, a Hungarian socialist whom Lukács admired, represented an analogous view. In 1914, he wrote: "By tendency, one can be a socialist or an anarchist, catholic or pro-feudal—and still be a great artist. But nobody can be a great artist whose works compare to the party programs of the social democrats, or the People's party, or the constitutionalists in such a way that one could state: 'They match excellently!' " [3]

Antonio Gramsci, a leading figure in the history of Italian Marxism, also counts among the serious supporters of this idea. Though he never diminished the importance of the intellectual and moral meaning of the literary work (what he called its "cultural value" in Pirandello's case),[4] neither did he deprecate the importance of impartial realism. An ideologically correct reflection of life was, in his opinion, no substitute for aesthetic values.[5] Since homogeneous and uniformly progressive societies do not exist, he wrote, an objective reflection of retrogressive tendencies, working even among the common people, is a prerequisite of realism. He mentioned as an example the passivity of the Italian peasant masses toward the movement for national unity.[6] Gramsci also established an interesting contrast between the politician (who thinks in nonfixed, fluid images and follows a practical political tactic) and the artist (whose outlook is more stable and nontimely), and used this to justify the frequent conflict between politics and poetry.[7] Unfortunately, the dichotomization of "fluid" and "fixed" world views, and the attribution of the latter to the poet, remained only an axiom which Gramsci did not adequately elaborate. Also, Lunacharsky preferred "great" art to "agitative" art,[8] and regarded the "heightened sensibility of the artist: his wish to interpret reality in images," as an attribute of greatness.[9] Furthermore, two personalities as different as chairman Mao and the Icelander Laxness agree that art is a more concentrated, qualitatively richer, representation of life than any biased social propaganda, and that the latter cannot substitute for genuine art.

On the other hand, there is a strong traditional opposition to the trend stressing impartiality and artistic values. For this other group of writers and critics the high degree of perception, which was the criterion of the genius for the first party, is negligible. Instead, they cultivate "class-conscious" writing, which they regard as superior to the probably aesthetically more valuable "bourgeois" writing. Also, the role of the party and a correct ideological outlook were premises they began with and never questioned.

The most famous of all the ideological critics was Bertolt Brecht. His literary views represent a qualitatively new phenomenon in socialist aesthetic theory. More recent applications of the Marxist concept of alienation to literary works—Adorno's, Marcuse's, and Ernst Bloch's interpretations of art—are all directly or indirectly related to Brecht's critical theory. For Brecht, the dialectical aspect of realism seemed to be more important than the materialistic. He based his "estrangement-effect," or the emotional distance created between stage and spectator, on the clearly Hegelian-Marxist epistemological pattern of "understanding-nonunderstanding-new understanding"; that is, on the necessity of constantly revaluating our concepts and ideas in order to attain new, better ones.[10]

It might sound paradoxical, but Brecht, who never was a party-member, always took a more political, practical, party-oriented "Leninist" stand than did the party-member Lukács. The two took issue with each other openly and frequently. Lukács never had a truly appreciative word for Brecht's dramas; Brecht attacked Lukács on four points, three of which are relevant in the present connection.

First, Brecht thoroughly disapproved of Lukács' method of separating the tendency of the author from the tendency of his work. Second, and more specifically, Brecht disapproved of Lukács' substituting sensualism for realism—obviously referring to Lukács' advocacy of "vivid imagery" and "concreteness."[11] Brecht did not believe that sensualism was a reliable literary criterion, as he thought one could also write realistic works on a nonsensual basis[12]—a method which Lukács condemned as abstract and dehumanizing. Third, for realism Brecht wanted to substitute rationalism—a concept which has been quite frequently (although unjustly) regarded as the opposite of "sensualism." In 1926, Brecht was still defining real proletarian art as something more "artistic" than "proletarian."[13] The next year, however, he was regarding the task of the socialist writer as that of breaking away from tradition and working for social change—which, he believed, aestheticians were unable to do.[14] In the early thirties this conviction grew increasingly stronger. Eventually Brecht would praise anything "contemporary" and condemn everything "traditional." As a whole, Brecht regarded Lukács' theory of realism as neither dialectical nor satisfactorily flexible in its particular terminology.

Brecht's aesthetic radicalism seems to be primarily a Russo-German phenomenon. Elsewhere only third-rate party theoreticians advocated it,—or rather, they expressed certain views which were as close to Zhdanov's as to Brecht's. In Germany, however, writers of leftist expressionism and documentarism, taking Brecht as their model, expressed their demand for political consciousness in writing.[15] The debate Lukács carried on with the German Ernst Ottwalt about Ottwalt's documentary novel on German legal practice (*Denn sie wissen, was sie tun: ein deutscher Justizroman*, 1931), illustrates at least one aspect of the controversy. While Lukács wanted the literary work to exist in past, present, and future, Ottwalt (and Brecht) emphasized its existence in the present. As Ottwalt said, it is true that an author should give something to the whole world and to the future, but still, his active contribution to the class struggle of his own age and society was equally, or rather more, important.[16] In the Soviet Union, the extreme formulations of socialist realism, like those forged by Gorky, and certainly by Zhdanov, show striking resemblances to Brecht's views.

The Brecht–Lukács controversy reveals what are probably the most problematic aspects of critical and socialist realism. According to Lukács, although the author's political consciousness may be ideologically incorrect, he can still create correct characters unintentionally. According to Brecht, the author's consciousness may be ideologically right and yet he still may create false characters intentionally, to attain a rational distance between his audience and his heroes. (Brecht regarded this creative device, this "intellectualizing through distancing," as an application of the Marxist idea of alienation to literature and the theater; he called it "estrangement.") While Lukács tends to forget that perception is already an integrated part of human consciousness, Brecht tends to forget that there is also "false consciousness," and that consciousness therefore cannot be evaluated solely in terms of itself. The controversy has its precedent in the Sickingen debate, in which Lassalle represented a view similar to Brecht's against Marx and Engels.

For a critic or reader brought up in the Western European tradition, the noncommitted, nonpolitical, "cold" observational position of Lukács may look attractive. On the other hand, Brecht's social or class consciousness is, in the final analysis, simply consciousness. If one denies the relevance of consciousness to creative writing, one throws out the whole respectable modern "literature of consciousness." The problem is just as relevant for non-Marxist as for Marxist criticism. It seems that, at least until now, no one has come up with any acceptable synthesis.

Though Lukács defines realism as critical by its essential nature, he still states that critical and socialist realism are ultimately identical. The above mentioned Ervin Szabó, whom the young Lukács' greatly admired, held the same view. "You can speak about proletarian poetry just as little as about proletarian science, proletarian philosophy, proletarian sociology, or proletarian technology," he wrote as early as 1914.[17] This is certainly a critique not only of the coming Proletkult and RAPP movements of the twenties, but also of the later long-prevailing, simplified definition of socialist realism. This third view, which rejects the relevance of the terms "critical" and "socialist" within the general concept of realism, is not widespread in Marxist criticism, but it is nevertheless of some significance.

2. The Realistic Method

The conflicting definitions of realism—reflection of life on the level of perception and reflection of life on the level of consciousness—deal equally with the question of what the author represents. Conveniently, both prefer to avoid, in the heat of the debate, the question of the "method"—how the writer shows his experience. This does not mean, however, that Marxist writers and critics have completely neglected this problem.

Though the word "method" itself seems to emphasize the intrinsic values of the work, it should not be confused with technique, form, style, or other concepts of Western European criticism. Method is close to some aesthetic epistemology or model theory, but is certainly radically different from style in the sense that numerous socialist critics have interpreted it, and as the Union of Soviet Writers has stated it since its founding in 1932.[18] Even quite recently, the "revisionist" Ernst Fischer himself defined socialist realism as a matter of attitude or method, but not style.[19]

In spite of the split between critical and socialist realism, most advocates of both agree on at least two basic characteristics of the realistic creative process: the creating of types, and the reflection of life in its totality.

The concentration of the writer's and reader's attention on an evolutionary process requires some limitation of scope. In order to accomplish this, the writer creates types. Connected to the type, is the question of how typical heroes and situations reflect elements of more general and more particular events or human features.

We may remember how Lukács established the theory of the "specific" in order to find an aesthetic category between the particular and the general that would correspond to the more practical critical concept of the type. Ralph Fox gave a different definition of the type. He identified it as the general element which had to be counterbalanced by individual elements. He did not use this concept as a dialectical synthesis but as one pole of an unreconciled dichotomy, corresponding to Lukács' concept of the "general." [20] Fox, however, agrees with Lukács that characterization should happen preferably through narrative.[21] Curiously, the dialectical spirit of Lukács' view of the typical is much more evident in Brecht's than in

Fox's definition: "Historically significant (typical) are those people and events which may not be the most frequent or striking ones, [but] nevertheless still appear to us as positive (desirable) or negative (undesirable) ones."[22]

Whether or not the artist can create a synthetic totality through typification (as Lukács claimed) or otherwise is debatable. More or less official statements on socialist realism emphasize the necessity of "width and depth." In some cases, however, the great emphasis on the necessity of selectivity contains a curious secondary meaning. Radek, for instance, seems to be just as much against a nonselective naturalism as Lukács, although his stress on the necessity of selection may indicate that he simply wants to cram the world into some narrow ideological box and discard whatever does not fit into it.[23] The Hungarian socialist poet Attila József in some sense speaks for creative individuality when he says that no artist can really reflect the totality of existence, since his existence and experiences are unique to him. Consequently, any claim of totality goes against the necessary concreteness of the literary work.[24] The eminent Hungarian party ideologist and literary critic József Révai criticized Lukács for his synthesizing tendencies when he stated that ". . . a writer does not become great by trying to 'dissolve' and synthesize the opposites at any price. On the contrary: a writer often becomes great by revealing these opposites, or at least pointing out their irreconcilable character."[25]

The development of the hero in modern literary realism raised a controversy over the interpretation of the socialist rather than the bourgeois hero. Very few significant Marxist critics have shared Gorky's complete intolerance of the bourgeois tradition; most of them agree with Lukács in viewing the earlier period of this tradition as progressive and the later one as regressive. Christopher Caudwell, for example, derives the heroic middle-class protagonists in literature from the tradition of *laissez-faire* individualism and progress; his interpretation stems from the premise that in the seventeenth century a new, differentiated, and complex view of the world appears. The dream of the bourgeois is of "the one man alone producing the phenomena of the world. He is Faust, Hamlet, Robinson Crusoe, Satan, and Prufrock." [26]

But then, as most critics agree with Lukács and Gorky, modern bourgeois culture is a decaying one. As early as 1907, Lunacharsky believed that since the time of Ibsen and Hauptmann, any hero appearing as a "social innovator" was condemned either to destruction or to expressing his protest only in "abstract and fantastic symbols." [27] To the figure of the social reformer, Ralph Fox adds two more heroes he finds missing in modern literature—the scientist and the businessman. He exploits their absence to illustrate the increasing distance between the escapistic norms of an aristocratic, esoteric art and the rest of society. Fox also discovers, just as Lukács does, the element of disillusionment in the heroes of great realists like Balzac and Stendhal. He traces the process from disillusionment to disintegration, until "in our modern novel both hero and villain have died." The destruction of the personality in the technological capitalist world corresponds to the destruction of the hero in the novel. The mechanized mass-man corresponds to the automated antiheroes of modern literature. If there are no individuals left with a consistent, distinct world outlook, neither can there be any heroes. [28]

The socialist hero is, of course, a different breed. But what kind? Can he assert his heroic inclinations by at the same time accepting collectivism? Theoretically, an Hegelian synthesis is of course possible. As we have seen, however, in practice Gorky became entangled in self-contradiction by trying to demonstrate the greatness of both the individual and society. He simply wanted to achieve this by representing man at one moment and the community at another moment, in dimensions which were out of proportion.

The debates on the socialist realist hero reveal the still-existing problems of social idealism and prediction, as applied to literary characters. Generally, Marxist critics outside of the Soviet Union reacted sceptically to Gorky's and Zhdanov's views of characterization. Though Brecht accepted Gorky's didacticism at least to some extent, he felt that he could well do without socialist pathos. The audience should have the opportunity to follow the hero's deeds with full awareness, instead of emotionally sympathizing or identifying itself with the hero.[29] Also, Fox criticized those Soviet and Western socialist writers who regarded the description of social and historical background and events as more important than molding clear, distinct characters. He especially found the characterization of revolutionaries to be unsatisfactory. In this respect, he said, even Sholokhov and Malraux failed.[30]

If we consider the most extreme claim of collectivistic descriptions and characterization, the idea that this trend comes from Jules Romains' unanimism (as the Czech Karel Teige stated it, proudly, and the American critic Philo M. Buck, disapprovingly),[31] seems to be justifiable. This cult of exaggerated collectivism forms a paradoxical contrast to the cult of overdimensioned heroes. What is common in both, however, is the quantitative, proportional distortion of reality. It is possible to trace the immediate history of this development at least as far back as the first decade of the century. In 1908 the Rumanian socialist critic Nicolae Cocea, for instance, believed that the narrow bourgeois class literature would eventually yield to grandiose novels of socialism, similar to the epic poem, recording a fighting, suffering, and victorious new epoch.[32] After the revolution, this relatively latent trend became overt: scores of socialist critics characterized the new culture as "monumental."

The most pathetic mouthpiece of "monumental realism" was Alexey Tolstoy. The idea first appeared in his writings in the early twenties, and soon became a leitmotif of his literary statements and also of his creative activity. In 1924, he provided a sort of manifesto of monumentalism.[33] In a tragicomical effort to create both giants and a monumental social picture, Tolstoy inevitably found himself in a paradox. After all, which is greater, the new man or the new world? If the proportions of both increase at equal rate, their mutual relationship still remains static.

In the same essay, Tolstoy pleaded for a new hero who would take the place of the hero of the great epic tradition. The task of Soviet literature, he thought, was to describe the new Great Man (*Bolshoy Chelovek*), which he wrote with capital letters so that the great man would seem bigger, too. At the same time, curiously, he did not attach too much importance to the complexity of descriptions and characterization. "We need not be afraid of clumsy or lengthy descriptions, or tedious characterizations: we need monumental realism!" This he repeated again, almost twenty years later.[34]

Alexey Tolstoy's consistent inconsistency also appears in his view of the social frame. Both in 1924 and in 1942, he emphasized that the author must also communicate "a gigantic idea." At the same time, the new hero steps out of the historical frame of his nation, which is "so large that the hero is not infrequently overshadowed by the construction works, so that a factory, a city, a dam, a mine become the real heroes."

These statements by the author of *Peter the Great* are not completely unprecedented in nineteenth- and early-twentieth-century nonsocialist literary practice. A variation of naturalism and naturalistic realism, peculiar to the literature of agrarian countries and therefore largely neglected by histories of "world literature" published in the West, often used fairy-tale-like elements as a device of characterization. This tendency is not unknown in Scandinavian literatures, as even the English title (a Biblical quote) of the Norwegian-American Rølvaag's famous novel, *Giants in the Earth* indicates. (The English title is not a literal translation of the original Norwegian one, but the author himself gave it to the American edition in 1927.) The case is similar in some East-Central European countries. The Hungarian Zsigmond Móricz was a true master of this mode of writing. Dani Turi, the hero of his novel *Gold Nugget* (Sárarany, 1910) is a good example. He is distinguished among the fellow-peasants by his extraordinary qualities—one of them is his immense sexual potency. Also, Maciej and Antek Boryna, the heroes of Wladyslaw Reymont's *Peasants* (Chlopi, 1904–1909), have several "monumental" features. The Italian *verismo* and probably late-nineteenth-century Spanish literature were not exempt from this tendency to look at characters through a magnifying glass.

Taking a concrete sociohistorical perspective, we may say that the Gorky-Zhdanovian excesses of overdimensioning appear at their worst in Alexey Tolstoy's remarks on literature. Romantic, or better yet fairy-tale, megalomania goes conveniently hand in hand here with the reification and depreciation of man. Lukács, as we have seen, repeatedly attacked both tendencies. The Soviet Mikhail Lifshits, Lukács' friend, also criticized monumentalism and *sbornost'* (creation of idols, fetishism) in art, in terms that were analogous with Lenin's critique of Gorky's *bogostroitelstvo*.[35] Also, Konstantin Simonov, in his contribution to the Second Soviet Writers' Congress, condemned shallow heroism and the creation of "giants of socialism" as methods employed by socialist realism.[36] However, the Soviet official establishment, overdimensioned itself, has always preferred overdimensioned art. Khrushchev himself reviled Stalinist architecture and sculpture, but paradoxically, he also confessed an admiration for monumental sculptures.[37]

History, however, proves that big powers at this point keep falling into the same pit. Juxtaposing quality and quantity ("bigger and better") is a recurring phenomenon of cultural imperialism. In this respect, Alexey Tolstoy, Stalin, and Khrushchev are but the scions of the Caesars and the Bonapartes, and the "artistic" monumentalism of the Lomonosov University in Moscow is but a belated parallel of the Eiffel Tower, Hitler's chancellery, and the Empire State Building.

3. Tradition and Innovation

As a symptom, even the idea of monumental realism demonstrates one further issue (already mentioned tangentially) relevant to this discussion: the function of *tradition* in modern society. Monumentalism is a naive, abortive attempt, among others, to continue classicism as a tradition, and also to synthesize the best of the artistic-intellectual achievements of the human mind.

The problem of the cultural tradition draws one more dividing line between Marxist critics. It is also an additional matter on which Lukács and Brecht held different views. The idea that socialist realism cannot simply discard the treasures of earlier cultures has been a theoretical undercurrent ever since the twenties, though it has often occured in controversial forms. In general, Lukács, Fox and Lifshits represent this view on a more sophisticated level. But it is not only these respected traditionalist representatives of the vanguard of the thirties who wrote in defense of past cultures. As we have seen, Marx and Engels had previously defended the relevance of the great past culture for the working class movement; so did later numerous other socialist ideologists.

The trend which views socialist realism as an heir of the great past is now dominant, even in the Soviet Union. To mention only one example, the Soviet scholar Ermilov regards Gorky's "socialist humanism" as a direct and organic development of a trend growing out of Tolstoy's *Resurrection* (an "indirectly social novel") through Chekhov's representation of the individual's social responsibility (e.g. in *Ward Number Six*).[38] Though this view clearly disregards Gorky's own later statements on the literary heritage and his particular dislike of *Resurrection,* one should welcome it as a positive search for a cultural umbilical cord.

Aside from the extreme views of the Proletkult and RAPP in the twenties, and the early excesses of the theory of socialist realism in the thirties and forties, the most ardent antitraditional attack came from a group of German communist writers. This group, followers of Brecht, during the thirties attacked Lukács on the issue of tradition as well as on the author's commitment. Brecht's critical essays are full of ironic, sarcastic, and usually intolerant comments on traditionalism. There are no "eternal aesthetic values," he says, since everything is changing: Shakespeare, Balzac, and Tolstoy are pathetically outdated. Brecht turned several of Lukács' concepts or arguments against him, in a slightly reinterpreted form. For example, he called Lukács' "assumed thesis" that a handful of nineteenth-century novels manifest the only workable method for realism, "formalism."[39] This assault is even more ironic in that Lukács repeatedly emphasized his belief that no formal category could define realism. Also, Brecht was as much opposed to fetishism as was Lukács, but he then called Balzac a writer of the age of fetishism. With reference to Lukács' dislike of montage, Brecht wrote: "No, Balzac does not employ montage. But he writes gigantic genealogies, marries the creatures of his fantasy like Napoleon did with his marshalls and brothers, follows the pleasures of families (fetishism of things) through generations. . . ."[40]

Becher, Seghers, Bloch and Eisler, along with other leftist German expressionists who later became communists, also expressed in one form or another the Brechtian idea that the old bourgeois tradition was dead and that a new, specifically socialist art must be established. More recently, the socialist Halldór Kiljan Laxness, who, like Brecht, never became a member of any communist party, showed a curiously intolerant attitude toward the past culture of mankind. In his essay

"Digtningens problematik i vor tid," he rejected the view that socialist realism descends either from the Greek cult of form and beauty (with the renaissance and classicism as its vehicles), or from nineteenth-century "orthodox" realism. While the basis of the Greek classical tradition is an idealistic Platonic view of the world, the foundation of recent literary realism is a down-to-earth "vulgar empiricism," and both are alien to Marxism.[41] Laxness was obviously carried away by the zeal of the creative artist in asserting his freedom and talent against aesthetic dogmas. Unfortunately, he did not distinguish realism from naturalism in the nineteenth-century tradition, as did Lukács. Nor did he consider whether or not aesthetic idealism and empiricism could become synthesized in the theory and practice of socilist realism.

There are a few Marxist critics who tried to find a dialectical synthesis between tradition and innovation. The Czech Karel Konrad, for instance, does not seem to find any dichotomic difference between the two. In rejecting the view of his countryman, Karel Teige, that socialist realism clings to "old-fashioned Balzacian and Tolstoian methods," Konrad lists works like Katayev's *Time Forward!*, Pilnyak's *The Volga Flows Into the Caspian Sea*, and Sholokhov's *Virgin Soil Upturned* as documents of a new artistic approach to a changing life.[42] Antonio Gramsci also made an interesting point when he derived the shifting appreciation of earlier cultures in different periods of history from the concrete and immediate social needs of these periods rather than from eternal aesthetic values.[43] This sociological approach to the problem closely follows Marx's view that more recent cultures inevitably reinterpret the past, and accept or reject it according to their own social and ideological needs. But again, as we may recall, Marx also wrote about an eternal interest in classicism throughout human history, and this is what Lukács, obviously in contrast to Gramsci, emphasized in his works.

We have already discussed the impact of classicism as a

major cultural movement on the Marxist theories of literary realism. The status of another large movement, romanticism, has also given rise to controversy. Though Lukács' consistency on this question is impressive, the majority of Marxist writers and critics have taken a position contrary to his. Perhaps an understandable yearning for fantasy, lyricism, and one form of commitment made several critics state, with Gorky, that there is no conflict between socialist realism and romanticism. Prior to Zhdanovism, Soviet functionaries (like Bukharin), writers (like Alexey Tolstoy and Fadeyev), more recently also some Western Marxist critics (like Finkelstein) shared this view.

Actually, the attempts either to reject or to defend romanticism are equally based on a shaky definition of this movement. The British Marxist critic Arnold Kettle openly stated his doubt that existing definitions of romanticism were even slightly satisfactory. Kettle did not believe that realistic exactitude could or should exclude fantasy. *Jane Eyre* and *Adam Bede* are, he said, basically realistic works, although tinged with romanticism, and *Gulliver's Travels* is, though full of fantasy, still a realistic work of art.[44] These uncertainties surrounding the definition of romanticism are as familiar to non-Marxist scholars of the West as they are to their Marxist colleagues in the socialist countries and elsewhere. Nevertheless, Kettle's doubts seem to justify the hypothesis that a more complex, tolerant, and dialectical view of the relationship between realism and romanticism than that of Lukács is highly desirable.

4. Realism and the Genres

We have already stated the problem of whether or not the Marxist theory of literary realism also fits genres other than prose. Lyric poetry, especially, seems to have been neglected in theoretical and analytical Marxist works. By 1914, Franz Mehring had already complained that "the history of the socialist lyric has not yet been written."[45] And in the thirties, Brecht plaintively asked: "How about the realism of the lyric, the drama?"[46]

An appropriate question indeed!

Lyric poetry has not yet received any specifically Marxist interpretation that could be compared to Lukács' or Fox's theories on the novel. But this does not mean that attempts are lacking. A sample of comments on lyric poetry proves that there is a basic difference between two groups of critics.

First, there are Marxist theorists who, although primarily concerned with finding valid norms for the novel, also are interested in comparing poetry with prose. Georg Lukács is our first example. In an essay on J. R. Becher written in 1951, he says that while the drama and the novel show the dialectic of existence in the finished form of the reflected reality, poetry shapes reality before our eyes, so that we observe the model of life *in statu nascendi*.[47]

Though Lukács did not make any other direct comment on the lyric as compared to prose, dozens of casual remarks about poetry appear in his writings. Shelley, Heine, Rilke, the French symbolists, and the Hungarians Petőfi, Ady, and Babits, are just some of the poets he discusses in passing. This has made several of Lukács' critics ask whether he also kept poetry in mind when he elaborated his theory of realism. The Swede Arnold Ljungdal attaches a great deal of significance to Lukács' lyric examples which (to him) indicate that a general theory of literature rather than just a theory of prose genres was Lukács' aim.[48] The Hungarian István Eörsi, himself a student of Lukács in his university years, begins one of his studies with the deductive assumption that Lukács' works, though primarily analyzing prose, do contain a potential core for a specific Marxist poetic theory.[49] Nevertheless, Ljungdal and Eörsi both fail to demonstrate their point. The former does not ask whether or not there are essential differences between poetic and prose genres, and if these differences modify the general theory of realism. The latter falls short of citing satisfactory evidence for even a core of some specifically *poetic* theory in Lukács. His examples are taken, without exception, from Lukács' writings on prose and (occasionally) drama. However, both critics seem to conclude with the same assumption, namely that Lukács' theory of realism is applicable to all genres.

A comparison of poetry and prose which is more general than that of Lukács, but still pathetically sketchy, occurs in Arnold Kettle, who uses several of Caudwell's statements on poetry. Caudwell, however, refrained from actually comparing prose and poetry in his *Illusion and Reality*. Kettle establishes three criteria for comparing the two genres: the function of creative consciousness, genetic chronology, and social practice. He finds that poetry is an expression of collective consciousness, and prose one of private consciousness; that poetry is older than prose—probably because the collective consciousness precedes the individual one; and, finally, that the origin of poetry is in magic and ritual, while that of prose is in the opposite—an attempt at conceptualization and rational reasoning.[50]

As we can see, all members of this first group either derive their interpretation of poetry from a theory of the novel, or feel compelled to constantly make comparisons between prose and poetry. Members of the more heterogeneous second group are less bound by the spell of the novel and its theories. Rather, they try to find laws valid for the poetic genre *per se*—laws derived from the peculiarities of the genre as consistently as some of the Marxist theories of the novel are.

One of the earliest statements on poetry after the Bolshevik revolution came from Otto Ville Kuusinen, leader of the communists in the Finnish civil war of 1918 and, later, a member of the Supreme Soviet. Kuusinen was an educated layman-aesthetician, and in three letters that he wrote to the Finno-Swedish poet Elmer Diktonius between 1919 and 1921, he listed these four characteristics of poetry:

—concreteness and "visual symbolism";
—an intellectual complexity full of tension;
—the centering around an idea and not around details or technical virtuosity;
—concentrated form.[51]

This characterization of lyric poetry is akin to Lukács' view of the realistic novel (which it preceded by more than ten years) in at least two respects. First, it seems to regard the Hegelian concrete universal—that is, the human experience expressed in concrete, yet symbolic, images—as an ideal, just as Lukács did. Second, the two tempting extremes one finds in modern poetry—subjectivism and uncontrolled emotion on the one hand, and objectivism or abstract intellectualism on the other—obviously do not occur as equally acceptable alternatives for Kuusinen; the same is true for both Hegel and Lukács.

Only a few Marxist critics dared to state openly that lyric poetry (except the most blatantly revolutionary kind) is more difficult to interpret in sociopolitical terms than the more rational and explicit prose genre. For cultural functionaries such as Bukharin, Zhdanov, or Khrushchev, the most important thing was to include poetry theoretically among the possible spheres of socialist realism. On the other hand, writers and critics such as Brecht and Caudwell admitted that the lyric genre poses special problems for the theory of socialist realism. At the same time, they also wanted to do something to clarify some of these problems.[52]

In *Illusion and Reality*, Caudwell reiterates the cultural anthropological view that poetry originally grew out of magic and the social demand for memorizing and perpetuating laws. The origin and the function of poetry mutually determine each other. Functionally, poetry is a form of primitive epistemology, and the same magic which gives birth to poetry also generates science.

Caudwell's and Brecht's views on some of the main characteristics of lyric poetry show an admirable concordance. Caudwell blatantly states that the essence of lyric poetry is irrational, not verifiable—that is, "illusion." Brecht, as a conscientious rationalist, avoids the word "irrational," yet must admit that, save for committed poetry, the lyric does not yield to any systematic proof. Both Caudwell and Brecht emphasize, however, that poetry still follows an "inner logic" of its own. This separation of external and internal logic reminds one of existentialistic epistemology, and therefore could well be labeled "irrational" from a Lukácsian point of view.

As a second characteristic of poetry, Caudwell lists its nonsymbolic, concrete feature. Again, Brecht concurs with this, and admits that the lyric creates emotions and moods, although this function of poetry clearly contradicts his own ideal of critical intellectualism and, on the stage, detachment through estrangement. As a third characteristic, Caudwell discusses the condensation of poetic expression. One difference here between the two critics is that while Caudwell emphasizes the originally conventional form of poetry and regards the free form as a conscious "rejection of all rhythm because of its social genesis," Brecht considers the question whether a poem is written in free or bound form irrelevant.

It is fairly clear that existing elaborated theories of socialist realism are not applicable to lyric poetry without undergoing radical transformations. The rules for these necessary transformations have not yet been established. One cannot judge the case with the *drama* exactly in the same manner, however, Brecht's theatrical achievements, for instance, organically belong together with the experimentations of a larger socialist realist scope. It is true that Brecht, who cultivates an "epic" technique in his dramas, gets support on this point from the general theory of realism which is based on the novelistic tradition. As a whole, however, this theory appears to be more suited, in almost all respects, to drama than to poetry.

The problem of the tragedy does pose some special difficulties. It is precisely the essence of the tragedy that is in conflict with the basic tenets of Marxism. This conflict is not necessarily unsolvable, but to this day the attempts to solve it have proved to be unsatisfactory. Georg Lukács' early preoccupation with the drama has nothing to do with Marxism, and consequently all attempts to discuss the Marxist concept of the drama which begin with the early Lukács (attempts like those of Goldmann or Bente Hansen) follow a false track. Some party critics believed they had found the essence of tragedy in spheres which are actually completely irelevant. The only recent full-length Soviet study on the tragedy, by Yury Borev, appeared in 1961. But this author seriously believes that the task of socialist realist tragedy is to show its heroes in the context of the world conflict of socialism and capitalism.[53] Such narrow-minded simplifications obviously discredit rather than constructively develop the general theory of socialist realism.

5. The Cultural Geography of a Concept

A survey of how far and how much Marxist theories of realism have penetrated the cultural sphere of the globe may indicate an impressive international influence. Yet, a recurring motif is the central place of Soviet literature and criticism in this international context. We may remember that Zhdanov openly (and Gorky implicitly) stated that Soviet literature was both the richest in ideas and the most advanced on earth. This culturally chauvinistic statement corresponds to Stalin's attempt to establish the Soviet Union as the leader of the international communist movement. This raises the question of whether the modern Marxist theory of realism is an ethnocentric theory, one which is ultimately rooted in *Soviet* Marxism-Leninism.

During the thirties and the forties, whenever tactical considerations demanded it, functionaries as well as critics in the Soviet Union referred to the intolerant attitude of the RAPP in a completely negative manner. The title of Zhdanov's congressional speech, however, clearly shows that there is indeed an unfortunate continuation of ethnocentrism in the Soviet cultural tradition. To illustrate the elitist character of the Soviet theory of socialist literature, the comparison of two documents will serve our purpose well.

The first document is a program from 1931 conceived by a group of emigrant Hungarian communist writers living in the Soviet Union. This clique of obscure scribblers with all seriousness compiled a collection of nonsense about what the socialist reflection of art should be. They next reviewed all of the possible literary orientations and refuted them one by one. This was not difficult as far as the "decadent bourgeois culture" was concerned; but when they discussed the activity of other emigrant communist writers' organizations, they bravely rejected these, too, as either right- or left-wing deviants. Hungarian writers within Hungary were but puppets of fascism, while those who were part of the Western emigration were constantly exposed to the temptations of the bourgeois world. Naturally, the only real representatives of Hungarian socialist literature were themselves—simply because they lived and worked in the Soviet Union.[54] On the same basis, Alexander Abusch criticized Hans Mayer in 1957 for discussing the literature of the German Democratic Republic within the framework of the total German culture. After all, according to Abusch, there is a radical difference between the socialist East

German and the bourgeois West German literature.[55] In the same way, many of Lukács' critics, such as Révai, Horváth, and Szigeti, demanded a greater appreciation of Soviet cultural superiority from him.

The other document in question is Laxness' essay on the problems of socialist literature, "Digtningens problematik i vor tid" (1954), which we have already quoted. In this essay, Laxness gave an interesting account of his recent meeting with a young Soviet painter. Laxness had to recognize, during their conversation, that for this artist, the Greek, Renaissance, and neoclassical culture of balanced, proportioned forms, and all of the subsequent aesthetic theories emerging from it, constituted the only way to look at the world. The Soviet painter furthermore believed that this classicist tendency was axiomatically and necessarily beautiful for everybody living on earth.

Laxness' critical observation reveals the great problem of realism. The tendency to generalize uncritically one's own limited experiences and values is a trap. Lukács fought against such generalizations, yet fell into the trap himself. His view of realism is determined by a refined Central European intellectual attitude toward life. Even this lofty spectatorial position has its disadvantages, however. Lukács is not only a Marxist scholar of wide scope and considerable education, but he is also a cosmopolitan. Incidentally, his overall view of Hungarian literature (expressed in numerous writings, the content and volume of which is largely unknown to the West) is built upon completely untenable, absurd assumptions.[56]

The recognition of social relativism and the importance of the roles of different national traditions in forming valid aesthetic norms is a tendency that has its origins in the thirties, supposedly as a reaction to the First Soviet Writers' Congress. Western European communist artists and intellectuals especially represent this trend. In 1937 Louis Aragon adopted a consciously national attitude toward the question of realism.

By rejecting the "bourgeois" accusation that socialist realism is a specifically Soviet Russian movement, Aragon soundly criticized Soviet cultural imperialism, too. First, he expressed his doubts about the value of a servile reflection of "the world." He then rejected any effort to imitate the achievements of Soviet literature. Finally, he thought that it was impossible to find any national tradition which was more exemplary than others. Aragon felt that even though the works of Pushkin, Gogol, and Tolstoy may fruitfully contribute to a Soviet concept of socialist realism, the French Marxists should "turn towards completely different masters" of their own country.[57] Brecht also expressed this view during the thirties. He felt that various concepts of the Soviet definitions of realism like "feelings," "synthesis," and others, were obscure and unreliable.[58]

During the forties and early fifties, this anti-Zhdanovist trend temporarily disappeared. Some of its earlier representatives, such as Ernst Ottwalt, who sought refuge from Nazism in the Soviet Union, died during the party purges. But after Stalin's death, national dissent reappeared. Besides Laxness, Aragon's renewed expressions of his dislike for Soviet cultural imperialism are especially notable. What the Soviet writers and critics call realism, said Aragon in 1959, cannot be a universal canon, especially since it was often merely down-to-earth realism, naturalism, naive populism, or no realism at all.[59] Significant modern Marxist critics have turned their interest to the heritage of their own cultures—Ernst Fischer to Kafka, Garaudy to Saint-John Perse and Picasso—instead of looking to the Soviet Union for ideals.

The same tendency to reject Soviet ethnocentrism seems to occur in other arts as well. We may refer here to Siqueiros' view of the Soviet variety of socialist realism, which he expressed in an interview.[60] Siqueiros was one of the most celebrated Mexican monumentalist painters, and he was at the same time a devoted communist who had been jailed several times for his political activity. He thus had the more right to maintain his own creative integrity and to criticize orthodox (and often incompetent) Soviet theoreticians who denounced modern art in general, and his own paintings in particular.

Speaking about the present situation in Marxist criticism, one cannot ignore the influence of Maoism on literary matters. The Chinese aesthetic literature which is available in translation leaves the impression of an archaic, earlier stage of socialist literary criticism. The spirit of the Proletkult and extreme Zhdanovism haunt the pages of the periodical *Chinese Literature*, however positively one may otherwise think of Maoism. This is no longer literary theory but literary policy. Until recently, it influenced cultural extremists around the world, but its impact was somewhat noticeable only in countries which did not have any strong and independent critical tradition of their own. In these countries, far-out statements of Maoist quasi-literati may have stirred occasional local storms, yet Maoist criticism represents a period long *passé* in the international history of socialist aesthetic theory.

As indicated earlier, the intention in undertaking this survey of the particular problems of the Marxist theories of realism was to apply the two models (Lukács' critical and Gorky's socialist realism) to a larger number of works in criticism. More recent achievements of the Marxist theories of realism appear in the reinterpretation of modern experimental literature, absurdity as a contemporary phenomenon, and interpretations of the "world of things" (reflected in literature by documentarism and the *roman nouveau*). Following chapters will analyze certain aspects of these issues. Investigations in these directions are inseparable from an increasing recognition among Marxists of the specific problems of our age of technology and science.

IV. Objectivism: Materialistic Realism or Left-Deviation?

1. Post-Hegelian Development: The Views of Marx, Engels, and Lenin

As we have already seen, the Hegelian-Marxist concept of realism emphasizes that the external (sociohistorical) and the internal (subjective-psychological) realities of an age should both have their places in the reflective process. Hegel attributed great importance to the dialectical synthesis of a series of opposing concepts when establishing his literary ideal. A partial list of these dichotomies would include: material-spiritual, sensuous-intellectual, concrete-abstract, particular-general, object-subject, individual-social. Georg Lukács aggressively defended this rigorously balanced characteristic of Hegelian aesthetics.

Hegel may well have brought the intellectual achievements of the preceding two hundred years—empiricism and philosophical idealism, classicism, and romanticism—to an impressive synthesis. After the defeat of the revolutions of 1848–49, however, a new epoch opened in the history of modern bourgeois society. There was a return to science, both natural and social. This tendency gained hold in philosophy in the form of the new positivistic trend, and in art in the naturalistic trend. The tremendous impetus of Darwin and Mendel, as well as the hardly less impressive later-time sociological achievements of Durkheim and Max Weber, yielded—in one interpretation of their findings—to a deterministic view of natural and social dynamics. After the turn of the century, new forms of communication and entertainment contributed favorably to the documentation of the numerically ever-increasing events of modern life, and to the diffusion of these events to an expanding, receptive public which was more and more interested in actual "facts," even if these were, by traditional standards of taste, either horrible or disgusting.

How did Marxist writers and critics react to the public demands of the new scientific-technological period? The wide variety of answers to this question deserves an entire chapter of its own, since it is directly related to the classical concept of realism and probably challenges it. Because of the high status of the "originators" of Marxist theory, let us first take a look again at Marx's, Engels' and Lenin's views.

In his letter to Miss Harkness, Engels considered Balzac "a far greater master of realism than all of the Zolas, past, present, or future." Lukács especially, but also present-day literary handbooks and textbooks, frequently quote this highly derogatory remark in arguing against naturalism. The statement is not unique to Marx's and Engels' taste. Lafargue also mentioned Marx's personal dislike of Zola, the Goncourts and Flaubert. Both Marx and Engels condemned that deterministic and reactionary view of "human nature" which they believed to have found in the anthropological speculations of such authors as the early-nineteenth-century philosopher of law, Gustav von Hugo, and their own contemporary Hermann Bahr.[1] Besides natural-anthropological determinism, social determinism also seemed unacceptable to Marx and Engels. In the Sickingen debate, they discredited Lassalle's view that the German peasants of the 1530s, owing to their class limitations, were reactionary adherents to archaic, medieval patriarchism.

The voluminous work of Marx and Engels, however, does not yield only to one interpretation of their views. In terms of subject matter, Engels especially was fairly close to a gutsy plebeian view of man's biological existence. It seems to have occurred to him, for example, that sexual drive may be a significant human motivating factor. In his essay on the German communist poet Georg Weerth (1883), Engels exclaimed: "When reading e.g. Freiligrath's poems, you really get the impression that people have no sexual organs at all. . . . It is high time that at least the German workers get accustomed to talking about things they practice daily or nightly themselves, about natural, unavoidable and highly pleasant things, just as openly as do the Romanic people, Homer and Plato, Horace and Juvenal, the Old Testament and the *Neue Rheinische Zeitung*."[2]

On the other hand, if we can believe Clara Zetkin, Lenin held an unfavorable opinion of sexuality. Zetkin describes Lenin as having disapproved of erotic passages in literature and as having regarded sexuality as a peripheral phenomenon of existence penetrated and guided by socioeconomic values.[3] Also, he condemned the nonselective documentarism of a Ukrainian novel, V. Vinnichenko's *Paternal Testaments*, which he regarded as a hand-picked collection of misery, social evil, and criminality—all easily recognizable elements, along with sexuality, of naturalistic entertainment literature around the turn of the century.[4] But, again, Lenin was a pragmatist, and whenever controversial imagery served him in explaining his thoughts, he adopted it willingly. For instance, he once referred to Zola's description of the pains of childbirth (most probably in chapter 10 of *La Joie de vivre*) in order to illustrate the painful process of social revolution with a vivid literary analogy.[5]

If references to realism are scarce in the writings of the most respected Marxist ideologists, they are almost completely missing with respect to naturalism and other related phenomena. The reason may be the relative newness of the latter movement. Engels' casual critical remark on Zola makes a very poor argument for Lukács in his ardent antinaturalist campaigns. Among recent leading ideologists, Zhdanov and Khrushchev also criticized naturalism, yet in practice they closed their eyes to its manifestations in socialist realism.

There were, however, scores of socialist writers and critics who held different opinions about naturalism, objectivism, and other new phenomena. Their observations are the more interesting, as they were relatively free from the compulsion of constantly referring to Marx's, Engels', and Lenin's remarks. The relationship between realism and naturalism should be especially notable for Anglo-American scholars, since in the critical tradition of the English-speaking world these two movements are not infrequently equated. Information gained from the Marxist debates may contribute to a revelation of the irrelevance of this leveling practice.

2. "Pro": Objectivism as a Form of Materialistic Realism

Lukács' and Gorky's theories of realism have already served to shape two models which could be compared to each other and to other views. Two other Marxist critics, Franz Mehring and Georgy Valentinovich Plekhanov, are appropriate for comparing a similar investigation of naturalism and its appearance in literary theory in the form of deterministic criticism. Both Mehring and Plekhanov were leading personalities of the Second International, and appear as archetypes of pronaturalist aesthetics in Lukács' view, as well as in current officially approved East-Central European handbooks on literature. Also, several literary scholars in the Western hemisphere have accepted this Lukácsian interpretation of Mehring's and Plekhanov's concept of realism.

At first sight it seems erroneous to tie Mehring to naturalism, as he explicitly and consistently criticized this movement. He regarded naturalism as a pseudo-scientific attempt by the bourgeoisie to assert its power. Moreover, in his view the idea that naturalist literature should describe "everyday life" turns out to be a justification used for describing bourgeois profit-making—that is, one superficial phenomenon of capitalist existence (*Gesammelte Schriften und Aufsätze*).[6] Though naturalism probably began as an attempt to emancipate man from capitalism, it stopped half-way. It describes misery and decay, but does not provide ideals or alternatives (2:110–11).[7]

This lack of ideals in naturalism is, in Mehring's opinion, merely the philosophical projection of the general lack of fantasy that one finds in the mainstream. This is, on the one hand, a result of man's slavish subordination to things, to the material world, in the naturalist ideology (*ibid.*).[8] Though Zola was a keen observer and an excellent psychologist too, he lacked creative genius, fantasy, and wit (2:304–7). Mehring asserts that naturalism also became the cause of modern decadence. It alienated imaginative poets and writers, who found the only escape from a world of things and rigid determinism in a dream-world of illusory subjectivism and "free" formal experimentation (2:111).

When reading Mehring's own critical writings it is, paradoxically, common to find rather unsophisticated examples of social determinism, which, together with natural determinism, was basic to naturalism. The best example is probably his *Die Lessing-Legende* (1893), the first part of which consists entirely of critical reviews of Lessing's bourgeois critics, descriptions of economic and social conditions, as well as historical events in Frederician Prussia. The second part analyzes Lessing's life and personality. Biographical references are abounding, especially sociocritical ones.

Of course, one may say that the danger of determinism, implicit also in nineteenth-century academic positivism, is not specifically an attribute of any Mehringian method. Yet, in Mehring, this goes hand in hand with an unattractive labelling of writers by their social origin. Thus, Gerhard Hauptmann "comes on father's and mother's side from . . . the proletarian stratum" (2:269), whereas Ibsen and Bjørnson derive from "a petty-bourgeois family" (2:315). Besides this labelling, Mehring reduces complex cultural movements to simplified single factors. He regards classicism, for instance, as "nothing else but" the struggle of the bourgeoisie for self-emancipation (2:104).

With respect to his controversial stand on naturalism, an extremely eclectic approach to concrete literary works emerges from Mehring's essays. He does not question the greatness of Homer, Aeschylus, Dante, Shakespeare, and Goethe. These were "universal poets, as their works admirably reflect the great changes of the world" (2:265). He also appreciates Dickens for his "excellent social types" (2:309). More problematic is his view of the period of what Lukács calls "great realism," since Mehring seems to discuss Balzac and Zola together as naturalists (who do not provide any ideals for the future) in at least two instances (2:58, 306). Moreover, there is no trace of the term "realism" in Mehring's writings.

Among his contemporaries, Hauptmann and Ibsen were especially troublesome for Mehring. Like Lukács, who called *Die Weber* a work marking a never-to-return, uniquely significant period in Hauptmann's work, Mehring also increasingly chided Hauptmann for turning away from his earlier sociocritical writings, which were tendentious in a positive sense (2:150). He strongly disapproved of Hauptmann's mood-evoking effects (like "a melodramatic simultaneity of music, light-effects and colorful costumes") in the symbolic and dreamplays, calling them unartistic methods (2:158). Up to this point, as we shall see, his critique corresponds to Lukács'. However, the differences between Mehring and Lukács lie deeper than their analogous views of dramatic technique. Writing about *Hanneles Himmelfahrt*, Mehring believes that the reports of the British parliamentary commissions reveal more authentically than Hauptmann's descriptions what proletarian children think of their life and world (2:159–60). This juxtaposition of literary genius and official documents, this undifferentiated view of the sources of social information, separates Mehring radically from Lukács.

A similar shift of opinion took place in Mehring's view of Ibsen, whose social critical plays he highly appreciated. But even among the dramas written in the critical period, Mehring disapproved of the particular method Ibsen used in *Ghosts*. In this play, Ibsen tried "to reconcile Moses and Darwin," and to present his audience with shallow moralizing in scientific disguise (2:262). The symbolism that entered Hauptmann's oeuvre with the dream plays also perverted Ibsen's works. Mehring discusses particularly *Rosmersholm* and *Little Eyolf* with critical dissatisfaction (2:321–22, 330).

All things considered, Mehring is a more controversial critic than Lukács believed. The characteristics Lukács attributed to Mehring—a Kantian separation of art and life, exalted enthusiasm for Schiller as opposed to Goethe, overestimation of the importance of German classicism[9]—are difficult to verify satisfactorily in Mehring's works. On the other hand, the reader may indeed find quite a few contradictions in Mehring.

Though in theory Mehring was against naturalism, in practice he widely exploited one of its basic theses: social determinism, which, if applied to literature, suggests that the author's social origin determines the literary work. Of dialectics and materialism, these twin foundations of Marxist thought, Mehring most willingly accepted materialism—that is, the thesis of the determining role of socioeconomic conditions in art. It is therefore hard to understand Lukács' high estimation of *Die Lessing-Legende*, which is a true manifestation of the deterministic outlook on art.

Mehring was willing to take a historical approach at times. His tracing the development of the social function of the bourgeoisie in *Die Lessing-Legende* from a progressive to a repressive force is clearly a Marxist achievement. However, the dialectical aspect of Marxism never entered his thinking. Human consciousness, both in its freedom and in its mutual connection with the natural sphere of existence, plays no role in Mehring. Lukács justly criticized him for this.

Mehring was probably right when he stated that literary history becomes "aesthetic-philological incompetence" if it fails to discuss economic and political conditions.[10] But he overdid this aspect of literary historicism himself. Because of his emphasis on biographical causality, he could not decipher the sophisticated life work of great poets, and he dichotomized the artistic development of such writers as Tolstoy, Ibsen, or Hauptmann. Since he underestimated creative consciousness, he was unable to analyze literary works with regard to their aesthetic values. Mehring was blind to the inner, created, integrated world of a work of art as one coordinated with, rather than subordinated to, economic realities.

Lukács also criticized Plekhanov for social determinism,[11] yet still believed that Hegelian philosophy found a more positive reception in this Russian Marxist than it did in Mehring.[12] It was probably because of the much lesser degree of mechanistic causality in Plekhanov's view of literature that Lukács slightly favored him over Mehring. For Mehring, society determined the author's views, which then determined the work; for Plekhanov, the author's mediating function between external reality and the internalized world of the work was more complex.

Like Mehring, Plekhanov also disliked naturalism. In *Art and Social Life* he noted that the cement for the foundation of this movement was only "naturalist-scientific materialism," and contained nothing of social history. The realists, these predecessors of naturalism, come out more favorably in the comparison Plekhanov establishes between the two movements. The realist generation created great works, based on their observation of the social environment, in spite of their frequently reactionary biases.[13]

Like Mehring, Plekhanov also yielded to social determinism, although to a form that differed from Mehring's. Mehring subordinated man to his created, material, "second nature" and to his social *conditions;* Plekhanov regarded social *activity,* the only Darwinian instinct of man he accepted, as the determining factor. The three first "letters" of his renowned "Unaddressed Letters" (Pisma bez adresa, pp. 19–139) especially elucidate his view of the origin, function, and definition of art.

In these aesthetic statements, Plekhanov first refutes the Darwinian idea of biological (inherited) aesthetic sense, and derives art from social needs and social activity. Then, he similarly rejects the imitative character of art and the rhythm-theory as views which find the essence of artistic creation in inherent biological factors, rather than social practice. Primitive people wear tiger or other skins neither for decoration nor for anthropomorphic-ritualistic reasons, but in order to assume the animal's power. Nothing comes from the inside; everything is socially determined (pp. 44ff). Therefore, the perception of reality is also a result of social conditioning.

Just as in Mehring, one cannot get rid of the notion of determinism when reading Plekhanov's writings. His arguments on why culture determines art (pp. 49ff) are nearly as hopeless as the following analogy between natural and social causality is ridiculous: "Just as an apple tree *must* produce apples and a pear tree pears, so must the artist who adopts the bourgeois standpoint be against the working-class movement" (p. 223). It is interesting, however, that Plekhanov's sociopolitical biases go along with a definition of art which opens the reader's vista to some challenging further problems.

Art is, in Plekhanov's opinion, "one of the means of spiritual communication between people." It is also one form of expression of feelings and thoughts "in living images and not abstractly" (pp. 183, 201). In other words, Plekhanov seems to define art as communication on three interrelated levels: emotional, intellectual, and spiritual. It is artistic imagery that separates art and literature from other, purely informative forms of communication.

How does the transformation of knowledge and experience into images happen in art? Plekhanov answers this question by examining a practical problem. If the upper classes no longer actively participate in the social productive process, how is it possible that their art and literature still reflect the economic basis of their society? Plekhanov believes that the process of reflection goes through several "intermediate links" (pp. 141–42). The sphere of mediation between external reality and its re-creation in the arts is the human psyche. Plekhanov clearly states that the author's mind translates the social experience into the language of the psyche, and consequently also seems to imply that this peculiar "language" takes shape in the work of art. Conversely, as he explains to us, the critic's task is to derive from this artistic psychosphere the original experience, the "sociological equivalent," by "translating the idea of a work of art *from the language of art to the language of sociology.*"[14]

To this "sociological" or "materialistic" criticism, Plekhanov contrasts the "philosophical" or "idealistic" trend in criticism which he, by reaching back to the Russian cultural tradition for examples, derives from Belinsky. While sociology says that nothing is absolute and everything is culturally conditioned (p. 165), philosophy assumes the existence of some absolute ideas or truths. Therefore, the philosophical critic believes that the writer or artist has hidden this kind of absolute idea in his work, and tries to decipher it by translating "truth from the language of art to the language of philosophy, from the language of images to the language of logic," and by seeking the general in particular details.[15]

It is probable that Plekhanov would have later criticized Lukács, too, for his philosophical method. Lukács felt the implicit antagonism between his ideas and Plekhanov's heritage, and therefore repeatedly emphasized his basic disagreement with Plekhanov. Undoubtedly, Plekhanov overestimates the impact of the temporary social message of the literary work, and underestimates its more permanent values, as well as the universal scope that it provides. However, Lukács and all those who accuse Plekhanov of "vulgar sociology" (English-speaking readers may find this standard Marxist term repulsive), seem to forget about one important factor. They all disregard the continuation of the essay (Plekhanov's introduction to the third edition of his collection *Za dvadsat' let*, 1908), in which the author set forth his definitions of sociological and philosophical criticism. Further on in this essay, Plekhanov wrote: "[Materialist] criticism, in its endeavor to find the social equivalent of a certain literary phenomenon, betrays itself unless it understands that the task cannot be limited to finding this equivalent, and that sociology cannot exclude aesthetics, but, just the opposite, must open the door to it. The second act of the true materialist critique—as well as of the idealist critique—must be judging the aesthetic values of the work analyzed." In other words, both sociological and philosophical criticism, though stemming from different premises, ought to work toward the same goal: to reveal the integrated, inner artistic values of the literary work.

In theory, this dialectical view of external conditions and the internal, created literary world sounds convincing and attractive. In practice, however, Plekhanov seldom entered the inner world. He rather looked at it from the outside, with a regrettable lack of understanding. His long essay on Ibsen is good evidence of this. Though containing valuable observations, it reveals the main weakness of Plekhanov's social deterministic view of literature—its mechanistically causal, simplified character. For example, Plekhanov identifies the hero with the general message of the work. He regards Brand, Ibsen's hero, as a symbol of an idea only, and does not see any personality in him. He also seems to identify Brand's and Dr. Stockmann's views with those of the writer, not noticing the critical distance between the two. Irony, wit, distance, and ambiguity evade Plekhanov. He also equates Ibsen's Kierkegaardian view of individual development with petty-bourgeois anarchism. Of course, all of Ibsen's shortcomings are results of his petty-bourgeois origin.[16]

Summarizing Mehring's and Plekhanov's views in comparison with those of Lukács, we find that even though the former two did not regard and define literature from the same perspective, both are at variance with Lukács' views. The significance that Plekhanov granted to the human psyche and the consequent indirect character of the mediation of social information to the arts separates him from Mehring; the great importance they both attributed to sociology and to social causality unites them. Neither of them considered the creative process and the reflection of reality as a dialectical interaction, as Lukács did. Lukács also believed, as the other two did not, that it is not only social information which shapes the author's consciousness. Finally, Lukács contended that references to social conditions appear in the literary work only in a philosophically generalized, universal form. Both Mehring and Plekhanov shied away from such a view in their practical criticism.

Whatever their individual shortcomings and differences, we can nevertheless derive from both Mehring's and Plekhanov's critical views a literary model that they regarded as ideal.

Though Mehring never and Plekhanov only occasionally

used the term realism for good modern writing, their model delineates one kind of realism. This realism almost exclusively reflects social, political, and historical conditions as they appear in the author's mind, in the form of some direct or indirect imprint. There is only a single channel, a one-way fixed relationship between society and man: socioeconomic conditions or actions come first, man comes next, and the former defines the latter. Man is less interesting than his work or society. This idea bears a conspicuous resemblance to Gorky's view of human labor.

Furthermore, literature is factually, scientifically informative. Whether the facts support the bourgeois system or instigate the readers (and the masses) to overthrow it seems to be the point at which the paths of naturalism and the Lukácsian-Marxist concept of realism diverge. Both Plekhanov and Mehring blame naturalism for not serving the cause of class-struggle. Also, both regard natural determinism—that other pillar of naturalism standing alongside social determinism—as irrelevant.

The author's creative talent is something Mehring and Plekhanov paid lip service to, but never really appreciated. A potential equation of artistic genius with scientific competence, or the craftman's skill, appears as a possibility from Mehring's and Plekhanov's points of view. Our two critics might have admired "inspiration," but they never defined or analyzed it. This *de facto* depreciation of artistic genius, of human consciousness and its interaction with the outside world, is a tendency Mehring and Plekhanov share with positivist critics and naturalist writers.

The problem is that elements of most of the assumptions we find in Mehring and Plekhanov also occur in Lukács in embryonic form, and in theorists of socialist realism as a potential. Social information is important for the whole Marxist tradition, as are "vividness," personal experience, and so forth. However, in Lukács, and even in Gorky, these assumptions appear as counterbalanced by other factors, or as syntheses of antithetic opposites. It would be hard to deny that the objectivistic trend does indeed tip the balance between "object" and "subject" in favor of the object—the external world of "facts," with all the possible consequences of this choice, which, however, are not necessarily as bad as Lukács believes.

Mehring's, and even more so Plekhanov's critical ideas, dominated the socialist cultural scene until the thirties, at which time Marx's and Engels' literary statements were published, Lukács introduced his Hegelian ideas into Marxist criticism, and socialist realism posed new problems. Two still-existing literary methods, social determinism and social documentation (both outcomes of Mehring's and Plekhanov's aesthetics), deserve our particular attention.

Social determinism and the tradition of the so-called "sociological criticism" stems from the time of the Second International. Several of Mehring's and Plekhanov's colleagues adopted the views of these two critics. Lafargue, Marx's son-in-law, considered writers as "slaves" [!] of their social environment; even though they might seemingly break out of that environment, it nevertheless enslaves them unconsciously.[17] Also, the question of whether or not socialist literature may exist without a preestablished socialist system stems from the decades of the Second International. Bebel's opinion that a social change must first take place so that literature might then gain a socialist character is but a forerunner of Vorovsky's and Trotsky's similar statements.[18] The implication is clearly deterministic: social changes condition the changes in the sphere of art and literature.

Furthermore, the importance of social psychology for evaluating literary works originates from the theoreticians of the Second International (Labriola, Lafargue, and of course, Plekhanov). The complex and dominating Soviet Marxist literary method of the 1920s, "sociological criticism," takes as the basis for its thesis the somewhat dichotomized and causally deterministic pattern of related sociological and psychological structures, which Plekhanov had established. Küppers is probably wrong when he attributes the later rejection of this tendency to the prejudices of one group of Marxists against methodologically specified and logically systematized research.[19] He seems to forget how clumsy and how pseudoscientific the phraseology of these critics was. On the other hand, it is true that the stubborn refusal to interpret the impact of science on man's spiritual culture gives an anachronistic, if not quixotic, feature to the writings of Lukács and other antisociological Hegelian Marxists, to whom we shall turn later. The achievements of Friche, Perevertsev, Sakulin and other representatives of sociologism during the twenties are, with all their errors, integrated parts of the Marxist literary-critical tradition. Their heritage, though in extreme forms, influenced the development of Marxist literary theory even in the later thirties.[20]

A less theoretical issue, but one closely connected to artistic technique, is that of literary documentation. The Czech communist critic Julius Fučik once made the observation that the documentary tendency in literature works in two ways—inductively, when the author collects, arranges, and presents facts for evaluation; and deductively, when the author attempts to illustrate his preconceived ideas ("hypotheses") with facts.[21] This is exactly the basis of Zola's enigma. Did he illustrate, with a vast number of observations and other first-hand sociological and second-hand natural scientific data, that "things cannot go on like this" (as Lafargue believes), or that "this is the way it is" (as Mehring and Lukács think)?

Documentation of sociohistorical facts, a maximal effort to create a journalistic rather than a literary report, found favorable ground in which to flourish in the Russian literature of the twenties, in Anglo-American Marxist criticism during the thirties, and in the theoretical and practical works of

Brecht, Ottwalt, Eisler, and Bloch during the same decade. Its principles undoubtedly contradict those of Lukács. For this reason, Lukács criticized documentarism for substituting story with description. (We shall return to Lukács' arguments.) The tendency of documentation, generally speaking, belongs to the realm of literary objectivism. Here, there is the same confidence in science, the same belief in "facts" and their omnipotent function in the modern world, as in naturalism.

How and why did objectivism or literary materialism divide Marxist theorists, and writers as well, is our next topic.

3. "Contra": Objectivism as Bourgeois Apology or Left-Deviation

Speaking in general terms, one may say that the critique of the overly materialistic outlook in the theory of realism has come from three different directions. The Hegelian Marxist critics objected to the upsetting of the precious balance between object and subject. Writers and critics committed either to formal experimentation or to different trends of philosophical individualism rejected, by virtue of the Western dualistic mind, the extremes of "dull naturalism" and "political propaganda." Finally, party critics attacked the "vulgar language," the shocking imagery, and other characteristics of the tendency already discussed, whether real or ascribed.

It was to be anticipated that the best developed and most comprehensive Hegelian critique would come from Georg Lukács. (We may remember how he disapproved of materialism without dialectics in Mehring.) Pure material determinism, the negation of the importance of active human consciousness, is probably Lukács' major argument against the objectivistic tendency he called naturalism, mechanistic materialism, vulgar sociologism, and other scarcely flattering names. He never believed, as Mehring did, that class origin determines class consciousness. If this were so, he asked, in an essay reprinted in his *Werke,* then how could even a part of the proletariat accept fascist ideology during the thirties?[22] He believed, however, that underdeveloped class consciousness was precisely the factor which facilitated the appearance of social determinism. If any class or individual cannot comprehend his existence, this existence appears to him as some abstract, universal fate (4:76). Therefore, speaking about "social necessities" becomes a convenient means by which to elude seeing and reflecting existence in all its complexity (4:288).

Above all, "social necessity" serves as a justification for established social systems and institutions. These appear as much in objectified, unchangeable, "fetishized" form as do any small parts or objects of nature or everyday life. People become things, and social institutions turn into immovable rocks around the impotent, insignificant individual. To illustrate the process that brought forth this world view, Lukács contrasts Balzac with Zola. In the former, social forces do not appear in superhuman, symbolic forms as they do in Zola (6:467). Zola's descriptive technique is admirable, but he presents social institutions not as the outcome of human relationships—like Balzac, Tolstoy, and Dickens—but rather as forces separated from, and imposed upon, man (6:518). One aspect of this fetishism in Lukács' view stems from an economic process Marx delineates in *Das Kapital*—namely, that the "reified" man and his institutions receive monetary values, the false exchange values of capitalism.

Besides making "things" of human beings and relations (*Verdinglichung*), the positivistic-naturalistic or documentary "realism" upsets the balance between the particular and the general, between detail and context (5:201; 6:469, 485). Particular things or events seen out of context take the place of overall coherence and the general theme. While Erich Auerbach seems to illustrate the roots of the naturalistic trend of modern realistic mimesis with what he sees as the retrospective and casual description of Odysseus' scar in Homer's epic, Lukács takes a different view of the Greek narrative. That the story of Achilles' weapons occurs at the functionally and structurally crucial part of the *Iliad* is by no means an accident (5:205). This consequently implies that modern realism, not modern naturalism, stems from the Greek epic. Again, Lukács contrasts the naturalistic method with that of Balzac, who could never possibly have accepted a "trivial photographic naturalism" (6:467). Finally, Lukács favorably contrasts the description of the horse race in *Anna Karenina* to that in *Nana*. Whereas in Zola this episode is but accidental and symbolic, in Tolstoy it receives a significant and concrete character. Zola merely describes his episode, whereas Tolstoy narrates through his (4:197–99; also 6:516).

Naturalism is an enemy of Lukács' sociophilosophical ideals. While the detailed description of death in Tolstoy's *The Death of Ivan Ilyich* stands for the death of a whole social class, in *Madame Bovary* it serves as nothing more than an analysis of physical decay, without any general applications (5:226). Not even Gerhard Hauptmann's social indignation satisfied Lukács. Owing to his naturalistic outlook, Hauptmann encourages his readers not to be against exploitation as such, but only one specific instance of exploitation (4:72). It is somewhat surprising to hear such an argument from a man who himself advocated the Hegelian "concrete universal" as eagerly as Lukács did.

In various works, Lukács states more specifically some of his objections against aesthetic manifestations of fetishism. One is the overestimation of quantity at the expense of quality. In literature, it means that the phenomenal, the grandiose, or an "authenticity" of otherwise nonfunctional details dominates over the psychological depth. People can be counted as numbers or things, but naturalism cannot reveal their essence. The "why" disappears, and only the "how," the observable changes on the surface, form the substance of art (6:168, 282).

Lukács also charges the naturalistic method with showing the incidental instead of the typical. He criticizes Zola, who commended Flaubert for building his works on the "harmonic evolution of incidents" (6:512). Though Lukács cannot deny the emotional effect of the description of particular happenings, he denies that these could be regarded as representative, "typical" events outside of their context (4:39–43). Lukács assures us that Zola himself never created a single character who grew to be a type (6:517), passing in silence over Nana, Gervaise, Etienne Lantier, and quite a few more of Zola's unforgettable characters. At times, however, Lukács seems to feel uneasy when confronted with Zola's literary views. After all, Zola, too, claimed to represent the "totality of objects." Lukács argues that this is true, but that in Zola's case, unlike Balzac, this totality remains only a nonevaluated, dead warehouse of man's produced world, his "second nature" (5:205).

The representation of the coincidental as well as the detail in naturalistic technique goes hand in hand, according to Lukács, with the ultimate acceptance and reflection of the average (5:201). Averaging out is the consequence of naturalistic descriptiveness, and the opposite of the truly analytical narrative (4:214). The average is the perversion of the typical (6:516). This process of the decomposition of the typical starts, as all of "new realism" or naturalism does, with Flaubert (6:512). While in great realism the "everyday" forms the theme, in naturalism, it becomes the creative norm (4:166).

Lukács criticizes the concept of the average for three reasons in particular. First, the average as a creative-aesthetic concept levels out individual and social conflicts. When thinking of "average" persons, the conflicts of an age appear in a smoothed-down, coincidental, noncharacteristic way (6:516; 10:221). Interpreting this in a less philosophical way, we may probably say that the average person by definition cannot reveal the complexity of individual and social existence. Second, averaging kills tragedy, as the mishaps of average heroes are coincidental and therefore sad, but not tragic (5:227). Third, since the average hero is filled with neither conflict nor tragedy, he simply becomes boring. To prove this, Lukács quotes Flaubert's frustrated lines on his realizing how boring his *Madame Bovary* was (5:223).

Leveling also deprives the hero of his specifically human (mostly moral) characteristics (6:516–17), and therefore ultimately works toward the deheroization of modern literature. This is Lukács' fourth argument against fetishism (6:514). Lukács condemns the killing of the hero both in naturalism (6:512, 520) and in the socialist documentary tendency of pre-Nazi German literature. In his critique of Ernst Ottwalt's *Denn sie wissen was sie tun,* Lukács reminds those zealous ultra-Marxists, who thought that psychologism was a bourgeois phenomenon, that several apologists for capitalism (notably Kipling) were not psychological writers at all (4:36–37). There are few places in Lukács' writings where the importance of the awareness of man's complex inner life is more emphatically stated than in his criticism of Ottwalt and the documentary tendency.

The social and psychological effects of fetishism (or its concrete literary manifestations, naturalism and documentation) are, however, more damaging in Lukács' opinion than are its aesthetic shortcomings. He lists three general arguments against fetishism.

First of all, fetishism in its political form is deductively propagandistic, as documentary literature proves. The author has a thesis which he merely illustrates, without any inner, organic plot or development of his characters (4:45). Lukács' positive antithesis to this deductive, "moralizing," "politicizing" tendency, which could obviously be paraphrased to an almost precise Brechtian definition of the epic theater, is, predictably, Balzac (6:477).

Second, Lukács believes that instead of a higher social consciousness, fetishism raises vague oppositional, and at times anarchistic feelings in the reader. The social sympathy for the poor appears as some philanthropic liberal-bourgeois attitude (4:71), and the criticism never leaves the phenomenal, superficial level; never takes a turn to investigate the vertical depth of social problems (4:165). This is the case with Flaubert and Zola, and also with Hauptmann who, whenever writing about organized, fighting masses (as in *Florian Geyer*), never sympathizes with these, but calls them "scum," and their leaders "demagogues" (4:74). Lukács finds one of the many links between naturalism and decadence in Huysmans, who no longer reflects conflicts between the individual and the social system, but between the individual and the environment (4:170).

Finally, Lukács uses his "big gun," his theory that description results in understanding, and that understanding in turn results in acceptance. This is probably the most important aspect of his condemnation of naturalism, as this problem has its extensions in Lukács' epistemological theory and in his overall view of science.

Briefly, the argument runs as follows: Since the naturalist author claims to be a non-participating observer of events, and since he only describes phenomena, all of the knowledge he provides for the reader is no more than a collection of uninterpreted "facts." However, "facts" are not the same as reality until they become "humanized"—integrated into human theory and practice (10:66). The only interpretation naturalism generates is that one must accept the existing world order—natural and social order—as given and unalterable. "Whatever is, is right," said Pope, and Lukács equates this teleological philosophy with that of naturalism, arguing that understanding brings reconciliation and acceptance. Naturalism brings a resigned, stoic submission to the supposedly unchangeable bourgeois reality (4:46–47, 256–60, 430–31; 5:122, 194), as science does to the "facts" of nature.

It would not serve the purpose of this study to discuss Lukács' sceptical view of the natural and social sciences very thoroughly. To him, science always remained quantitative, statistical, petrifying, phenomenal, and something exalting "necessity" and urging acceptance of the existing conditions. Above all, science was "disanthropomorphic"—nonmoral and not man-centered.[23] This is, of course, a supreme bias, to which we shall repeatedly return.

In order to illustrate how naturalism transfers the temporary social order into the sphere of the eternal and natural (4:282), Lukács points out the process of how socially pathological figures in earlier nineteenth-century realism (like Hulot in Balzac's *La Cousine Bette*) turned into psychologically pathological figures (as in Zola and Taine, 6:514). Of course, one may argue that Lukács irrelevantly separates social and individual psychology. But it is only by this device that he is able to demonstrate his formidable thesis that Zola was "an apologist of the *bourgeois* social order" (6:510, 517). The same holds true for Hauptmann (4:71), whose dramas are "seemingly artistic generalizations of bourgeois triviality" (4:69). Their antithesis is—who else?—Balzac, whose writings, unlike those of Zola, are "never dry" (6:475).

Particular periods of cultural history (especially the early, Newtonian phase of the English, and perhaps also the French Enlightenment) may support Lukács' view that temporary social phenomena tend to become transformed into eternal laws in human consciousness. Nevertheless his basic argument that understanding equals approval is completely speculative. Marx, Zola, and Lenin agree that understanding is also the basis of criticism and change, not only of acceptance. The rejection of systematic empirical knowledge is a pathetic undercurrent of Lukács' ideology, which he inherited from German idealism and which breaks through most vehemently in his view of naturalism. It also manifests itself in his condemnation of "avant-garde" literature, as we shall see later.

It should be necessary, however, to point out a particular major paradox in Lukács' theory of naturalism. At first, it appears as self-contradictory that Lukács equally condemns "submissive" naturalism and "politicizing" documentarism. If one speculates about the possible reasons, it seems that Lukács is speaking about two equally possible reactions to such objectivistic literature—one inciting the individual to anarchistic or philanthropic action, the other restraining him to acceptance. We can only hypothesize that Lukács regarded the two different forms of reaction as equally probable and, consequently, hardly predictable. Social backgrounds and milieus ("more aggressive" and "less aggressive") might have played some role in individual decisions; but Lukács most probably would not have taken "choleric," "phlegmatic," and other temperamental dispositions into consideration. It should be emphasized, however, that Lukács is not even stating the implicit dichotomy of the two effects of "objectivism," let alone analyzing the conditions which may influence the character of the reaction in individual cases.

Where did literary fetishism come from, and what direction did it take? Lukács attempts to find the roots of naturalism and documentarism in Kantian philosophy.[24] Specifically, he criticizes the emphasis on the limited character of empirical cognition, and the separation of art and social reality in Kantian aesthetics. He develops his criticism of the phenomenal character and the deliberate negation of the aesthetic element in naturalism, documentarism, and sociological criticism from a theoretical-philosophical investigation of the Kantian tradition (4:26–28).

Lukács believes that the causes of literary positivism are to be found in the failure of the revolutions of 1848–49. In the second half of the century, the Hegelian balance which had characterized the realism of the earlier decades was uprooted (5:186–87). One extreme, with its emphasis on the externalized, reified world, comes from Flaubert and reaches its climax in Zola, with Maupassant as a connecting link between the two (5:193–96). Flaubert was still able to create individualized characters like the Bovarys, but this was no longer possible for Zola, who became a great writer in spite of, and not by virtue of, his literary program. Lukács calls this one-sided perversion of realism in the nineteenth century "new realism" or naturalism, two concepts as synonymous for him as "great" and "bourgeois" realism (6:515–17).

The paradox of Lukács' view of naturalism is similar to that of his theory of realism. Both systems have highly vulnerable points at their very bases. But the structures—the arguments—erected over the bases show (at least at first sight) such an elaborated order and such a high degree of acquaintance with literature that scores of Marxist critics blindly adopted them without ever examining them deeply enough to discover the basic logical lacunae. Current handbook-interpretations of naturalism in the socialist countries reflect Lukács' influence just as much as does the rejection of literary and critical scientism by his Western disciples such as the Brazilians Konder and Coutinho.[25]

For us, it should be more interesting to consider other trends in the Marxist rejection of naturalism, which preceded Lukács' critical view or developed independently from it, but which still demonstrated striking analogies with it. These analogies are the more remarkable for their occurrence in critics who often held views on realism that were very different from those of Lukács.

Before World War I, a large group of socialist critics disagreed with naturalistic objectivism, and expressed their disagreement in less controversial form than Mehring did. Lunacharsky, for example, accused naturalism of objectifying human beings, and of sacrificing the literary hero as a false concession to populism. He also rejected naturalistic literature for taking its subject matter from the bottom of society, and for substituting the subjective perspective not with socialist theory or practice but with philanthropism.[26] To paraphrase this, naturalism is deheroizing, atypical, paralyzing, and submissive. The proximity of these views to those of Lukács is the more surprising as Lukács never referred to this controversial, but highly educated, Soviet critic-functionary in his writings.

After the cultural turbulence of the 1920s in Soviet Russia, which also brought a revival of objectivistic tendencies in literature, there were numerous critics who reacted disapprovingly to this kind of neonaturalism. In a speech given at the first congress of the RAPP in 1928, Fadeyev expressed his dislike of the journalistic social propaganda art which a so-called "Lef" movement represented at that time, at least in Fadeyev's opinion. He blamed the "Lef"-ists for a "vulgar-empirical and metaphysical" contrast of facts and art. In Fadeyev's view, the real task of art was to reveal deeper correspondences, dynamism beneath the surface of events, and not simply to increase the surface described. Clearly, Lukács' critique of the quantification of reality in naturalism, at the expense of a qualitatively new and artistic re-creation of it, is the issue that Fadeyev, too, raises. Lukács' preoccupation with the role of consciousness also appears in Fadeyev's warning: it is the uniquely organized perception of man, not some impassionate programmed machine, which selects and records so-called "facts."[27] The target is, as in Lukács, the pseudo-scientific "objectivism" of the different neonaturalistic movements.

In literary criticism, the reaction against social or biographical determinism overlaps the rejection of naturalism. In the early years of the century, the Hungarian socialist-sympathizer Lajos Biró appropriately summarized the general attitude of the Hegelian Marxists toward a scientific view of art. Biró reproached Plekhanov for the distorted picture he drew of Ibsen. Plekhanov "is not using the method of historical materialism to establish aesthetic values, but asks Ibsen in the stern, accounting voice of the socialist politician: 'Do you know that our aim is the nationalization of the means of production, and our future is the classless society?' "[28]

The so-called "sociological criticism," this projection of objectivism into literary theory, has been met with hostility by Hegelian Marxist critics throughout its existence. In the early thirties, Lunacharsky himself denounced the practice of labeling individual writers by their class origin, since there was no possibility of considering any class homogeneously. One could not call the poet Alexander Blok an ideologist of the Russian nobility, as he hated his own class.[29] In the later thirties, of particular significance are Lifshits' and Rozenthal's contributions to the heated debates with the so-called "Red Professors," a group of completely incompetent Bolshevik officials whom the party appointed to key academic positions, and who represented an utterly perverted, nonsensical variant of sociological criticism in literary scholarship.[30]

4. The Recent Situation

Taking a look at the present scene in socialist literature and criticism, we find that the heat of the debates for or against naturalism is cooling off. We may speculate as to whether or not a necessary recognition of some objective, factual, reporting technique in the process of informing and educating the masses is a result of the increasing scientific and technological priorities and prestige of the socialist world. If so, we might say that a greater tolerance toward a more objective form of realism is an indirect outcome of the sputniks and of Gagarin's space flight.

Numerous recent works reflect the positive reinterpretation of naturalism in the socialist countries. In 1962, Alexander Abusch, while trying to revaluate Hauptmann, emphasized the significance of the potential revolutionary element in naturalism.[31] In a collection of essays published some years later by the Soviet Academy of Sciences, the editors paid tribute to the importance of the artistically valuable documentary and journalistic tradition of the twentieth century in its shaping of socialist realist theory and practice. They cited as examples Egon Erwin Kisch, Julius Fučik, and Mikhail Koltsov.[32] There have been attempts to revaluate and possibly remove the derogatory label of "vulgarized sociology" from the sociological trend of Soviet literary criticism of the twenties and thirties. Currently, it is rather in Western European socialist criticism that we find elements of the earlier controversy between Hegelian and scientifically oriented theorists.

There are two significant and controversial critics who more or less claim to be Marxists, and whose whole activity shows strong influence of scientifism, notably positivism, both in its Cartesian-rationalistic and in its empirical form. These are the French-Rumanian Lucien Goldmann and the Italian Galvano Della Volpe. Both are recently deceased.

The myth of Goldmann as a proto-Marxist literary sociologist was, and still is, widely accepted in Europe and North America, showing an unfortunately indiscriminating and uninformed attitude among the intellectuals toward the main problems, terms, and nuances of the Marxist theory of literature. Goldmann himself had two bases for repeatedly stating that he was influenced by Marxism. One is his constant reference to Lukács' early work, *Die Theorie des Romans*. This influence, however, can be discarded as a Marxist one. Lukács wrote this work well before his theoretical acquaintance with Marxism. Goldmann, with his strong interest in structuralism, could have found a sound theoretical influence in Lukács' speculative neo-Hegelian *mental* structures, but this is something far removed from Marxism.

Goldmann's other claim to Marxism is his use of the

basis-superstructure relationship in the analysis of literary works, which he utilized particularly in his *Pour une sociologie du roman*. In his theory that the psychological structures of literary heroes are analogous to social economic structures, he supersedes in no respect the practice of the Soviet sociological critics, except that he never refers to this tradition. He writes: "There is a *rigorous homology* between the novel form . . . and the relation of people to their products in the respective age, and secondarily, also between the novel form and the human relations of the merchandising society."[33]

The result of this sociologism is that, historically speaking, Goldmann is merely repackaging an old tradition in a fashionable mixture of structuralistic, existentialistic, and psychoanalytical jargon. Let me illustrate the eclectic "genetic-structuralistic method" with the random example of Goldmann's analysis of Malraux's *Les Conquérants*. The hero's sickness "does not constitute a static structure" (structuralist jargon), but something "shaped by the relation between action and nothingness" (existentialist jargon). Women characters in the novel are interpreted as symbolic objects, standing for the complex ambitions of the individual; therefore sexual fulfillment also means existential gratification (libido, i.e. psychoanalytical jargon).[34] The general message is nonsensical.

The only instance of originality in Goldmann's sociological theory is his application of Marx's value theory to literature. While dwelling on different literary works, he tries to point out the process by which the fetishized values of exchange (or created values) increasingly dominate the moral consciousness of the alienated man at the expense of the values of use (or original values)—a process that Marx thoroughly analyzed, both in his early writings and in *Das Kapital*. This analogy between economic and moral values, though of course deterministic enough, would still be Goldmann's only relevant contribution to a discussion on literary realism, if it did not restrict the consideration of how social reality is reflected in literature to only *one* sphere of the superstructure—ethics. Besides, Goldmann is looking only for analogies in different works, and never discusses (since his method is unfit for this) the variety of the *forms* of expression produced by the same social structure. Whatever profound influence Goldmann otherwise might have had on Western literary scholarship, his views represent, when put in the historical frame of Marxist criticism, as outdated a phase of socialist literary theory as those of Maoist critics.

The other significant Marxist critic who appears to have been strongly influenced by positivism is Galvano Della Volpe. His *Critica del gusto* (1960) analyzes a score of renowned works of world literature from a perspective which is quite unusual in Marxist literary criticism: semantics. In demonstrating the process through which social structures and social consciousness are reflected in the literary work, he also arrives at some noteworthy conclusions.

Della Volpe's opposition to the Hegelian tradition, and particularly to Lukács, is explicit. He has only adverse remarks to make about Lukács, whom he mentions several times. He dismisses the Hegelian-Marxist assumptions that words do not carry intellectual elements, and that in poetic language words tend rather to communicate truth in a sensuous way, as no more than "mysticism" and "romantic relics." Instead, he claims that words do carry intellectual elements, and that they reflect the level of knowledge of a given society, thereby also representing "truth"—that is, they reproduce the objective world.[35] In a purely deductive argument Della Volpe maintains not only that images do not receive primacy in any communication process, but also that historically they are simply the results of rational knowledge.[36] According to Leandro Konder, this argument restricts the function of art entirely to information and documentation.[37]

While extending this deductive, rational determinism (which assumes that social conditions define the content of verbal communication), Della Volpe reveals his indebtedness to the Soviet sociological critics, whom he, like Goldmann, never refers to. It is the "sociological character" of the poetic work he intends to investigate. In analyzing Sophocles' *Antigone*, he maintains that the literary work has *only* a historically determined and explicable existence, owing to its close connection with the superstructure.[38]

Della Volpe's critical statements suffer from inconsistency considerably more than do Lukács' or even Gorky's arguments. For example, he separates intuitive and rational knowledge more than Lukács does (and he reproaches Lukács for doing so), but at the same time pretentiously states that science and art are mutually interchangeable.[39] Lukács, as we may remember, avoided *this* paradox by consistently separating these two fields of knowledge. Also, the only difference between Della Volpe's and Plekhanov's determinism is that the latter gave an empirical ("practice determines culture") tint to it, while the former gave it a rational ("knowledge determines culture") tint. The motivation for Plekhanov was the nineteenth-century empirical positivism of the natural and social sciences; for Della Volpe, the more philosophical twentieth-century forms of positivism—notably the linguistic positivism of Sapir and Whorf, and the unique logical philosophy of Wittgenstein. Della Volpe's claims to "dialectical semantics," and "concrete" or "sociological" stylistics are, in the formulation he gave them, pure nonsense. The essence of dialectics, the interaction between language and knowledge, is not an element of Della Volpe's semantic theory, because he never says that language expands knowledge. Furthermore, the "sociological" character of his "stylistics" manifests itself only in his linking of art works to certain historical periods in a deterministic way.

It is true that Della Volpe attempts to point out subtly realistic reflections of modern life in poets like T. S. Eliot or Ezra Pound, whom most Marxist critics, including Lukács, regard as apologists of decadence. Yet, he discredits others like Auden, Dylan Thomas, Rilke, Valéry or Yeats. Why? In part, because they return to different "archaic" forms of consciousness (such as myth or folklore), and in part because they express themselves in images. Certainly, ahistoricity and depreciation of the subjective element of poetic consciousness are pillars of the social deterministic tradition. But are they more useful criteria of realism than those which Lukács established? Ultimately, both Lukács and Della Volpe give up when confronted with the question of how they could possibly and objectively justify their subjective literary preferences and dislikes.

Like Goldmann, Della Volpe was also a controversial figure in cultural discussions. From Konder's essay and from Rocco Musolino's study on Italian Marxist criticism, it appears that Della Volpe's anti-Hegelian attitude had a strong appeal to both Italian and French intellectuals.[40] This fact might be due to the great impact of rationalism, the structuralistic frenzy, and the popularity of Fichte's speculative, abstract system in the Franco-Italian tradition. In other parts of the Latin cultural sphere, however, Della Volpe seems to be less influential. Konder generally disapproves of his method, and another Brazilian critic, C. N. Coutinho, believes that even Stalin showed greater insight into the problems of language than Della Volpe.[41]

Those theorists of Marxism and Leninism who are at all outstanding in some respect regard the original tradition not as dead, ossified material, but as one which constantly changes with, and must be modified according to, the new needs of the passing times. Also, the scientific, "sociological" tendency, the theories of documentation and information in literary criticsm are in themselves relevant and challenging, and therefore should be reevaluated and further developed. It seems, however, that Goldmann's and Della Volpe's attempts do not open any new vistas. Wherever they are Marxists, they slavishly follow the tradition of Soviet Russian sociological criticism without avoiding its pitfalls. Wherever they contribute, especially in details, to general literary scholarship, they are not specifically Marxists.

V. Subjectivism: Dialectical Realism or Right-Deviation?

1. Problemata

The traditional European view of the world dictates that if there is a left side there must be a right side too. In Marxist aesthetics, the projection of the social deterministic extremity, which Lenin called "left deviation," is supposed to be the naturalistic, documentary, or blatantly social propagandistic trend. The opposite of this usually appears in modern Marxist terminology as "revisionism." The philosophical projection of this tendency is the suggestion that Marx's and Engels' theories be revised in light of the changes which have taken place in human society and knowledge during the past hundred years. The socioeconomic projection of revisionism is the theory of a peaceful coexistence between socialist and capitalist countries, though since Khrushchev only ideological coexistence is recognized as revisionism, while the necessity of a political coexistence is accepted. Two further revisionistic ideas are that socialism can organically and peacefully develop out of the existing conditions in capitalist societies, without the necessity of class struggle, and that this peaceful pattern of socialization is the typical pattern for the future.

If we can believe Lukács, Plekhanov, Lunacharsky, and other Marxist critics who condemned several phenomena in contemporary literature, this "rightism" or "revisionism" also had aesthetic projections. The arguments underlying aesthetic revisionism run, briefly and in paraphrased form, as follows:

Since the time of Marx and Engels, radical changes have taken place in human society and knowledge. Capitalism, although having arrived at its imperialist phase, has demonstrated unforeseen flexibility in resolving parts of its contradictions. Mass media, mass society, and the welfare-state model have created new problems which the theory of socialism has to cope with. In science the discovery of microparticles and relativity, and in technology the application of electricity and atomic energy, have revolutionized both society and human consciousness. Consequently, if realism is a complete and truthful reflection of an age, modern art and its theory should develop so that it will be able to express the changing times. In short, while the objectivistic tendency emphasized (and supposedly overemphasized) the Marxist heritage of *materialism,* the theory of a distinct twentieth-century realism, in addition to underlining the importance of individual perception and psychology, also asserted itself as a *dialectical* outlook on an ever-changing reality.

The interpretation of present-day literature, and the reinterpretation of the European literary heritage, are matters of controversy more complex and problematic than the issue of positivistic realism. The question of the preservation and the renovation of the literary heritage, as well as of the Marxist critical concepts and terminology, are in the focus of the debates on modern literature. These debates are especially bitter and unresolved because the two parties are unable to use any of Marx's and Engels' statements on literature, since all the scientific, technological, and social issues which necessitated and developed both a qualitatively new literature and a new critical approach to this literature have come after the death of Marx and Engels. Engels made no recorded comments whatever on the pre-Raphaelites, impressionism, symbolism, or any other early "modernist" movements that he possibly could have witnessed. Also, Lenin virtually never stated any opinions on the nonconventional literary movements or styles of his age. To be sure, he did once express his dislike of the poet Vladimir Mayakovsky, but added that he regarded himself as no "competent judge in this respect."[1]

In short, the renowned statements of the classics of Marxism never touch on the questions of modern literature, and therefore they are irrelevant here. As opposed to those who still cling to the principle of some mythical respect for Marx and Engels, Brecht argued that these two "never learned about the technique of writing novels,"[2] and Aragon warned that the ideas of the two "founding fathers" should only be models and inspiring examples, but never fixed, definite dogmas for today's writers and critics.[3]

In this chapter, again, I shall summarize the two different viewpoints by analyzing two contrasting theoretical models. Among those modern Marxist critics who urge their comrades to revaluate the traditional socialist view of realistic writing, I chose Roger Garaudy and Ernst Fischer. Although their references to each other in their writings are surprisingly few, the development of their views, as well as the price they had to pay for them, are so analogous that, unlike the case of Mehring and Plekhanov, it would be inappropriate to discuss them separately.

Roger Garaudy stood for decades as the ideological pillar of the French Communist Party. In the Stalin era, he joined the party campaign against "bourgeois" literature. In his *Une Littérature de fossoyeurs* (1947), he debunked, in the servile idioms of the official party view, Sartre's existentialism, Mauriac's bourgeois Catholicism, Malraux's "narcissism," and Koestler's anti-Soviet writings. After Stalin's death, however, a slow but basic change occurred in Garaudy's outlook. His sympathetic understanding in discussing the importance of surrealism for Aragon's artistic development makes his *Du surréalisme au monde réel* (1961) a connecting link between his early views and those expressed in his *D'un réalisme sans rivages* (1963)—a work which will serve as the basis of his realism model. During the sixties, Garaudy initiated a debate between French communist and Catholic theoreticians, radically questioned the contemporary Marxist practice (in his *Marxisme du XXe siècle*, 1966), established a new theory of the place of technological intellectuals in modern society, and condemned the Russian intervention in Czechoslovakia. As a result of this increasingly "revisionistic" activity, he, a lifelong party and Politburo member, was ousted from the party in 1970.

The recently deceased Ernst Fischer suffered a similar fate. Son of an Austro-Hungarian army officer who turned from social democracy to communism in 1934, and who served for a short period in the first postwar Austrian government as Secretary of State for Education, Fischer never wrote any work comparable in intolerance to Garaudy's *Une Littérature de fossoyeurs*. But his essays, even during the late fifties, show the mark of a very partisan judgment of literature. His *Von der Notwendigkeit der Kunst* (1959—hereafter cited as *NK*) is a fascinating mixture of a traditional dogmatic view of art, and of a simultaneous inner dissatisfaction with that outlook. His contributions to the Kafka debate in the early sixties, and his *Kunst und Koexistenz* (1966—hereafter cited as *KK*), however, are clear manifestations of his deepening conviction that Marxist literary theory and terminology badly needed a radical updating. Fischer, too, was expelled from the Austrian communist party in 1969, and in the more dogmatic socialist countries his works, like those of Lukács after 1956, have become the object of hysterical attacks. Relevant parts of his controversial *Von der Notwendigkeit der Kunst* and *Kunst und Koexistenz*, and of his statements on Kafka, will serve as material for constructing the model of his theory of realism.

As a counter-example, again, it seems to be rewarding to use Georg Lukács' view of several modern literary phenomena as right-deviations and evidence of the decay of the bourgeois class. Hundreds of Soviet, East German, and other literary theoreticians have done more to discredit bourgeois "decadence" than Lukács did—in terms of rhetoric, but much less in terms of preparedness, competence, and relatively consistent logic. Therefore, the innumerable journalistic attacks on "rotten Western modernism" are an obscure part of past and even present dogmatic-Marxist literary practice and are not worthy of serious consideration.

2. "Pro": The Theory of a Dialectical Realism

Let us consider first how the argument for the reinterpretation of literary (and artistic) realism appears in Garaudy and Fischer.

Like the interesting, eclectic quasi-Marxist German critic Walter Benjamin, who influenced Garaudy and Fischer in several respects, both use the discovery and perfection of photography as a central argument in favor of the reinterpretation of modern art. Prior to the late nineteenth century, art and literature were the only ways of reproducing human life "as it is." Therefore, mimetic reproduction was their essential function. The introduction of photography challenged the whole Aristotelian tradition, as well as later theories of realism based on this tradition. Photography took over the function of reproducing static reality, and therefore art had to go one step further—it had to search for the underlying dynamism of existence. Garaudy and Fischer apparently believe that this process exemplifies the interaction of art and technology: art must flexibly ("dialectically") extend and modify its methods and its approach to life, whenever challenged by the passing times.[4]

What are the means of the new artistic approach to life? Garaudy, with obvious critical reference to Lukács' theory of realism, argues that the function of art ceased to be putting abstract ideas into concrete images. Consequently, the topic represented does not in itself define the content (or message) of the work.[5] Both Garaudy and Fischer condone the experienced, personal character of contemporary realism, which Garaudy places somewhere between old-fashioned imitation and Kandinsky's completely introverted abstractions (pp. 108–9). Still, the abstraction and generalization of experience, or the abstracted patterns of its structure, are relevant as long as they have reference to social reality. By using the analytical devices of Campbell's and Frye's mythological approaches to literature, Garaudy establishes "the Animal," "the Search," and "the Unfinished," as three of Kafka's "great themes" (p. 220).

The examination of technique, the "how" of processes, occupies a high status in the consciousness of the modern technological age. Consequently, both Garaudy and Fischer devote considerable space to the problems of artistic expression. Notable are Garaudy's analysis of Picasso's painting technique, and Fischer's observations about Beckett's dramatic technique in *Kunst und Koexistenz*. Though they both emphasize the view that realism is not a matter of artistic technique, but one of a certain attitude toward life[6] (and this happens to be a view that they share with Lukács), they do not exclude stylization and distortion from the arsenal of possible realistic devices. Garaudy reminds us that distortion is neither evidence of the disintegration of realism, nor of the decay of capitalism, since it was a widely employed device during the Renaissance and the Baroque period. It is rather a form of reinterpreting conventional realism, a modification of an old concept so that it may cope with the changes in reality itself (pp. 48–49). Also, Fischer's great preoccupation with the realism of primitive art (especially in *NK*) shows the same concern for discovering the complex reality of social existence behind the stylized and distorted shape.

Abstraction, distortion, and a return to the subjective and the primitive, constitute no danger per se in the eyes of our two critics. From abstraction, a new concreteness emerges; from subjectivism, a new social awareness. Fischer states that just as in nature there is no final, perfect stage of development, so there is none in art either (NK, p. 99).[7] Garaudy adds to this statement that changes in art cannot be criticized a priori, but that only the direction of these changes, depending on whether they lead to revolution or escapism, can be criticized (p. 58). The controversial movements of the earlier decades of the century (like "expressionism, futurism, surrealism," NK, p. 74), not only nurtured, but also buried decadence and contributed to social-intellectual revolutionary fomentation. The only shortcoming of those who see and reflect the dialectics of the changing times in their works may be, as Garaudy notices in Kafka, their inability to see how to control the dialectical processes (p. 228). Their questioning of man's alienation from existence, their inquiry into what is taking place in the social sphere and why, is, however, the first step toward a new consciousness and revolt (pp. 127, 225). This is also the main contribution of painters like Picasso, poets like Saint-John Perse, writers like Kafka, and dramatists like Beckett, to the modern form of realism and to the redefinition of that concept.

If abstraction, distortion, stylization, and the reflection of alienation, are not necessarily antirealistic, what are we to think of the traditional classical-Hegelian definition of realism? Garaudy does not believe that classicism has any inherent inner value. Whenever it appears, "warmed over," in different periods of human history, it does so as an incarnation of the demands and values of a specific society, rather than as a vehicle of unaltered, suprahistorical aesthetic values (pp. 60–61). Fischer, for his part, reminds us that it is precisely decadence which frequently appears in the guise of "health" and classicism. His example is Nazism, this extreme and ultimate form of capitalism,[8] which cherished pseudo-classicism and denounced "decadent" modern art (*KK*, pp. 166–68). Also, Fischer singles out the old-fashioned theory of an "objective," "balanced" realism as the basis of a morally and historically false teleology (Stalinism, that is), which forced its claim of "optimism" on the Eastern European literary tradition and criticism (*KK*, p. 21).

The function of modern art, in the view of these two critics, is not to embrace abstract aesthetic norms, but to contribute to man's "de-alienation"—to his return from a world of things and reified values to mankind and human consciousness—by analyzing the process and essence of alienation and reification with any artistic means available. Both critics believe that poetic creation is a major weapon in overcoming alienation (Garaudy, p. 171; Fischer, *NK*, pp. 5, 34ff, 43ff). The assertion of an active and beneficial wealth of experienced knowledge ties both of them to Marxism (society can be changed), but also to existentialism (the individual can change himself). In Kafka's prose, Garaudy discovers about as much will to overcome alienation as authenticity in representing it (p. 153). Fischer, in turn, discusses the typical "realist" objection to Hamm's keeping his maimed parents in ashbins (in Beckett's *Endgame*). It is, of course, absurd and abnormal, he says, but so is slaughtering children in Auschwitz (*KK*, p. 15). On this point, Fischer seems to adopt Dürrenmatt's view that it is modern life which is absurd, and that the "absurd" theater simply reflects this life realistically.

When analyzing Picasso's *Guernica*, Garaudy dismisses as a lie the widespread pseudo-populistic assumption that such works are inaccessible to the masses in general (p. 89). The depreciation of the taste of the modern public may happen for two reasons: in order to feed the masses on cheap, low-quality literary products, or to assert forcibly the thesis that it is only on a "rational" (in the eighteenth-century sense) level that communication may take place. The reinterpretation of the sources of literary information takes three concrete and distinct shapes in Garaudy's and Fischer's critical writings.

The first and still the least exploited level is the semantic one. Here, the criticism of the idea that language has only rational aesthetic elements is relevant for us. Garaudy, for instance, does not believe that one could profitably study the explicit message of Kafka's parables, as he sees no imaginable literary correspondence between the concrete symbol and its abstract meaning (pp. 232–33). Nothing shows the tripartite division between the Hegelian "middle way" and the positivistic and modernistic extremes more clearly than the comparison of Garaudy's opinion with those of Della Volpe and Lukács. Della Volpe, as we have seen, excludes all "irrational" elements from language, while Lukács cautiously admits that there are *some* emotional, subjective communicative elements in language; he thereby takes a balanced, "linking" position between Della Volpe, who insists on a rational message only, and Garaudy, who seems to discard entirely the rational interpretability of the literary language, at least in its parabolic form.

The two further points Garaudy and Fischer make in contributing to the reinterpretation of rationalism show definite revisions of Marx's views on the issues of the interpretation of the primitive, and of the myth.

Marx, more than either Engels or Lenin, held a view of progress versus primitivism which can be called ethnocentric at best. The Europe-centered character of the original Marxist theory comes from two sources. One is the assumption that technological development is a prerequisite of socialism. Europe, therefore—as the technologically and thus also culturally most advanced continent—is closest to the possibility of realizing a socialist order. The other source is the idea of internationalism. Just as capitalism already embraces and unites the Earth, so socialism will also gradually expand beyond national borders and spread around the entire globe.

Consequently, the separatism of small nationalities, their struggle for political and cultural autonomy, was anachronistic in Marx's eyes. He, and to a lesser extent Engels, ridiculed the nationalism of the Swiss, the Danes, and the non-Russian Slavic peoples, and gave a teleological, almost sympathetic, interpretation of the British colonial presence in India.

The views of Marx and Engels on mythology show the same condescending cultural superiority in historical terms which their idea of the great, expansive civilizations demonstrates at a more present-oriented, geographical level. Though both Marx and Engels appreciated mythology (especially Greek mythology), they regarded the age of myths as an irrevocably completed, pre-scientific period of human history. "All mythology masters and dominates and shapes the forces of nature in and through the imagination; hence it disappears as soon as man gains mastery over the forces of nature," wrote Marx in 1857.[9]

Garaudy and Fischer attempted to do away with the conventional Marxist ethnocentrism which also penetrated the completely Europe-centered aesthetics of Lukács. Garaudy regards the recent interest in African and Polynesian art (especially cultic sculpture) as a discovery of ancient representations of alienation (pp. 62–63). The only difference he sees between this "primitive" art and Franz Kafka is that while the idols manifest man's alienation from the forces of nature, Kafka reflects man's alienation from modern society and from himself (p. 235). Fischer, whose understanding of primitive realism has already been mentioned, cannot comprehend, unlike Lukács, why earlier, socially determined and explicable, primitive forms of "barbarism," or an interest in these, are signs of decadence (KK, p. 169).

Primitive art, then, has a relevant "message" and contributes to the reinterpretation of the modern concept of realism. The same is the case with myth. Garaudy and Fischer feel that authenticity, copying, and reproduction are concepts which no longer hold for the true function of modern art. They believe that modern society, too, favors the creation of myth, and that the age of enlightenment, rationalism, and science did not put an end to man's expressing himself in mythological forms. Garaudy emphasizes his view that the novel is not an idea expressed in metaphoric form, but rather a myth (p. 155), and that Kafka, too, builds myth instead of copying reality (p. 239). Likewise, Fischer seems to believe that myth is a better expression of the totality of life, and also of the as-yet-unrationalized world outlook of modern man, than is "authenticity."

The reinterpretation of the primitive and the myth shows, besides the attempt to redefine concepts like the "rational" and the "irrational," an effort to revaluate the Marxist critical terminology as well. Garaudy's preoccupation with model theory has already been mentioned. His writings about Kafka emphasize that Kafka is in his prose building models of human relations, much as scientists do in their fields (p. 239). Garaudy seems to believe that a model gives a more dimensioned and testable image than the imprint, copy, or other of the metaphors used earlier for realism, which somehow all suggest authenticity, and a fixed and ultimate knowledge.

As for Fischer, he revises the very concept of "decadence," which he actually wants to preserve in order to indicate different phases within social systems, rather than to identify their final decay. He believes that within a bigger developmental cycle there are numerous smaller ones. In other words, capitalist culture goes through crises, yet is still able to renew itself (KK, pp. 152–53). Fischer's other attempts to depoliticize the Marxist literary critical vocabulary (by substituting the sincerity of personal experience for partisanship, or fantasy for ideological correctness) are laudable signs of his ideological tolerance, but at times go so far as to deprive

Marxist criticism of its specific character and method, thereby pushing it into the realm of the most basic terminology of general literary theory.

The revision of the term "decadence" results in a radical reinterpretation of "bourgeois" art in Garaudy and Fischer. The art of the capitalist world is neither reproductive, epigonistic, nor psychopathological by historical necessity or by definition. Ernst Fischer compares decadent Roman literature to modern Western literature and finds that traces of the dying Roman culture (such as the petrified world, the cult of the horrible and the grotesque, the mask, the feeling of aimlessness and the temporary, the escape from chaos to privacy) are missing in Western culture. Instead, the literature and art of modern bourgeois society are dynamic, as the examples of impressionism and cubism show (*KK*, pp. 150–53). Fischer can detect no "decadence" at the social level either: the Western social pattern, far from being stagnant, demonstrates such great degree of dynamism that it even absorbs such general axioms of the initial socialist program as a planned economy and general employment.

The conclusion at which both Garaudy and Fischer arrive is precisely what the title of Garaudy's book indicates—that realism is "shoreless" (*sans rivages*). "We can define neither reality nor realism for all future ages," Garaudy adds in another essay, since reality keeps overflowing its shores, and so does literary realism. A socialist conception of realism, in Garaudy's view, is not the most limited, but is precisely the most comprehensive and generous view of the realistic tradition. Its totality embraces all of the marvels of the past cultures, "from the friezes of Phidias to the mosaics of Ravenna, from Poussin to Cézanne or Picasso." Also, such reflections of human moods as still life, landscape, or eternal human feelings (like "joy, love, rebellion") should be relevant for a socialist realist outlook, says Garaudy,[10] in obvious opposition to Lukács' objection to descriptive and metaphysical art. Fischer, for his part, defined realism at the Czechoslovakian Kafka-congress in 1963 (the same year in which *D'un réalisme sans rivages* was published) in a way that sounds like a paraphrase of Garaudy's view.[11]

Garaudy became a Marxist literary iconoclast by reevaluating Kafka (and in such a way to have made any rigid rejection of Kafka among even the most dogmatic communist literary circles impossible after 1963). Fischer went one step further in his *Kunst und Koexistenz*. It should be noted that Lukács, in his *Die Gegenwartsbedeutung des kritischen Realismus* (1957), did give some indication of his appreciation of Kafka, but at the same time he, with disgust, dismissed Samuel Beckett as a pathological portrayer of creeping imbeciles.[12]

Fischer, though without mentioning Lukács by name, took issue with him on Beckett. Fischer thought it was fallacious to classify Beckett with the literature of the absurd, provided that one defines this tradition as a literature beyond social relations. He argues that the relation of Clov and Hamm is not cosmic, but rather grows out of a society of property and class conflicts between masters and servants. He also singles out, as a realistic element, Hamm's great psychological talent in dominating and "convincing" others. Subsequently, he compares *Endgame* to Solzhenitsyn's *One Day in the Life of Ivan Denisovich* (a novel Lukács hailed as an example of the purest realism), precisely to show that the deformation of man and his simultaneous struggle against this phenomenon, as well as the coexistence of human dignity and moral supremacy with physical impotence, are the common subjects of both works (*KK*, pp. 8–15).

The "revisionistic" idea of the "shoreless" realism is certainly an attractive, tolerant view of modern literature, although not without some fundamental inner contradictions. Before examining these contradictions we shall, however, turn to the theory of realism, as it appears in Garaudy and Fischer, in order to see how their interpretation is related to similar interpretations of the specific realism of modern literature.

As in the case of Lukács, Gorky, Mehring, and Plekhanov, we find here that the demand to renew the socialist concept of realism appeared in Marxist criticism long before it took its most consistent and vociferous shape in the models analyzed. During the thirties, Lukács' German opponents used the arguments of "changing times" and "technological advancement" fairly frequently. According to Brecht, it was only natural that the steam engine, microscope, dynamo, oil companies, Rockefeller Institute, and film industry had to enter the world of literature, and had in turn to elicit new devices of expression.[13] Bloch and Eisler, among others, echoed the same idea. Earlier, during the Soviet literary debates of the twenties, Bogdanov had urged "proletarian" artists to employ new technical devices of Western art "like photography, spatial representation, movies, spectral colors, or the recording of sounds."[14] Again in the Soviet debates of the twenties, the program of the "New Lef" (one of whose leaders was Mayakovsky) sarcastically denounced the anachronism of using prerevolutionary forms to express postrevolutionary content. The program contends that the old icon-painters now paint the face of a Red soldier under the helmet of Saint George the Dragon-killer, or call an idyllic picture showing peasant girls "Komsomol-girls."[15] In the "thaw-period" after the twentieth congress of the Soviet communist party, several other writer-critics, among them Ilya Ehrenburg, turned to similarly ridiculous examples to convey a message identical to that of the "New Lef."

In one instance, Brecht gave a list of modernistic devices he considered as being useful for socialist literature: interior monologue and shifting style (as in Joyce), dissociation of elements (Döblin, Dos Passos), free association technique

(Joyce, Döblin), montage (Dos Passos), and alienation (Kafka).[16] Earlier, Otto Ville Kuusinen made some observations on the abstracted rhythmic structures of modern poetry,[17] which persuaded one of his recent critics to tie him closely to the Russian formalistic critical tradition of the twenties. The argument in favor of formal expression, abstraction, and a greater stress on technique continues throughout the history of Marxist literary criticism. The Marxist debates on music as the most abstract, patternized form of expression (from Lunacharsky's sensible comments to Zhdanov's down-to-earth claim of "socialist realist music") could serve as enlightening supporting materials to the discussion of formalism.

The fact that realism and stylization were not incompatible was something which Lunacharsky, too, recognized. In 1931, he used Aristophanes' example to illustrate how "caricature, hyperbole, and deformation" may all serve a higher realistic conception of the author.[18] On the other hand (as several critics of the same decade recognized as clearly as Fischer would thirty years later), it was precisely fascism which tried to appear in the disguise of classicism. Ernst Bloch, especially, emphasized this in his polemic against Lukács and other critics in the so-called "expressionism debate" among Marxist literary theorists.[19]

Bloch was also the promulgator of the idea that modern literature expresses the dialectics of man and history. In polemicizing against Lukács, he maintained that the diagnosis of decay does not mean approval of decay, and even if it did, approval may be positive in a dialectical sense, as destruction necessarily precedes construction.[20] In 1921, Antonio Gramsci expressed an almost identical view of Italian futurism—although he changed his mind soon thereafter and condemned the futurists.[21] In the late thirties, the Hungarian József Révai reminded his ideologist comrades that the dialectic of history should serve as a basis for the consideration of literary phenomena. If a poet in Hitler's Germany were to have written pessimistic poems, these would more likely have been documents of a revolt against Nazi barbarism than of bourgeois decadence.[22]

In addition to emphasizing the dialectical *character* of modern literature, several Marxist critics have pointed out its de-alienating *function* as well. During the thirties, the Czech socialist critic Václavek cited a growing yearning for a new collectivism as the essence of modern poetry. The age of the bourgeois "aesthetics of preciseness" was over, and poetry was about to return to man, to human consciousness. Václavek regarded the breaking of the rule of objects over man as the first task of socialist literature. He thought that modern realism was characterized by the reorganization and reflection of the elements of human life "according to the order of human sensibility," which is not the same as logical order.[23] More recently, the Swede Arnold Ljungdal extended the view of de-alienation to poetic language as well, when he said that this language has been a protest against the "verbal alienation" of capitalism (i.e. clichés, jargon, stereotypes) since the time of Baudelaire.[24] That the masses demand and understand the new art was an idea which won the support of several pro-modernist socialist critics and writers.

The dissatisfaction with the traditional definition of rationalism as an indispensable feature of literary realism is a relatively new phenomenon, probably generated by the existentialist wave after World War II. But between the two wars, Gramsci had already emphasized that language also has a nonrational communicative function, which is especially significant for poets.[25] Moreover, as early as the turn of the century, Labriola had regarded myth as evidence of some "natural constant" in man, and therefore indispensable.[26]

While these critics challenged the conventionally derogatory Marxist concepts of "irrationalism" and the "metaphysical," Brecht did the same with formalism. By giving a sophistic (he would have called it "dialectical") turn to the interpretation of the term "formalism," he accused Lukács and other traditionalists clinging to outdated nineteenth-century ways of expression, of formalism.[27] In the fifties, in a more serious mood, he too rejected the formalistic idea that only formal categories provide the values of the work, but at the same time he defended the privilege of the artist to constantly give new shapes to new ideas, as "a factor without which art is no art."[28] Also, during the thirties, the Hungarian socialist poet Attila József, who had earlier been strongly influenced by Benedetto Croce, maintained—against the arguments of emigrant Hungarian dogmatic communist scribblers—that modern bourgeois literature was not simply a collage of mechanically reproduced formal clichés. He insisted that a mechanical reproduction of the form was impossible, as the form was the product of the dynamism of the soul, and this dynamism was not mechanical, but both dialectical and unique.[29]

This discussion of form and irrationality leads us once more to the evaluation of modern "bourgeois" literature. Rejecting the assumed epigonistic character of bourgeois art, Arnold Ljungdal believes that after 1900, instead of disintegration, modern Western art and literature entered a phase of growth.[30] Other critics defend the "mental soundness" of modern artists. Even before World War I, a debate focusing on this issue stirred Hungarian liberal and socialist intellectuals. The debate started with Sándor Csizmadia, who, in the social democratic newspaper *Népszava,* branded an otherwise insignificant young poet as a representative of lunatic bourgeois decadent poetry. Another socialist, Emil Bresztovszky, took issue with Csizmadia and defended, if not the young poet himself, certainly his right to formal experiments and an ideologically nonconformist modern poetic outlook.[31]

The Hungarian discussion on the relevance of modern bourgeois poetry for the cause of socialism continued from

1909 to the eve of World War I, and became a prototype for innumerable later discussions of the same kind. Between the two wars, the interpretation of Joyce especially divided Marxist critics. Brecht himself admired *Ulysses* as a "great satirical novel." He noted an analogy between the attacks on the novel by certain petty bourgeois critics and by Marxist critics, all of whom claimed the book was pornographic, sick, or immoral.[32] At the First Soviet Writers' Congress, Wieland Herzfelde defended Joyce as the respresentative of a thinking, suffering, and protesting (not yet mechanized and cynical) part of the bourgeoisie, and as an innovator who creates "microscopic realism" in his novels.[33] (For his pains, Herzfelde was viciously attacked by Radek.)

Finally, we have arrived at the idea of "shoreless realism." As early as the thirties, Brecht wanted to interpret the concept of realism "more widely, more generously, indeed, more realistically" than his Marxist contemporaries did.[34] In 1938, Anna Seghers asked Lukács polemically whether there were any work of art that did not represent at least some elements of life.[35] In 1935, Aragon had already interpreted realism so broadly that practically everyone from Hugo, through the symbolists, to Mayakovsky and the Russian futurists was included.[36] Already at this time Aragon adumbrated a view which later became conceptualized in *J'abats mon jeu* and in his introduction to Garaudy's *D'un réalisme sans rivages*, namely that socialist realism is not a rigid concept, but an open, nondogmatic one which lets the author reflect the world in his own way.

Actually, the urge to reinterpret realism and to enrich it with the formal virtuosity of "bourgeois" literature, seems to have been widespread during the thirties, although not within the Soviet Union. If Květoslav Chvatik can be trusted, the significance of the pro-modernist Czech socialist critic Bedřich Václavek lies in the fact that he attempted to synthesize the ideological values of proletarian realism with the expressive-formal values of the bourgeois avant-garde in his concept of socialist realism.[37] Paradoxically, Václavek could freely express this view in Masaryk's "bourgeois" Czechoslovakia, whereas in most of the postwar Eastern European socialist countries, such opinions were not allowed to reappear until the sixties. In other parts of Europe, socialist critics did manage to keep this tradition alive throughout the forties and fifties. In the forties, for example, the American Sidney Finkelstein, who was generally critical of bourgeois art, nevertheless appreciated and spoke well of Proust, Joyce, Eliot, and Dylan Thomas.[38] In the fifties, H. K. Laxness considered realism as a "floating concept," and cited Brecht, Neruda, Eliot, Picasso, and Chaplin as the masters of modern realism.[39]

As we have observed, in Eastern Europe the sixties brought a critical revision of the traditional concept of socialist realism in favor of modernistic movements. The Hungarian Lajos Nyirö, for instance, has recently suggested that even poets such as Anna Akhmatova and Marina Tsvetayeva should be considered as socialist realists.[40] But if we call all "good" literature "realistic," does this serve the definition of the term "realism" well? This is a dilemma which Lukács and other opponents of modernistic literary tendencies carefully exploited.

3. "Contra": The Theory of a Decadent Irrationalism

There were different motivations behind the rejection of naturalism, and the same is true in the case of the rejection of modernistic literature. The basic argument to which all of the others can be reduced is as follows: The bourgeois mode of production, and the bourgeoisie as a social class, have been in a state of decay approximately since the revolutions of 1848–49. Similarly, bourgeois culture still makes vain efforts to appear interesting and progressive, although that culture has been degenerating. One of the two major forms these pro-

gressive attempts take is the socially "harmless" modernization of the devices of expression (as in the experimental styles
of Joyce, for example). The other form is the reinterpretation
of modern reality—the rejuvenation of the message of the literary work (as in Kafka, or in the literature of existentialism
and the absurd). As we can see, the target of these critiques
is, ultimately, the ideological content of modern literature.

Among the diverse critical opinions concerning modern
bourgeois literature (which are often contradictory in themselves) Georg Lukács' arguments are, relatively speaking, the
most solid, and the arguments of others can acceptably be ar-
ranged around his. Although Lukács assures us that not all
modern bourgeois works are necessarily decadent, the majority of twentieth-century Western European authors and their
writings appear in his essays as evidences of the moribundity
of the middle classes.

The term Lukács used for radical modernization and experimentation of thought and form is "avant-garde" or
"avant-gardism." Its most succinct definition is reminiscent of
Lukács' view (found in *Werke* 4:324) of naturalism: the chaotic
phenomena of life represented in their disorder, without the
mediation of concrete, realistic art. (We shall return to this
analogy between naturalism and the literary avant-garde.)
Lukács assumes that for the avant-garde artist, essence is
comprehensible only when it is detached from its "chaotic"
context, in an intuitive-irrational way (4:137–38). This phenomenon is, according to Lukács, a result of the impossibility
of the "triumph of realism" in the modern age. The decay of
the bourgeois class has advanced to the point at which moral
and artistic sincerity no longer appear *in spite of* the illusions
of the writer (as in Balzac) but rather precisely *because of* the
illusions of the writer. One of Lukács' examples is Gregers
Werle, a hero of Ibsen's *Wild Duck*. He claims that this play
could have turned into a great satire of the bourgeois world,
but that it did not because Ibsen kept sympathizing with the

absurdly idealist young Werle. The same is true, he believes, of such other Ibsen heroes as Solness, Rosmer, or Hedda Gabler (4:290–94).

Lukács' general insensitivity to any subtle irony in modern literature is perhaps the only explanation for this completely untenable view of *The Wild Duck*. This play occupies a particularly important place in Ibsen's work precisely because it is a drama in which, for the first time, he does away with illusions. However, Lukács uses the same "bed of Procrustes" for the work of other writers, too. He believes, for instance, that in Hauptmann there is no break between the earlier and the later dramas. The differences only reflect the ideological development of the liberal German bourgeoisie—from *Sunrise* to *Sunset*, as Lukács says, referring to two dramas by Hauptmann (4:71). It is probably easier to appreciate Lukács' pun, than his view of Hauptmann's development.

What are the characteristics of the avant-garde in Lukács' opinion? In the first place, its basis is irrationalism. Lukács, whose definition of rationalism follows the nineteenth-century Hegelian-Marxist view fairly closely, devoted an entire volume to a dissection of existential philosophy as the typical bourgeois ideology of imperialism (*Die Zerstörung der Vernunft*, 1954; *Werke*, 9). He thinks that irrationalism is the transcendence of problems which are unanswerable within a given socioideological structure. Of course, irrationalism is incompatible with any realistic method of literature, which presupposes the possibility of systematic, objective, rational knowledge and reflection. Furthermore, Lukács states, irrationalism means submission to "mental or biological fatalism" (4:75) in establishing still another analogy between naturalism and avant-gardism.

Lukács blames the narcissistic subjectivism of the avant-garde, another characteristic of this mode of writing, on the division of labor which led some modern artists and intellectuals to "specialize" in the depth and subtleties of the human soul, or in the "eternal mysteries" of existence (4:260). Finally, the antidialectical dichotomy of "ideal" and "real" also evokes Lukács' criticism in a philosophical form. According to Lukács, avant-gardism dualizes the possible (*Möglichkeit*) and the real (*Wirklichkeit*) and, since the possible is abstract and therefore always richer than the real [?], avant-gardism cultivates that at the expense of reality (4:472). (It is the same Georg Lukács, who, on other occasions, praises the "richness" of reality and condemns the "poverty" of abstractions in art.)

The particularization of the world, the static absolutizing of individual experience, the cult of the psyche and (in philosophy) of the probable, are, as we can see, aspects of the Lukácsian characterization of modern literature. Indeed, Lukács emphasizes that avant-gardism is a matter of world outlook (*Weltanschauung*), not of style (4:467–68, 501). He defines world outlook as human content, and derives modern formalism from the loss of this content in the literature of the age of imperialism. Formalism, therefore, is not an evil in itself, but only a phenomenon, a sign of the loss of anything human in avant-garde literature, and an attempt to compensate to the reader for this with technical surrogates.

Lukács illustrates the presence and absence of the human content in a renowned comparison of Joyce's and Mann's interior monologues. He finds that in Joyce the very technique of the interior monologue is an end in itself, whereas in Mann it is only the means of revealing the many-sided relationship of the individual to his society. In Joyce, these human connections are casual and static, while in Mann they are constantly changing and dynamic, just as Mann's whole narrative composition is (4:467–68).

It is precisely these findings which are tragic evidence of Lukács' contempt for "technique." Since he consciously denies the relevance of formal, textual analysis of literary works, he himself is unfamiliar with the elementary devices of how to convince a reader with concrete evidence. The conclusions he draws from the comparison of Joyce's and Mann's interior monologues are illuminating when considered as hypotheses, but arbitrary when considered as theses. They certainly in no way satisfy the criteria of a systematic, textual-interpretative approach to literature.

There are further shortcomings to Lukács' depreciation of the impact of science and technique (or technology) which Marxist defenders of modern literature have constantly referred to. Lukács derives Joyce's world outlook from his prose technique and finds a constant oscillation between the details, a permanent but aimless and accidental dynamism of the whole, and the stasis of the total structure itself (4:468). He lists these features of the Joycean world as characteristics of irrationalism and of a decadent world outlook.

Lukács never asks the question, however, of whether or not these very same characteristics could be those of a new realism of the scientific age. Lukács' description of Joyce's image of the world conspicuously reminds one of the structure of the atom. What he says about the "aimlessness" of dynamism is almost analogous to Heisenberg's and Eddington's findings on the movement of micro- and macro-particles elaborated during the twenties (the same decade during which *Ulysses* was published). Lukács, who was pathetically unfamiliar with everything which had anything to do with the natural, abstract, and quantitative sciences, had no idea of how much his description of Joyce's world and the label of irrationalism which he attached to its creator contradicted each other. The question is not whether the reflection of physical laws should be an especially tempting goal for writers, or whether scientific ideologies conceived half a century ago are still satisfactory today, but whether literary critics should take scientific and technological issues into account whenever they are making generalized judgments about the ideological spectrum of certain historical ages.

Lukács' early devotion to Kant, and his constant indebtedness to Hegel, determined his separation of the social and
natural sciences, and his depreciation of the latter (as well as
of several branches of the social sciences) throughout his life.
Nevertheless, he lavishly made critical references to the negative impact of the sciences and technology on modern literature, and blamed these for the dehumanizing and abstract
tendencies in avant-garde arts. It is the idea of the domination
of the sociohistorical content which Lukács constantly op-
poses to the argument that the new experiences of life need
new channels of artistic expression.

Stylization and distortion are not the only signs of decadence in modern literature; so, even more ominously, are
symbols and allegories. Lukács' aversion to symbolism stems
from his platonic assumption that symbols have meanings
which are detached from objective, tangible existence (4:217).
To him, symbols and allegories were escapist attempts to
overcome a schizophrenic world by means of the transcenden-
tal (4:493). Furthermore, symbols could also be vehicles of the
author's illusions. Ibsen, for instance, should have seen the
"base, repulsive, nay, ridiculous" character of some of his
heroes (like Gregers Werle, Rosmer, or Borkman), but still he
idealized them by attaching symbolic meaning to their ca-
prices (4:293).

Ultimately, however, Lukács does not believe that any
kind of stylistic device could, by itself, make a work decadent.
He illustrates his thesis that absurdity does not equal fantasy
with the example of Kafka, in whom all of the details correspond to the criteria of conventional realism, while the whole
work is still absurd.

Lukács answers his opponents by asserting that modern
avant-garde art, far from being more dialectical than
nineteenth-century realism, is antidialectical in its roots. It is
either anarchistic (in an abstract way) and pseudo-radical
(4:110, 120, 125), or escapist, idealistic, antisocialist (which

Lukács calls "romantic anticapitalism," 4:126, 138), or ahistoric, since it shows alienation as an unalterable, eternal "human condition" (4:142). Though more cautious in his judgment than most other critics of a like mind, Lukács was one of those who emphasized the potential contribution of avant-garde literature to fascism rather than the well-known destruction of "degenerate art" by the Nazis (4:146-49). The two poets he occasionally mentioned as examples of this phenomenon were Marinetti and Gottfried Benn.

Lukács never used the argument that avant-garde literature is inaccessible to the larger reading masses, or that it is sick or mad. He left such complaints to literary "specialists" like Zhdanov, Khrushchev, and the innumerable scribbler-"critics" in the socialist countries. For him, avant-garde literature on the whole was, as a social phenomenon, explicable on a philosophical level. But his summary labeling as "irrationalism" vast parts of modern art and philosophy which recognize and reflect the complexity of twentieth-century life shows the same escape from the problems and scope of contemporary existence as that of the party ideologists.

Irrationalism is also the name for the discovery of the primitive and the mythological tendencies of modern literature. The old Europe-centered view of civilization as opposed to "lower" forms of culture was, in spite of its evident absurdity, a reality for Lukács even in the 1960s. Therefore, he regarded any return to earlier forms of culture along the path of the socio-economic development of mankind as a sign of degeneration, or else simply snobbery. African sculpture and the sculpture of Phidias, the drawings of schizophrenics and those of Rembrandt, are incompatible (4:361) unless one simply submits oneself to the cosmopolitan frenzy of petty-bourgeois snobbery during the age of imperialism (4:337). Lukács also believes that authentic folk literature is realistic and communicative, unlike the writings of Joyce and others who claim to return to the folk tradition and tales (4:338-41).

Lukács did not participate actively in the political labeling of defenders of modern literature as revisionists. Nevertheless he too regarded avant-gardism as a deviation from the classical terms and values of Marxist aesthetics. As such, the avant-garde was an ally of its opposite—naturalism. Both naturalism and avant-gardism reflect details of life detached from the larger context, cultivate the atypical, disregard the balance between object and subject, and rely on the immediate subjective perception (4:70, 77, 322, 442, 465ff, 486–87). The idea that both naturalism and the avant-garde are two genetically identical, equally "bourgeois," movements is analogous to the relationship which Marxist historians of philosophy establish between Berkeley's and Hume's subjectivized empiricism (or its nineteenth-century outcome, positivism), and the cult of objectivized irrationalism in phenomenology and existentialism. In both philosophical systems, the existence of any objectively verifiable and meaningful reality ceases where individual experience ends (4:112ff). Both regard existence as chaotic and unknowable. Knowledge is an illusion; the individual can know only himself. Translate this to "the language of literature" and the conclusion is that neither naturalism nor avant-gardism reflect the essential and the universal ("typical") in man's social existence; instead, they reproduce an atypical and incoherent individual existence.

Ultimately, Lukács thinks that both naturalism and avant-gardism "liquidate" realism (4:314). Chronologically, as he believes, naturalism precedes the avant-garde. Next, it is impressionism in which the phenomenal "objectivity" of naturalism takes a subjective character. Third, symbolism separates the expression of human moods even from this superficially conceived environment. Finally, expressionism, being preoccupied only with a subjective "essence," liquidates even the last internalized traces of external social reality (14:139–40). In other instances Lukács presented somewhat differing interpretations of the stages of this process (e.g. 4:486), but his essential message is consistently the same.

All thing considered, Lukács regards avant-garde literature as a pathological and perverted product of the no-longer-viable modern bourgeoisie. As has already been mentioned, he maintains, in certain essays, that the most progressive elements of the bourgeoisie can still produce great realistic works. This is what separates Lukács from the more intolerant Gorkian and official party line. Lukács believes, however, that modern realism is great precisely because it grows organically out of the nineteenth-century realistic tradition. We have also considered Lukács' theory of how social pathology becomes individual pathology in the naturalist tradition. He proposes the same thesis (unfortunately even more dogmatically) for avant-garde literature as well (4:483–84). This complete dissolution of the sciences in biased philosophized speculations evoked Brecht's criticism during the thirties. In one of his sarcastic remarks, Brecht recommended the knowledge of modern psychology to certain critics who were badly in need of it.[41]

In spite of the fallacies of the argument, we find again an admirable consistency in Lukács. For him, "shoreless realism" is nonsense, a sign of the revival of ahistorical romanticism blended with pseudo-Marxism (6:13). He believed that realism *had* its shores, and he also believed, probably with better reason, that it was he who had reinforced these shores most solidly.

What Lukács called avant-gardism and condemned as such was the same phenomenon that Lunacharsky, Gorky, and Caudwell described as "formalism." It was also the same literary phenomenon which has more recently been taken up in the Eastern European debates of the fifties and sixties under the rubric of "modernism." Even if Lukács is somewhat unusual with respect to the term he uses, he is not alone in condemning the phenomenon itself.

For Mehring, the main criterion for separating bourgeois and proletarian literature was its outlook on the future. Whereas proletarian literature was optimistic, bourgeois literature, though at times indeed reflecting life realistically, was still a literature of decay because of its pessimistic lack of hope in the future.[42] As we can observe, Mehring too emphasized not so much the formal experimental trend in modernism in this view as the decadent world outlook of one generation of artists around the turn of the century. Later other Marxist critics, from Zetkin and Lunacharsky through Ziegler, to Révai, Abusch, and Băleanu, also noted that the decadent, cynical attitude of the bourgeoisie, as reflected in its literature, became a chronic phenomenon. All of these critics emphasized that this "formalist" tendency was a matter of ideology and not of technique—which leaves the question open why so many of them called this tendency "formalist." Generally speaking, the characteristics which socialist critics have used to label modern European literature are varied, but only a few of them complement Lukács' criticism in any respect.

One view that several Marxist critics seem to share is that modern bourgeois literature provides a reflection of a world in which the individual alone seems to constitute a solid basis. In analyzing Freud's effect on modern literature, Fox and Caudwell argue that this reliance on the perceiving and thinking ego is a return to the futile Western cult of individualism.[43] Other critics, however, warn us that individualism should not be confused with subjectivism. One of these critics, József Révai, separates the subjectivism of the "realist" poet from the individualism of the "symbolist." The realist lyricist speaks about his world even while speaking of himself, whereas the symbolist lyricist looks inside in order to transcend his reality and escape from it into an irrational and mystical sphere of existence.[44] Just how to draw a dividing line between the two attitudes is a question which Révai, like Lukács, does not answer, thereby leaving the reader with the unpleasant feeling that the ultimate criterion for categorizing poets is the critic's personal taste or political commitment.

Lukács' idea that modern literature is metaphysical rather than dialectical in its escape from the great sociohistorical problems of the times has its precedent in Plekhanov's writings. Plekhanov thinks that art for art's sake is an indication of the writer's disaccord with his social environment. This denial of a reactionary society is, however, appreciable only as long as there is no alternative available to the artist. In modern times, socialism is the light which disappointed poets should see, or else their poetry cannot avoid the pitfall of a futile *l'art pour l'art*.[45] Fox and Caudwell adopted essentially the same view of artistic isolationism in different ages. According to Lunacharsky, bourgeois society is fairly receptive to formalistic art simply because it senses the harmless character of this art. For that reason, too, the same society is hostile to socialist ambitions in literature.[46]

Two particular forms of taking refuge in the irrational are the aforementioned cult of the primitive and the mythologization of existence. Others joined Lukács in his denunciation of modernism from the bastion of Marxian Europeanism. As if with one voice Clara Zetkin, Bukharin, Băleanu, and Hans Koch condemn the "primitivism" and "barbarism" of bourgeois art for maintaining any interest in "Bushman drawings" and "Negro dances." They all equate this interest with decay, degeneration, and escapism. "Hermann Hesse writes Indian poems, Pechstein paints Negro sculptures, Barlach carves icons." With these words, Ziegler summarized and buried primitivistic bourgeois decadence during the thirties.[47] The problem seemed to survive, however, and has caused, together with Garaudy's and Fischer's attempts to revive myth and magic as bases for art, a considerable amount of ideological headaches for dogmatic Marxist theoreticians.

Mehring, Plekhanov, Lunacharsky, and Ralph Fox—as did Lukács—saw the nineteenth-century disintegration of realism into naturalism, impressionism, and symbolism, as intermediary stages of its progress to modern decadence. But unlike Lukács, these critics (especially of the Soviet and party-line variety, Gorky and Lunacharsky included) quite distinctly spelled out their belief that modernistic literature was, by definition, epigonistic and of inferior aesthetic value. Similarly, the charge that modernistic literature (far from containing even a few grains of reality) is irrational, "morbid and obscure," and even "mad," has been expresed even more vociferously by other critics than Lukács.[48]

Of course, we cannot derive all of the accusations of Marxist critics against modernism from the Lukácsian model. One of the most interesting points Lukács never made is that modernism rejects the essence of genres and dissolves them. Both Franz Mehring, in analyzing Hauptmann's *Hanneles Himmelfahrt,* and Antonio Gramsci, in discussing Pirandello's plays, attempted to show how experimental technique de-dramatized the drama.[49] Analogously, Ralph Fox believed that the de-heroization of the novel character in modernistic prose dissolved the novel itself as a genre.[50]

4. Recent Developments. An Example: The Kafka Debate. Problems of "Shorelessness"

The debate on "modernism," unlike the one on naturalism, is far from over. Nevertheless, signs of concessions are abundant in recent East-Central European pronouncements on literary issues. As some articles from the sixties show, the cry for a reinterpretation of the concept of realism has been uttered often, even in so dogmatic a critical milieu as the Soviet Union. In 1965, Yezuitov, like Garaudy, urged a "historical" view of the term "socialist realism"—one which could not be fixed for once and all, since reality itself was changing.[51] It is, again, Garaudy's and Fischer's views of the realistic creative process which M. S. Kagan, another Soviet scholar, expressed in 1966. He emphasized the human character of the literary model, which is a dialectical embodiment of things in the author's consciousness.[52]

Traditionally, as we have seen, Soviet officials called upon the socialist authors of the world to follow an ethnocentric (and for a Western European artist unacceptable) Russian cultural and artistic pattern as the prototype for socialist realism.

Modern Western Marxist interpretations of realism, grounded in a technologically and scientifically more advanced cultural tradition than the Russian one, have as one of their bases a call for decentralization; and even in the Soviet Union, literary scholars have recently admitted the failure of the old practice. During the sixties, the Soviet Academy of Sciences itself undertook the task of editing and publishing numerous collections of essays on the interrelationship between national traditions and the concept of socialist realism.[53]

The event that irreversibly did away with the Khrushchevian and earlier conservatism was the reinterpretation of Franz Kafka during the sixties. I shall summarize the stages of this process, which is important because of its unprecedented and thorough character and because since then it has served as a model for reinterpreting other figures of modern literature.[54]

By the early sixties, Kafka had not yet even been published in the Soviet Union, nor had his works appeared in any of the people's republics between 1947 and 1956. In 1956, Poland began publishing his works, and in the next year Hungarian and Czechoslovakian translations followed. In 1962, at the World Peace Congress in Moscow, Sartre himself urged Marxists to finally pay tribute to Kafka's genius. In the same year, Viktor Nekrasov, one of the Russian literary black sheep in Khrushchev's eyes, advocated this in his memoirs. In the meantime, Garaudy and Fischer began to discuss Kafka with great understanding.

On May 27 and 28, 1963, Kafka scholars gathered in the little Czech town of Liblice to exchange their views. Czechoslovakian, East and West German, Polish, Hungarian, and Yugoslavian scholars attended the meeting. Garaudy and Fischer were also present, but Soviet critics and scholars from the Balkan people's republics were absent, as were those from most of Western Europe.

The congress became polarized between the liberal Czechoslovakian and the conservative East German views. It turned out to be of decisive importance for Kafka's interpretation from that time on. Not even the Soviet literary view of Kafka has been left unaffected, as Zatonsky's book of Kafka (1965), for example, proves. Several of the congressional speeches dealt with Kafka's influence on other European literatures (like the Yugoslavian, the Hungarian, and the Scandinavian), thus proving the universal character of his work.

At the congress itself there were two general attitudes toward Kafka. One was the critically appreciative attitude, best represented by Paul Reimann, one of the main speakers. Though critics belonging to this group did not regard Kafka as an example relevant in any way to socialist realism, they were still willing to admit his "significance" to modern world literature. The other attitude went further, believing Kafka could be made relevant to the socialist tradition. Eduard Goldstücker, the other main speaker of the congress, and several other Czechoslovakian critics (Kautman and Kusák) represented this view.

Taking into consideration the approaches to Kafka's works, we find two dominant interpretations which are independent of the discussions about the relevance of Kafka to socialist and nonsocialist literature. Most of the critics discussed Kafka in the light of the specific historical and social experiences of his time. They emphasized the impact of the atmosphere of the Austrian-Hungarian Monarchy, of Kafka's German-speaking Jewish minority background, of his job as an insurance official for low-income people. Goldstücker himself took this approach. A very small group, however, whose views were most clearly spelled out by Jiří Hájek, looked at Kafka in more general, almost existential, philosophical terms. They saw him as the universal author of alienation and unchangeable "human conditions."

Hájek's group accused Goldstücker's group of simplistic "sociologism." This seems valid only to a point. It certainly is true that Hájek offered a more radical interpretation of Kafka than Goldstücker did. On the other hand, it is also true that Goldstücker, in emphasizing the socio-historical experience in Kafka's works, stayed closer to the socialist literary tradition, and obviously wanted first to do away with the accusation that Kafka's work was a product of psychosis. He and his group apparently intended to point out, by using the methods of Marxist criticism, how Kafka's works belong to the realistic tradition in a new way and in a new sense.

Returning to Garaudy and Fischer, and to their idea of a "shoreless" realism, we should first refer to the critical reaction it received from two distinct sources. The less interesting of these is the official rejection of the whole idea as "revisionism." The Soviet and East German journalistic-critical "subculture" has been particularly generous with this type of accusation. For us, however, the Lukácsian opposition seems to be considerably more intelligent and willing to deal with specific issues.

Besides Lukács, Coutinho and Konder have also accused Garaudy of faulty logic and epistemological relativism in stating that realism has no shores.[55] By rejecting the possibility of defining it, one is certainly led to the dissolution of a concept. If one does not define realism, calling a literary work realistic would be subjective far beyond Lukács' biases in accepting and rejecting literary works as realistic or anti-realistic. Lukács is quite willing to define his concepts, while Garaudy's scepticism of objective human knowledge makes him dismiss human concepts. We cannot define anything, he says, since our knowledge is always changing, and therefore limited.

Coutinho calls Garaudy's idea of shorelessness a manifestation of impressionistic criticism. Subjectivistic criticism would probably be a better term. Garaudy and Fischer certainly acknowledge the irrational-subjective sources of literary information. These are theoretically acceptable, but objectively not verifiable. Only the existentialistic tradition attempts some systematic verification, and indeed, there is a definite affinity between Garaudy and the existentialists. The clash between the ideas of shoreless and definable realism reflect the still very real gap between the philosophy of existence and the philosophy of science.

As long as efforts are made to describe and define the still "irrational" channels of literary reflection and experience, Coutinho's condemnation of the Garaudy-Fischer view seems to be hasty and intolerant. If, however, the Garaudy circle ever gives up its efforts, Coutinho will be right. Furthermore, this would be an event not only failing to serve the interests of Marxism, but contradicting precisely this very group's admiration of modern technology and science, which are ultimately products of a "rational," objective, controlled, and applied knowledge.

Conclusion

1. Models

The selection of Marxist literary theorists discussed in this book reflects fairly closely the priorities of scholars of socialist criticism. In terms of quality, scope, relative consistency, and impact, Lukács, Gorky, Mehring, Plekhanov, Garaudy, and Fischer form the vanguard of Marxist literary theory. In the second rank, we might include Brecht (as the only non-party member of this group), Caudwell, Finkelstein, Fox, Gramsci, and Lunacharsky.

There are three additional groups whose knowledge is indispensable, but only in an illustrative-documentary sense. The first of these is made up of Marx, Engels, and Lenin themselves. The second group consists of officials who meddle with cultural politics (Bukharin, Radek, Trotsky, Zhdanov, and Khrushchev). The third is a problematic and extremely heterogeneous group of quasi-Marxist critics, which was mentioned briefly in our Introduction, and whose ideas overlap with those of truly socialist critics but never constitute all of the essential aspects of Marxism.

When categorizing the different Marxist models of realism, Lukács' triparite division—a more descriptive, externalizing model and a more psychological, internalizing variant, with an ideal, dominating mainstream in between which synthesizes the extremes—

seems to be a relevant and clear-cut one. Although such three-fold attempts to bridge the classical gap between Aristotelian-Horatian and Platonic-Plotinian aesthetics could hardly be traced farther back in time than Hegel, it should be mentioned in all fairness that the Marxist line, to which Lukács belongs, has not been the only one operating with such tripartite aesthetic-epistemological conceptions. Charles S. Peirce's terms—indexical, iconical, and symbolical—for instance, show a great similarity with Lukács' terms and system.

The tripartite structure, aside from being persuasively convenient for classifying purposes, also makes it possible to conceive the Marxist views of realism within the framework of model theory. In this case, of course, four sets of models should be established. Two of these sets are primary: Lukács' and Gorky's synthetic definitions of realism as being "critical" or "socialist." The other two sets are secondary, since they are less synthetic in their exaggerated emphasis of one of the two parts of the object-subject relationship. These sets constitute, respectively, Mehring and Plekhanov's, and Garaudy and Fischer's, theories.

Let us summarize the characteristics of any model as listed in the beginning of chapter 2, section 2: re-creation of the dimensions and function of any system, usually for the purpose of an experiment or for the verification of an hypothesis, built from the perceptual angle of one particular observer. The two first criteria are closely related to the model itself (describing it qualitatively as well as quantitatively), whereas the two last criteria refer to the purpose the model serves, and to the goals (social or scholarly), and even to the personality, of the modeler.

If the model is the reproduction of an original system in corresponding dimensions, then Lukács' Hegelian assumption that the literary work is a drop of the sea, that the specific and the typical are microcosmic reflections of the macrocosm, convey the same definition in a more poetic way. At the same time, Lukács emphasizes that only unique and relatively high stages of civilization can develop this sophisticated synthesizing artistic quality which is ultimately the result of a heightened consciousness. Whereas Lukács' model of realism is a reproduction of *conscious* existence, Gorky's model reproduces the process and organization of human *labor*. Some kind of activity is certainly as much an essential attribute of man as is some kind of conscious existence—hence the two complementary definitions of man as *Homo sapiens* and *Homo faber*. Unlike Lukács, however, Gorky tends to limit aesthetically relevant human action to ethically positive and socially beneficial action.

Although in Lukács and Gorky two aspects of existence (the meditative and the active) got somewhat greater emphasis, in the two secondary models these aspects attain almost dichotomic dimensions. The key word in both is *need*. But whereas in Mehring and Plekhanov, man's elementary material needs define his consciousness and its literary reflection, in Garaudy and Fischer, an existential rejection of these dehumanizing elementary needs motivates man. Both secondary models appear fairly ahistoric and anthropologically motivated as compared to the primary ones, but Mehring and Plekhanov are extreme materialists (magic is a means to attaining food), Garaudy and Fischer extreme rationalists (magic is a means to higher awareness and self-knowledge). This overdimensioning of either of the two factors appears in our secondary models as the reflection of the age-old dichotomy of empiricism and rationalism in European thought, which also affected Marxism.

By using a somewhat simplified typology, we can call the two primary models synthetic, with a relative lean toward, respectively, dialectical rationalism and less dialectical, economically motivated materialism; whereas in the secondary models, the two "antithetic" characteristics dominate the respective models.

Qualitatively, the function of our four models shows distinct traces of the sociocultural systems they reproduce. Also, hypothetically, they might in the future appear particularly applicable to systems analogous to the reproduced ones. It is, of course, impossible to determine exactly which models suit which cultural areas most appropriately. Yet, there is some relevance in speculating at least in terms of the spheres of culture the models reproduce.

Lukács' model of realism appears as one growing out of the soil of, and applicable mostly to, the literary tradition of culturally sophisticated, economically more or less self-sufficient, socially differentiated countries where, at the same time, the reeducation of the society and the preservation of one part of the tradition were primary tasks. This "preservative change" also appears in the social theoretical model Lukács presented in 1928 in his "Blum-theses": the idea that an evolutionary, long-range, democratic way to socialization might be more feasible and desirable in certain countries than a Leninist Bolshevik dictatorship. Hungary, Austria, Czechoslovakia, West Germany, and the Scandinavian countries have appeared particularly receptive to this Lukácsian model. But the very same model seems to have satisfied certain needs and tendencies implicit in the cultural traditions of France, Italy, and parts of South America (especially Argentina and Brazil) as well, and has analogies in the works of the British Fox and Caudwell.

Gorky's model is related to a very different cultural milieu and needs. With its emphasis on "correct" consciousness and human productivity, it is based on the circumstances of either turbulent times of national or class wars, or times when major collective social efforts were needed for strengthening national economy. There is quite often a continuity of these developments, as in the Soviet Union, China, Albania, or Cuba. Indeed, the Gorkian model characterizes the cultural mood, and most certainly the literary policy, of all these countries; but is not alien to certain East German tendencies, either. By and large, this literary model reproduces an industrially underdeveloped, ideologically authoritarian and feudal-conservative social system in which, owing to the little-differentiated character of the class structure, the mobilization of the relatively homogeneous and professionally unspecialized masses for collective efforts, or for a collective appreciation of the arts, is not improbable.

Of the secondary models, Mehring and Plekhanov's shows features akin to Gorky's, whereas Garaudy and Fischer's bears distant resemblance to Lukács' model. Mehring and Plekhanov's model is based on the doctrinaire principal guidelines of party politicizing. Without any self-confident, "omniscient," extensive Marxist organizational bureaucracy, similar to those supporting the structure of the Second International, of Stalinist Soviet Russia, of East Germany (where Mehring is highly esteemed) or of the American labor movement during the thirties, the deterministic materialism would never appear as a distinct model of any trend of realism.

Another kind of self-confidence is reflected in the model provided by Garaudy and Fischer—that of strong communist parties which function in a democratic parliamentary system, and try to attain domination while accepting the laws of this system. (The fact that the Austrian communist party, to which Fischer belonged, is not particularly strong, does not invalidate this characterization of the joint Garaudy-Fischer model.) The tactic is, of course, to involve more and more individuals in a communist-directed, but ideologically lenient, mass movement (a "popular front") until a safe parliamentary majority is attained. This is why Garaudy and Fischer claim so many "outsiders" for their concept of realism; this is why they constantly emphasize the importance of awareness. France, Italy, potentially also Austria, or the politically communist but culturally pluralistic Poland and Yugoslavia, are among those receptive to this most inclusive model of literary realism.

To summarize, the qualitative aspects of the four Marxist models of realism can be labeled as "democratic" (Lukács), "populist-collectivistic" (Gorky), "party bureaucratic" (Mehring and Plekhanov), and "popular front" (Garaudy and Fischer).

The experiments that the constructors of the four models carry out are inseparable from the conditions they are modeling. Lukács' whole theory of realism seems to be an attempt to provide continuity between the great literature of the past and that of the future. Gorky, too, is preserving one aspect of the past (popular culture taking the shape of folklore and myth); but he wants to start the future with a slate clean of the signs of upper-class culture, and his whole model of socialist realism is built to support this attempt. Mehring and Plekhanov's model demonstrates an experiment in positivistic infallibility. These men made their model extremely exclusive. From a position of supreme certainty, they observed one by one the literary works of past and present to see whether they fit into the box of their idea of realism (most of them don't). Garaudy and Fischer are, on the other hand, carrying out an experiment in dialectics, finding pleasure in their own generosity in extending the limits of the term "realism."

The fact that there are no unique models could be best demonstrated by comparing these four to other examples; for instance, Lukács to Ralph Fox, or Gorky to Brecht. Such biographically based, psychologically oriented, and, in a condensed form, unavoidably simplifying or speculative enterprise is beyond our ambitions at this time, however.

There is one important fact to be mentioned: all four modelers are Europe-centered in their views. With the exception of colonized, white North America, the applicability of realism to the arts of other continents has not yet been attempted, nor was the hypothesis that it was applicable ever stated reassuringly enough. When reading Lukács, one almost gets the impression that literature and art have existed in not more than a dozen countries during the past four thousand years of human civilization. Without one's knowing the arrogance of Central European urban middle-class intellectuals toward folk ("peasant") and non-European ("primitive") art, Lukács' attitude can hardly be understood. Garaudy and Fischer assure their readers that they are all-encompassing and universal, but they discuss only what they feel they know best: modern European literature and art.

In Gorky and the materialist critics, the situation is somewhat different. Seemingly, there is a greater appreciation of the folk tradition of European literature and art, as well as of the literature of the people of other continents. At the same time, the deterministic idea that only an advanced form of economic production can bring forth a degree of consciousness high enough to make man master of his future results in a firm belief that socialist literature is superior to all other previous or present forms of literature. Giving up the aesthetic and artistic criteria is quite legitimate in the view of this tendency. It is equally obvious that the ultimate ideal is a European one for these critics too—although in Gorky, there is enough evidence to suppose that the ideal literature did not grow out of a European but solely of a Soviet Russian soil. Whereas in Lukács it was the superiority of the European cultural heritage that justified the ethnocentric model, in Gorky and the materialistic model it was the supremacy of European socio-economic patterns that served the same purpose.

Taking an evaluative look at the models, one finds that, among all of the Marxist critics, it is Georg Lukács whose works on literary problems surpass in volume, scope, and consistency those of any other outstanding socialist critic. The *essential* problems concerning the term "realism" can be derived without exception from Lukács' work. These may be summarized by pointing to various contradictions in his writing on the subject of realism:

1. *Is realism a historical term (period), or an ahistoric one (method)*? If it is a historical term, Lukács and his followers are anti-dialectical by not admitting the necessity of developing other, newer, and eventually radically different forms of expression. If realism is an ahistorical term, then Lukács seems to contradict his own principle of historicism. If both are true, how can we develop a dialectical definition which would reconcile these two fairly remote definitional possibilities?

2. *Is realism a descriptive or an evaluative term?* (This question is unrelated to the previous one, as both a historical and an ahistorical definition can be either descriptive or evaluative.) If realism is a descriptive term, why does Lukács often evaluate literary works by historically outdated standards? If it is an evaluative term, how can he possibly cope with the concrete problem of the existence of other movements?

As our comparison of the two hypothetical models (representing realism as method and as movement respectively), demonstrates, at present realism as a historical *movement* seems to be more easily definable. As such, it appears as one of the major literary trends of the complex nineteenth- and twentieth-century scientific-technological Western world, of the age of mass-man and mass-media, class conflicts and class reconciliations. Its philosophical basis is wider than that of naturalism, its formal-technical criteria more vague than those delineated in the manifestoes of the different modernistic "isms." However, it is precisely these wider borderlines that make realism perhaps a more problematic, yet more inclusive and more typical, movement of the modern age than the others mentioned. At the same time, it should not be forgotten that nineteenth-century realism demonstrated considerable overlappings with other movements (especially with romanticism, naturalism, and symbolism) in all those countries where it appeared as a significant tendency.

Still, realism could at some future time be used in a limited sense to label a *method,* by referring to a certain kind of mimesis, similar to the one we find in nineteenth-century European prose. But first, Marxist epistemology should develop a more consistent stand on the relationship between nature and human consciousness. The issue is not, as Lukács believed, whether one should give up or preserve rationalism; rather, it seems unavoidable that one must screen out whatever is outdated or biased in the nineteenth-century views of Marx and Engels, or in that inclusive Hegelian idealism Lukács inherited from the teachers and idols of his youth. The impact of science and technology on modern consciousness; the occasionally immense autonomy of the psyche from social conditions; the epistemological relevance of myth, religion, or other manifestations of "false consciousness"; the acceptance of non-European cultural patterns as well as the cultures of European ethnic minorities; the coping with the existence of social evil and individual unhappiness in the socialist system; the tolerance toward deviations—as long as Marxist aesthetic theory is unable to sincerely face these epistemological, social, and artistic-thematic problems, there can be no solid basis for considering realism as a method from a socialist point of view.

Another philosophical and aesthetic problem is the haunting spirit of social determinism that penetrates all existing Marxist models of realism. Instead of accepting the two original Marxist ideas of the uneven development of social conditions (that it is impossible to conceive any social development free of relapses, and that the sphere of consciousness is "relatively" independent of the sphere of economically productive human interaction), even outstanding socialist theorists tended to apologize for assumed direct, unfortunately deterministic, connections between literature and so-cial conditions. The thesis of Mehring, Plekhanov, and Gorky, and one of the two interpretations of realism in Lukács, all state that in modern times, the bourgeois class turned deca-dent; therefore its positive and objective self-reflection in the form of a "great realism" became impossible. Clearly, this is a social-deterministic principle built on the speculative axiom that the bourgeoisie is rigid and unable to regenerate itself. Garaudy and Fischer recognized and criticized this, and ascer-tained that the bourgeoisie was *not* decadent, mostly in order to defend modernism in literature and art. By doing so, how-ever, they gave as much evidence of a belief in art being socially determined as did the group they were challenging.

Although the possibility of using the term "realism" to describe a method cannot be excluded, there are no solid arguments for using this term as a value judgment. Should it happen that the works of Zola and Flaubert, Faulkner and Dürrenmatt, Robbe-Grillet and Beckett do not satisfy the cri-teria of realism either as a period or a method, we still do not have any reason to call them inferior authors, since not even the most outstanding Marxist critics have convincingly proven the superior value of realism to other literary methods.

In short, we may say that realism is a valid term when used for a historical period; it might become a valid term when applied to a supra-historical method; but it is not, and should never be, valid in any qualitative aesthetic "value" judgment of works and authors.

While we still must live with the epistemological dichot-omy of the consciousness-oriented, historical tradition and the pro-scientific, agnostic, and ahistorical theory of Garaudy, Fischer, and other neo-Marxists, we could at least attempt to talk about two concepts of realism as a creative method. "Realism 1" could be the Lukácsian ideal of classical nineteenth-century realism, in the most traditional meaning of the word. In this "primary realism," which denotes both a creative method and a historical period, not the transposition of the experience in the author's consciousness, but the experienced subject matter itself, is the factor that may or may not capture the reader. "Realism 2," on the other hand, could be the Garaudyan method of building models analogous to social reality, yet transposing it into spheres of consciousness where the reader may or may not be able to follow the writer. This "secondary realism" is a basically ahistorical concept, and identifies a creative method only. The so-called "ideological criticism" (*Ideologiekritik*), an approach which unifies Marxism, structuralism, and history of ideas and is particularly widespread in West Germany and the Scandinavian countries, seems to be especially well suited for decoding the social background of works written by the methods of "Realism 2."

Such a distinction between two "realisms" would unify the creative mind, and at the same time it would satisfactorily separate the creative mode of a Balzac or a Thomas Mann on the one hand from a Blake or a Kafka on the other. Still, such division between two concepts of realism is problematic and not wholly desirable. Even if accepted as a method, the earliest occurrences of realism would be hard to trace; nor would there be any easy answer provided to such valid question as how different forms of documentarism (not necessarily consisting of the documentary novel only) could be described as specific modes of realism. Nevertheless, the temporary division of the term seems to be the only acceptable way to further investigations into its dimensions.

2. Significations

By establishing the different Marxist models of literary realism, the goal of our study has been reached. Yet the scholarly results may leave one who is interested in the general context and relevance of these models dissatisfied. The value of theoretical findings is not necessarily self-evident. Therefore, the second section of this conclusion is devoted to an investigation into some farther-reaching implications of our models of realism.

One may ask, in the first place, which characteristics of the various Marxist theories of realism are unique. Looking back at a more than hundred-year-long development, we may venture the statement that, with all its contradictions and shortcomings, relatively speaking, Marxist aesthetics has made the most consistent and unabrupted efforts to establish an epistemological foundation for literature—that is, to regard literature as an element of active human knowledge. Naturally, Marxist aesthetics shares this basis, for better or worse, with Marxist philosophy. There seem to be only two other identifiable modern ideological trends which have developed epistemologies with a somewhat permanent, active influence on literature: existentialism (in overlapping with phenomenology), and Jungian anthropological "myth-criticism." Existentialism, however, exalts rationalism in a dualized relationship of the subject and object of knowledge, whereas mythological criticism postulates the existence of timeless, metaphysical symbols. In opposition to both, the Marxist line gives a more immediate and outreaching interpretation of the process of gaining knowledge for, and from, artistic creation. The method by which this contextual view of literature is attained is dialectics which, in addition to the new perspectives it opens up for literature, also facilitates an integrating utilization of different relevant non-Marxist theories. In spite of the protest against basic axioms or conclusions of Freudian psychology or existentialist philosophy, Georg Lukács and other eminent Marxist critics themselves rely on particular ideas or achievements of "bourgeois" psychology, philosophy, or sociology.

Also, in the definitions of the concept of realism, Marxists may have found inspiration in the theories of non-Marxist contemporaries or predecessors. Georg Lukács' indebtedness to Hegel, and a basic similarity between his and Peirce's aesthetic system, have already been mentioned. We have seen as well how Marx and Engels utilized the dramatic ideas of Otto Ludwig, in addition to Hegel's aesthetics. Actually, Ludwig quite clearly influenced Lukács too, and preceded him by almost a century in stating that the existential superiority of Shakespeare's characters is spelled out by his contrasting them with characters who exist parallel to the protagonist.[1] Ludwig may have given additional impulses to Lukács through his repeated praise of the individualization of expression in the realistic literary work;[2] and by placing realism (the "artistic middle-way") perhaps as early as the 1840s, in between two extremes of idealism and naturalism.[3] Ludwig's claim of "totality" for realism, as well as his compatriot Friedrich Spielhagen's claim, some decades later, of "breadth and width," are additional terminological and conceptual analogies between these two nineteenth-century critics and Lukács.[4] It should be noted that while Lukács repeatedly referred in his works to Ludwig's and Spielhagen's literary activity, at the same time he left their critical studies unmentioned, although there is hardly any reason to doubt that he knew of them.

Influenced as Lukács always remained by the critical idols of his youth, writings of more recent Marxist literary theorists demonstrate a greater impact of different twentieth-century critical views. The Jungian influence on Garaudy and Fischer has already been mentioned; and the attempts of these two, in particular, to establish various levels of consciousness may not be greatly different from similar structuralistic endeavors. Among theories of literary realism, Erich Auerbach's and Richard Brinkmann's are akin to Garaudy's ideas. Auerbach's well-known thesis of a concentrated, episodic variation of realism which chooses extreme existential situations for its themes, and Brinkmann's conception of realism as an externalization of the mind, are identical with the ideas on which Garaudy based his critical analyses of Kafka's, Picasso's, and Saint-John Perse's works.[5]

No major movement has ever arisen without having its roots in the past, however. In all fairness, it should be emphasized again that even if several elements of the Marxist theories of literary realism are not particularly original, they are still integrated into a dialectical and historical texture which is, in spite of its shortcomings, among the most inclusive and best structured of its kind.

A second question one may ask is: Which conclusions are of permanent value for literary criticism? The Marxist models of realism demonstrate, I believe, that the need to consider rationally literary projections of the human experience in its multifaceted social context is still among the first tasks of criticism. By now, the slaughtering of such sacred cows of yesteryear as "New Criticism" no longer belongs among the heroic tasks. Yet it is impossible to forget how a technically interpretative, text-centered view of literature, while certainly producing respectable achievements, dominated American and Western European critical and educational practice for decades, and in certain countries virtually eradicated any attempts to use other methods. It is equally impossible to disregard from the continuation of text fetishism in several now-fashionable trends, such as certain directions in structuralistic, anthropological, and sociological criticism.

Although the Platonic spheres of "illusion and reality," of "object and subject" can be dichotomized (as they usually are) for the purpose of analysis, this dichotomy should, however, later be superseded by synthesis in the process of observing literary phenomena in their totality and development. The focus of any meaningful criticism is ultimately on a synthetic human encounter with life witnessed in the work of art. The comparative method, aiming at finding out how different sociocultural contexts modified analogous human experiences and shaped them in quite various ways, seems to be a basic method of the most successful Marxist investigations.

Another conclusion we may gain from the Marxist models and can regard as one surviving the changing fashions of times is the need for literature to have some rational communicative function. With a good degree of sophism, one can naturally view tendentious noncommunication as one form of communication—an evidence of frustration, of nihilism, of the existentialistic recognition of "nothingness," and so on. Yet as a whole, extreme noncommunicative experimental trends of modern literature (such as dada, onomatopoetic experimental poetry, certain offshots of surrealism, and the "concrete" literature of the early 1960s) are already regarded as antiquated phenomena. Their genesis is socially or psychologically explicable, but their literary documents no longer bridge the times past to reach the subjective sphere of experience and evoke the curiosity of modern readers. In the final analysis, the particular meaning of individual works, not only the phenomenal meaning of collective artistic tendencies, is the true criterion of the survival of art. This is, perhaps, an element of what Hegel and Lukács called the "human content" of literature.

A third question, and one more concretely related to the history of the development of the Marxist models is this: What do the "infightings," the ideological party hassles, reveal about various socialist concepts of realism, and about the background and genesis of these concepts?

Concentrating on party politics has been a favorite approach of books which attempted to explain literary phenomena from the perspective of political science or modern history. Curiously enough, whereas political scientists have long noticed clearly pluralistic tendencies in Marxist ideology, this phenomenon has not yet been pointed out in socialist literary theory. Throughout this book, I have tried to stress the culturally pluralistic character of Marxist interpretations of literary realism.

Recent political events, which might be seemingly not at

all related to literary critical developments, provide welcome supporting arguments to several of my points. Although one of the first things Georges Marchais did in 1970, as the new acting general secretary of the French Communist Party, was to denounce Roger Garaudy, the very same Marchais became one of the leaders of the Atlantic-Mediterranean communist dissent at the international Berlin conference of the communist parties in 1976. The implications of this conference are far-reaching. Aragon's, Fischer's, Garaudy's, and Siqueiros' pioneering claims for the freedom of socialist art and criticism from the central dogmas of *one* communist party, is now finally supported by the program of *several* communist parties. Clearly, pluralistic tendencies in Marxist views on literary realism have gained a well-structured, identifiable political presence in the programs of communist parties throughout the world. Although the history of literary criticism is by no means an extension of political controversies and struggles, it does not exist completely independent from them. Significantly, debates on realism several decades ago foreshadowed quite recent political and ideological controversies.

It would be pretentious to equate the Marxist views on literary realism with Marxist literary theory, or to regard them as being revelatory of all essential theses of Marxist aesthetics, not to mention philosophy. Similarly, it would be an extreme simplification to use the debates over literary realism to understand modern political history. Certain discriminations are imperative when implications of intricate interrelations are observed. But the interrelations nevertheless exist. Our models of realism open challenging vistas to as yet unresearched, larger problems of socialist ideology, such as the methodological pluralism of general Marxist theory or the cultural pluralism of the established socialist world order. Investigations in all these directions would be ultimately beneficial for Marxist aesthetics as well, since they would further qualify and shape the concept of realism itself.

Notes

In the text, all quotations appear in English translation, with the indication of their source in the Notes. Wherever no source is indicated, the translation is my own.

In the documentation, Russian transliterations follow the Board of Geographic Names (BGN) recommendations, except for names ending with -iy, where the conventional English -y ending is preserved (e.g. Gorky, Lunacharsky); and in names where the phonemic connection -ks- is traditionally transliterated as -x- (e.g. Alexey, Maxim).

Introduction

1. H. Mayer, "Karl Marx und die Literatur," in *Marxismus und Literatur*, ed. F. J. Raddatz (Reinbek b. Hamburg: Rowohlt, 1969), 3:335.

2. "What Is Socialist Literature?" in *The Modern Polish Mind*, ed. M. Kuncewicz (New York: Grosset & Dunlap, 1962), p. 368.

3. Particularly useful are the following works: M. H. Abrams, *The Mirror And The Lamp* (New York: Norton, 1953); *Osnovy marksistsko-leninskoy estetiki* (Moskva: Gospolitizdat, 1960); "Realism," in *Literaturnaya entsiklopediya*, eds. V. M. Friche and A. V. Lunacharsky (Moskva, 1929–39); R. Wellek, "The Concept of Realism in Literary Scholarship," *Neophilologus*, 1961, pp. 1–20; Wellek, *A History of Modern Criticism*, 4 vols. (New Haven: Yale University Press, 1955–).

I. The Classics And The Bureaucrats

1. See *Hegel-Lexikon*, vols. 23–24, in Hegel, *Sämtliche Werke: Jubiläumsausgabe*, ed. H. Glockner (Stuttgart: Frommann, 1927–39). Subsequent references to this edition will appear in the text.

2. Cf. also Lukács' interpretation in his *Werke* (Neuwied: Luchterhand, 1962–), 10:446.

3. *Ibid.*, p. 126.

4. *Ibid.*, p. 238.

5. The original English letter is lost. Our source is K. Marx and F. Engels, *Literature and Art* (New York: International Publishers, 1947), p. 41. Hereafter cited as *LA*.

6. H. Mayer, "Karl Marx und die Literatur," in *Marxismus und* Literatur, ed. F. J. Raddatz (Reinbek b. Hamburg: Rowohlt, 1969), 3:329.

7. K. Marx and F. Engels, *Werke* (Berlin: Dietz, 1957–), 13:9. Hereafter cited as *MEW*. Trans.: *LA*, p. 1.

8. *Ibid.*

9. *MEW*, 23:192–93.

10. *MEW*, 25:828.

11. *MEW*, 37:463. Trans.: P. Demetz, *Marx, Engels, and the Poets* (Chicago: The University of Chicago Press, 1967), p. 142. Trans. in brackets mine.

12. *MEW*, 13:640. Trans.: *LA*, p. 18.

13. *MEW*, 26(1):257. Trans.: *LA*, p. 28. Trans. in brackets mine, owing to mistranslation in *LA*.

14. *MEW*, 13:641–42.

15. *MEW*, 28:246–47.

16. *MEW*, 21:102–106.

17. *Ibid.*, pp. 65–66.

18. *Ibid.*, pp. 475–76.

19. *Ibid.*, pp. 72–73.

20. *MEW*, 23:90–93.

21. *Ibid.*, pp. 145–47; see also *MEW*, *Ergänzungsband*, 1:562–67.

22. *MEW*, 25:49.

23. See J-P. Sartre, *Situations* (Paris: Gallimard, 1949), 3:157ff; P. Demetz, *Marx, Engels und die Dichter* (Stuttgart: Deutsche Verlags-Anstalt, 1959), p. 104; R. Barilli, *La barriera del naturalismo* (Milano: Mursia, 1961), pp. 134–35; R. Barthes, *Le Degré zéro de l'écriture* (Paris: Gonthier, 1964), pp. 61–64; G. Steiner, *Language and Silence* (New York: Athenaeum, 1967), p. 328.

24. *MEW*, 2:59.

25. *Ibid.*, pp. 60–62.

26. *Ibid.*, pp. 70–71.

27. *Ibid.*, pp. 172–99.

28. See Lukács, *Werke*, 10:243.

29. F. Lassalle, *Nachgelassene Briefe und Schriften*, ed. G. Mayer (Stuttgart, Berlin: Deutsche Verlags-Anstalt, 1921–24), 3:185–213; refs. to pp. 151, 204.

30. See Lukács, *Werke*, 10:475.

31. See their letters in *MEW*, 29:590–93, 600–605. Subsequent quotations and references related to the Sickingen-debate are from these pages. Trans.: *LA*, pp. 45–56.

32. G. Büchner, *Werke und Briefe: Gesamtausgabe* (Wiesbaden: Insel Verlag, 1958), p. 400.

33. See O. Ludwig, *Gesammelte Schriften*, ed. A. Stern (Leipzig: Grunow, 1891), 5:259, 525, 532, etc.

34. Three convenient surveys and collections of nineteenth- and twentieth-century debates on realism are *The Age of Realism*, ed. F. W. J. Hemmings (Harmondsworth, England: Penguin Books, 1974); *Begriffsbestimmung des literarischen Realismus*, ed. R. Brinkmann (Darmstadt: Wissenschaftliche Buchgesellschaft, 1969); *Documents of Modern Literary Realism*, ed. G. J. Becker (Princeton: Princeton University Press, 1963).

35. *MEW*, 36:394.

36. *MEW*, 37:465.

37. *MEW*, 39:206.

38. *MEW*, 37:493.

39. *MEW*, 37:436–37.

40. *MEW*, 37:413.

41. *Marx, Engels und die Dichter*, p. 203.

42. *MEW*, 35:460. Trans.: Demetz, *Marx, Engels, and the Poets*, pp. 138–39.

43. V. G. Belinsky, *Polnoye sobranie sochineniy* (Moskva: Akad. nauk SSSR, 1953–56), 12:69. Trans.: his *Selected Philosophical Essays* (Moskva: Foreign Languages Publishing House, 1948), p. 163.

44. Cf. *MEW*, 16:407–408; 18:540, 664–66; 32:521; 33:540.

45. N. G. Chernishevsky, *Polnoye sobranie sochineniy* (Moskva: Goskhudizdat, 1939–53), 2:10–11.

46. N. A. Dobrolyubov, *Sobranie sochineniy* (Moskva, Leningrad: Goskhudizdat, 1961–64), 2:260.

47. For more about the populism of the revolutionary democrats, see G. Bisztray, " 'With the People, Through A Thousand Dangers': East-Central European Literary Populism," *Mosaic*, 6, no. 4 (1973):39–49.

48. V. I. Lenin, *Collected Works* (Moskva: Foreign Languages Publishing House, 1960–), 10:44–49. Hereafter cited as CW.

49. Cf. *Druzhba narodov*, 4, 1960.

50. The so-called Russian formalist critics, for instance, wrote a series of essays on Lenin's language and style in the 1920s and 1930s. Collected in German translation: *Sprache und Stil Lenins*, ed. F. Mierau. München: Hanser, 1970.

51. Lukács, *Werke*, 10:65–66.

52. D. Zoltai, " Elidegenedés és művészet," *A Magyar Tudományos Akadémia Nyelv-és Irodalomtörténeti Osztályának Közleményei*, 25 (1968):60–79.

53. Works in English providing a general summary of literary debates, theoretical programs, party decisions etc. in the Soviet Union after 1917 are the following: H. Ermolaev, *Soviet Literary Theories 1917–1934* (Berkeley: University of California Press, 1963); A. Philipov, *Origin and Principles of Soviet Aesthetics until N. Khrushchev* (New York: Pageant Press, 1964); G. Struve, *Russian Literature Under Lenin And Stalin, 1917–1953* (Norman: University of Oklahoma Press, 1963). See also a German source: P. W. Neumann, "Sowjetrussische Literaturtheorien seit 1917." *Europa-Archiv*, 1952, pp. 5333–36.

54. According to Ermolaev, it was Ivan Gronsky, editor of the periodical *Izvestiya*, who used the term "socialist realism" first in a speech to Moscow writers on May 20, 1932 (*Soviet Literary Theories*, p. 144).

55. In *Problems of Soviet Literature* (Moskva, Leningrad: Co-op. Publishing Soc. of Foreign Workers, 1935), pp. 13–24. Subsequent references to the congressional speeches of Zhdanov, Gorky, Radek, and Bukharin, all published in this volume, will appear in the text.

56. See Ermolaev's repeated favorable references to Trotsky, and his appreciation of Bukharin's congressional speech (p. 143); Struve's repeated references to Bukharin's and Radek's "most interesting" congressional speeches; Victor Erlich on Trotsky in *Russian Formalism: History, Doctrine* ('s Gravenhage: Mouton, 1965), pp. 100, 105.

57. Yury Olesha, "Speech to the First Congress of Soviet Writers," *Envy and Other Works* (New York: Doubleday, 1967), p. 217.

58. E. Zola, "Proudhon et Courbet," *Oeuvres complètes* (Paris: Cercle du livre précieux, 1962–), 10:35–46.

59. See A. A. Zhdanov, *Essays on Literature, Philosophy, and Music* (New York: International Publishers, 1950), pp. 15–44.

60. Yo. V. Stalin, *Marksizm i voprosy yazykoznaniya* (Moskva: Gospolitizdat, 1950), English trans. 1951.

61. *MEW*, 3:30–31.

62. Lukács, *Werke*, 10:433–58.

63. See his *The Great Mission of Literature and Art* (Moskva: Progress Publishers, 1964). Subsequent references to this work will appear in the text.

64. Cf. P. Ludz, "Vorwort," G. Lukács, *Schriften zur Literatursoziologie* (Neuwied: Luchterhand, 1961), p. 22; A. Ljungdal, *Georg Lukács och marxismens estetik* (Stockholm: Bonnier, 1967), p. 22; G. Steiner, *Language and Silence*, pp. 340–41; H. Mayer, "Karl Marx und die Literatur," in *Marxismus und Literatur*, 3:333; V. Žmegač, "Einleitung," *Marxistische Literaturkritik* (Bad Homburg: Athenäum, 1970), p. 8.

65. See his introduction to Marx and Engels, *Über Kunst und Literatur* (Berlin: Henschel Verlag, 1953), pp. 10–13.

66. Cf. *Marx, Engels und die Dichter*, pp. 154ff., and *Marx, Engels, and the Poets*, p. 232.

67. See Lukács, *Werke*, 10:205; B. Hansen, *Den marxistiske litteraturkritik* (København: Reitzel, 1967), pp. 10, 16; L. Konder, *Os marxistas e a arte* (Rio de Janeiro: Civilização brasileira, 1967), p. 2.

68. *Marx, Engels und die Dichter*, pp. 99–100.

69. See *LA*, p. 139.

70. R. Garaudy, *Karl Marx* (Paris: Seghers, 1964), pp. 16–17.

71. E. Fromm, Introduction to *Socialist Humanism*, ed. Fromm (Garden City, N.Y.: Doubleday, 1965), pp. viii–ix.

II. Critical and Socialist Realism: Terminology and Models

1. P. Demetz, *Marx, Engels und die Dichter* (Stuttgart: Deutsche Verlags-Anstalt, 1959), pp. 178–85.

2. R. Wellek, "The Concept of Realism in Literary Scholarship," *Neophilologus*, 1961, p. 11.

3. H. Levin, "On the Dissemination of Realism," *Proceedings of the Fifth Congress of the International Comparative Literature Association* (Belgrade: University of Belgrade, n.d.), pp. 239, 241.

4. See their congressional speeches in *Problems of Soviet Literature* (Moskva, Leningrad: Co-op. Publishing Soc. of Foreign Workers, 1935).

5. See, e.g., Lukács, "On Socialist Realism," *International Literature*, April 1939, p. 87; his *Werke* (Neuwied: Luchterhand, 1962–), 5:9–10; P. Demetz, *Marx, Engels und die Dichter*, pp. 178–81; A. Hansen, *Arbeideren i norsk diktning* (Oslo: Tiden, 1960), pp. 10ff; G. Gunnarson, *Litteratur och samhälle*, unprinted study (ref. in A. Hansen, p. 13).

6. *Problems of Soviet Literature*, p. 65.

7. *Questions d'art et de littérature* (Paris: Calmann-Lévy, 1878), pp. 98–109.

8. *Oeuvres complètes de Charles Baudelaire*, ed. F. F. Gautier (Paris: Ed. N.R.F., 1918–31), 4:60.

9. "[elle] non seulement . . . constate, mais elle répare," *ibid.*

10. W. Morris, "How I Became a Socialist?" *Collected Works* (London: Longmans Green & Co., 1910–15), 23:281.

11. "Le Roman expérimental," *Oeuvres complètes*, ed. H. Mitterand (Paris: Cercle du livre précieux, 1962–   ), p. 148.

12. H. Feigl, "The Philosophy of Science," in *The Great Ideas Today 1969*, eds. R. M. Hutchins and M. J. Adler (Chicago: Encyclopaedia Britannica, 1969), p. 148.

13. J. G. Kemeny, *A Philosopher Looks At Science* (Princeton: Van Nostrand, 1959), p. 165.

14. See Marx and Engels, *Literature and Art* (New York: International Publishers, 1947), p. 139.

15. A. V. Lunacharsky, *Sobranie sochineniy* (Moskva: Khudlit, 1963–67), II, 63.

16. G. Lukács, *Werke* (Neuwied: Luchterhand, 1962–   ), 4:278. Subsequent references to this edition will appear in the text. These references to Lukács' works cannot claim to contain all occurrences of the issues in question; they should be regarded only as examples. By now, a laudably large number of Lukács' writings are available in English translation. It appeared necessary, however, to avoid the use of two sets of references (one to the German, another to the translated English sources), in order to keep the large reference material under control. Many of Lukács' statements referred to in this book, can be found in two English collections of his essays: *Studies in European Realism*, ed. A. Kazin (New York: Grosset & Dunlap, 1964); and *Writer and Critic, and Other Essays*, ed. and trans. A. D. Kahn (New York: Grosset & Dunlap, 1970). Several of the studies Lukács wrote on German literature, especially on Goethe and Thomas Mann, are available in two further volumes: *Essays on Thomas Mann*, trans. S. Mitchell (New York: Grosset & Dunlap, 1965); and *Goethe and His Age*, trans. R. Anchor (New York: Grosset & Dunlap, 1969). His two studies on Solzhenitsyn appeared in *Solzhenitsyn*, trans. W. D. Graf (Cambridge, Mass.: The MIT Press, 1971).

17. See esp. his "Über die Besonderheit als Kategorie der Ästhetik," *Werke*, 10:537–789; also 12:193–266. For further discussion of the category, see G. H. R. Parkinson, "Georg Lukács on the Central Category of Aesthetics," in *Georg Lukács*, ed. Parkinson (London: Weidenfeld and Nicolson, 1970), pp. 109–46.

18. In addition, Parkinson refers to some further analogies between the romantic critical tradition and Lukács' views; Parkinson, *ibid.*, pp. 138–39.

19. See Lukács, "On Socialist Realism," p. 87; and ch. 3 of his "Die Gegenwartsbedeutung des kritischen Realismus," *Werke*, 4:551–603.

20. M. Gorky, *On Literature* (Moskva: Foreign Languages Publishing House, n.d.), p. 360. Subsequent references to this edition will appear in the text.

21. L. Trotsky, *On Literature and Art* (New York: Pathfinder Press, 1970), p. 219.

22. M. Gorky, *O literature* (Moskva: Goskhudizdat, 1961), pp. 63–64.

23. *Ibid.*, p. 493.

24. *Ibid.*, p. 218.

25. A. Tolstoy, *Sobranie sochineniy* (Moskva: Goskhudizdat, 1958–61), 10:77.

26. N. S. Khrushchev, *The Great Mission of Literature and Art* (Moskva: Progress Publishers, 1964), p. 10.

27. According to B. Küppers, Gorky got this idea from the renowned Russian writer Korolenko (*Die Theorie vom Typischen in der Literatur*, München: Sagner, 1966; p. 10).

28. See also *O literature*, pp. 218–19.

29. "On the Dissemination of Realism," p. 239.

30. Basel: Verlag für Recht und Gesellschaft, 1953; see esp. pp. 160–65.

31. *CW*, 5:509.

32. *MEW*, 4:391–98.

33. *MEW*, 7:266.

34. *CW*, 35:144.

35. *CW*, 29:509; see also p. 518.

36. *Die Theorie vom Typischen in der Literatur*, pp. 10, 12–13.

37. *Ibid.*, p. 235.

38. See his two articles "O karamazovshchine" and "Yeshcho o karamazovshchine," *O literature*, pp. 66–75.

39. See *MEW*, 36:392–94; interpreted by Lukács, *Werke*, 10:224–25.

40. Marx and Engels, *Literature and Art*, pp. 42–43.

41. *MEW*, 36:314–15.

42. The sources of Lenin's five articles on Tolstoy are: *CW*, 15:202–209; 16:323–27, 330–32, 353–54; 17:49–53.

43. The sources of Lenin's statements on Turgenev are: *CW*, 13:56; 18:29; 20:72; 27:274.

44. *CW*, 23:334.

45. *CW*, 33:125–26.

46. Though the essay in which this statement appears is printed in Lunachars-ky's *Sobranie sochineniy*, 7:422–25, this particular utterance was omitted from that edition. For the source, see *Rabochiy put'*, 291 (Dec. 21, 1924).

47. "Parteidichtung" (1945), "Freie oder gelenkte Kunst?" (1947), in *Schriften zur Ideologie und Politik*, ed. P. Ludz (Neuwied: Luchterhand, 1967), pp. 376–403, 434–463. (Both originally published in Hungarian.)

48. *O literature*, p. 64.

49. *Os marxistas e a arte* (Rio de Janeiro: Civilização brasileira, 1967), p. 31.

III. Problems Of The Two Realisms: Variations And Developments

1. See, e.g., Werner Mittenzwei, "Die Brecht-Lukács Debatte," *Kritik in der Zeit*, ed. K. Jarmatz (Halle: Mitteldeutscher Verlag, 1970), pp. 786–812; V. Žmegač, *Kunst und Wirklichkeit: zur Literaturtheorie bei Brecht, Lukács und Broch* (Bad Homburg: Gehlen, 1969).

2. See Soyuz sovetskikh pisateley, *Pervy vsesoyuzny s'ezd* (Moskva, 1934); *Vtoroy vsesoyuzny s'ezd* (Moskva, 1956).

3. See *A szocialista realizmus* (Budapest: Gondolat, 1970), 1:253.

4. *Letteratura e vita nazionale* (Torino: Einaudi, 1966), pp. 11, 47, 52.

5. *Ibid.*, pp. 6, 11.

6. *Ibid.*, p. 58.

7. *Ibid.*, p. 13.

8. *Sobranie sochineniy* (Moskva: Khudlit, 1963–67), 7:424–25.

9. *Ibid.*, p. 163.

10. B. Brecht, *Gesammelte Werke* (Frankfurt: Suhrkamp, 1967), 7:250–52.

11. *Ibid.*, 8:314, 353.

12. *Ibid.*, p. 326.

13. *Ibid.*, 7:66.

14. *Ibid.*, pp. 126–29.

15. See, e.g., A. Seghers in Lukács, *Werke* (Neuwied: Luchterhand, 1962–), 4:347 –48; or Friedrich Wolf's exalted confession, "Kunst ist Waffe:eine Fest-stellung," in *Marxismus und Literatur*, ed. F. J. Raddatz (Reinbek b. Hamburg: Rowohlt, 1970), 2:250–62.

16. See Lukács, "Reportage oder Gestaltung?" and "Aus der Not eine Tugend," *Werke*, 4:35–68; and E. Ottwalt, " 'Tatsachenroman' und Formexperiment," in *Marxismus und Literatur*, 2:159–65.

17. See *A szocialista realizmus*, 1:253.

18. See V. Kirpotin, "Nakanune pervogo s'ezda," *Voprosy literatury*, 11, no. 5 (May 1967):38–39.

19. *Von der Notwendigkeit der Kunst* (Dresden: Verlag der Kunst, 1959), pp. 86–87.

20. See R. Fox, *The Novel and The People* (London: Lawrence & Wishart, 1937), pp. 24–25.

21. *Ibid.*, p. 66.

22. B. Brecht, *Gesammelte Werke*, 8:531.

23. See *Problems of Soviet Literature* (Moskva, Leningrad: Co-op. Publishing Soc. of Foreign Workers, 1935), p. 181.

24. A. József, *Összes művei* (Budapest: Akadémiai Kiadó, 1952–58), 3:215.

25. J. Révai, *Válogatott irodalmi tanulmányok* (Budapest: Kossuth Kiadó, 1968), p. 294.

26. C. Caudwell, *Illusion and Reality* (London: Macmillan, 1937), p. 58.

27. *Sobranie sochineniy*, 7:162.

28. *The Novel and The People*, pp. 90–97.

29. B. Brecht, *Gesammelte Werke*, 7:813–14.

30. R. Fox, *The Novel and the People*, pp. 107, 114.

31. K. Teige, "Neue proletarische Kunst," in *Marxismus und Literatur*, 3:90; P. M. Buck, "The Marxian Formula: M. Sholokhov," in *Directions in Contemporary Literature* (New York: Oxford University Press, 1942), pp. 243, 258.

32. N. Cocea, "Spre arta viitoare," *Scrieri* (Bucuresti: Minerva, 1970), 2:316.

33. "Zadachi literatury: literaturnye zametki," *Sobranie sochineniy* (Moskva: Goskhudizdat, 1958–61), 10:70–79.

34. *Ibid.*, pp. 540–41.

35. See his introduction to *Karl Marx und die Ästhetik* (Dresden: Verlag der Kunst, 1960).

36. Soyuz sovetskikh pisateley, *Vtoroy vsesoyuzny s'ezd*, pp. 86–91.

37. See his praise of Y. V. Vuchetich, one of Stalin's favorite sculptors, in *The Great Mission of Literature and Art* (Moskva: Progress Publishers, 1964), p. 147.

38. "O russkoy literature kanuna i nachala sotsialisticheskogo realizma," in Akademiya nauk SSSR, Institut mirovoy literatury, *Sotsialisticheskiy realizm i khudozhestvennoe razvitie chelovechestva* (Moskva: Nauka, 1966), pp. 22–81.

39. See e.g. his *Gesammelte Werke*, 7:126–29, 147; 8:298–99, 303, 309, 311, 317, 326, 339–40, 349.

40. *Ibid.*, 8:311–12.

41. H. K. Laxness, *Dagur í senn* (Reykjavik: Helgafell, 1955), pp. 219–42.

42. K. Konrad, "O socialistickém realizmu," in K. Chvatik, *Bedřich Václavek a vývoj marxistické estetiký* (Praha: Nakl. Čs. akademia ved, 1962), pp. 335–36.

43. *Letteratura e vita nazionale*, pp. 13–14.

44. *An Introduction to the English Novel* (London: Hutchinson, 1951), 1:26–30.

45. *Gesammelte Schriften und Aufsätze*, ed. E. Fuchs (Berlin: Soziologische Verlagsanstalt, 1929–), 1:327.

46. *Gesammelte Werke*, 8:299.

47. See his postscript to J. R. Becher's *Abschied* (Berlin: Aufbau, 1952); quoted by I. Eörsi, "György Lukács and the Theory of Lyric Poetry," *The New Hungarian Quarterly*, 6, no. 18 (Summer 1965):35.

48. *Georg Lukács och marxismens estetik* (Stockholm: Bonnier, 1967), pp. 58–63.

49. Eörsi, "Lukács and Lyric Poetry," pp. 33–46.

50. A. Kettle, *An Introduction to the English Novel*, 1:33–35.

51. Discussed and partially quoted by Olof Enckell in *Den unge Diktonius* (Stockholm: Wahlström & Widstrand, 1946), pp. 60–80.

52. The following discussion of Brecht's and Caudwell's views on poetry is based on their statements in Brecht, *Gesammelte Werke*, 8:385–91, 403; Caudwell, *Illusion and Reality*, pp. 3, 25–28, 131, 135–48.

53. Y. Borev, *O tragicheskom* (Moskva: Sovetskiy pisatel', 1961), p. 223.

54. "A magyar proletárirodalom platformtervezete," in A. József, *Összes müvei*, 3:431–36.

55. A. Abusch, *Humanismus und Realismus in der Literatur* (Leipzig: Reclam, 1966), pp. 146ff.

56. See the critical account of Lukács' view of Hungarian literature by Zoltán Kenyeres, "Lukács György és a magyar kultúra," *Kritika*, no. 12 (1970):1–10 and no. 3 (1971):4–15.

57. L. Aragon, "Réalisme socialiste et réalisme française," *Europe*, 46, no. 183 (March 1938):290–92.

58. *Gesammelte Werke*, 8:444–45.

59. L. Aragon, *J'abats mon jeu* (Paris: Éd. Français Réunis, 1959), pp. 138–39.

60. Cf. *La Nouvelle critique*, 168 (July–Aug. 1965):46–55.

IV. Objectivism: Materialistic Realism Or Left-Deviation?

1. Cf. *MEW*, 2:78–82; 37:413.

2. *MEW*, 21:8.

3. C. Zetkin, *Erinnerungen an Lenin* (Berlin: Dietz, 1957), pp. 65–68; see also Henri Lefebvre, *La Pensée de Lénine* (Paris: Bordas, 1957), pp. 339–40.

4. *CW*, 35:144–45.

5. *CW*, 27:497–98.

6. F. Mehring, *Gesammelte Schriften und Aufsätze*, ed. E. Fuchs (Berlin: Soziologische Verlagsanstalt, 1929–   ), 2:58. Subsequent references to this edition will appear in the text.

7. See also Mehring, *Die Lessing-Legende* (Stuttgart: Dietz, 1893), p. 420.

8. See also Mehring, "Kunst und Proletariat," in *Marxismus und Literatur*, ed. F. J. Raddatz (Reinbek b. Hamburg: Rowohlt, 1969), 1:203.

9. G. Lukács, "Franz Mehring," *Werke* (Neuwied: Luchterhand, 1962–   ), 10:341–432; see esp. pp. 351, 370, 379–80, 390–95.

10. *Die Lessing-Legende*, p. 200.

11. *Werke*, 10:351, 379, 491, 776.

12. *Ibid.*, p. 139.

13. Plekhanov, *Art and Social Life* (London: Lawrence & Wishart, 1953), pp. 188–92. Subsequent references to this edition will appear in the text.

14. Plekhanov, *Sochineniya* (Moskva: Gosizdat, 1923–27), 14:183.

15. *Ibid.*; see also 5:355–57; 10:259–61, 285–86, 294–95, 303–304.

16. *Ibid.*, 14:193–237. Trans.: F. Engels et al., *Ibsen*, ed. A. Flores (New York: Critics Group, 1937), pp. 35–92.

17. "Les Origins du romantisme," *Le Devenir social*, 7 (1898):606.

18. A. F. Bebel, *Die Frau und der Sozialismus* (Stuttgart: Dietz, 1913), pp. 458–60.

19. B. Küppers, *Die Theorie vom Typischen in der Literatur* (München: Sagner, 1966), p. 212.

20. Recent recognitions of this fact are not exactly numerous, but at least fairly explicit; see, e.g., Pál Miklós, "A marxista irodalomelmélet történetéhez," *A Magyar Tudományos Akadémia Nyelv- és Irodalomtörténeti Osztályának Közleményei*, 25, nos. 1–4 (1960):92.

21. J. Fučik, *Literarische Kritiken, Polemiken und Studien* (Berlin: Dietz, 1958), p. 289.

22. See his *Werke*, 4:463. Subsequent references to this edition will appear in the text.

23. Lukács used this term only in his *Ästhetik,* but he had already delineated the idea itself in his earliest writings.

24. The three major essays in which Lukács explained his objections to Kantianism are: "Zur Ästhetik Schillers," *Werke,* 10:17–106; "Hegels Ästhetik," *ibid.,* 107–46, "Karl Marx und Friedrich Theodor Vischer," *ibid.,* 233–306.

25. See Konder on Mehring, Plekhanov, and Bukharin in *Os marxistas e a arte* (Rio de Janeiro: Civilização brasileira, 1967); Coutinho on Trotsky and Della Volpe, *Literatura e humanismo* (Rio de Janeiro: Paz e terra, 1967), pp. 102–103.

26. A. V. Lunacharsky, *Sobranie sochineniy* (Moskva: Khudlit, 1963–67), 7:159–61.

27. A. A. Fadeyev, *Sobranie sochineniy* (Moskva: Goskhudizdat, 1959–61), 4:25–27.

28. L. Biró, "Leszámolás Ibsennel," *Nyugat,* 1908, pp. 778–86.

29. Lunacharsky, *On Literature and Art* (Moskva: Progress Publishers, 1965), pp. 159–60.

30. See *Literature and Marxism,* ed. A. Flores (New York: Critics Group, 1938), pp. 7–15, 23–31, 43–51, 74–95.

31. A. Abusch, *Humanismus und Realismus in der Literatur* (Leipzig: Reclam, 1966), p. 89.

32. Akademiya nauk SSSR, Institut mirovoy literatury, *Sotsialisticheskiy realizm i khudozhestvennoe razvitie chelovechestva* (Moskva: Nauka, 1966), p. 11.

33. L. Goldmann, *Pour une sociologie du roman* (Paris: Gallimard, 1964), p. 36.

34. *Ibid.,* pp. 122, 126.

35. Our source is the 1966 ed. of *Critica del gusto* by Milano: Feltrinelli; pp. 1–2, 55.

36. *Ibid.,* p. 4.

37. *Os marxistas e a arte,* p. 205.

38. *Critica del gusto,* p. 11.

39. *Ibid.,* pp. 1–8, 55.

40. Konder, *Os marxistas e a arte,* pp. 199–206; R. Musolino, *Marxismo ed estetica in Italia* (Roma: Riuniti, 1963), pp. 49–78.

41. *Literature e humanismo,* pp. 102–103.

V. Subjectivism: Dialectical Realism Or Right-Deviation?

1. Lenin, *CW*, 33:223.

2. B. Brecht, *Gesammelte Werke* (Frankfurt: Suhrkamp, 1967), 8:308.

3. See his preface to Garaudy's *D'un réalisme sans rivages* (Paris: Plon, 1963), p. 14, 16.

4. Cf. Garaudy, *D'un réalisme sans rivages*, pp. 41–42; Fischer, *Von der Notwendigkeit der Kunst* (Dresden: Verlag der Kunst, 1959), p. 70. Subsequent references to the works discussed will appear in the text, with the following codes:

> Garaudy, *D'un réalisme sans rivages:* page reference only.
> Fischer, *Von der Notwendigkeit der Kunst: NK,* followed by page reference.
> Fischer, *Kunst und Koexistenz* (Reinbek b. Hamburg: Rowohlt, 1966): *KK,* followed by page reference.

5. See his contribution to the symposium "Semaine de la pensée marxiste," *Europe,* 42:419–20 (March–April, 1964), 336–37.

6. *Ibid.,* 341; Fischer, *KK,* pp. 136–38.

7. This statement is fairly close to the view of Yevgeny Zamyatin who, in his essay "O literature, revolyutsii i entropii" (On Literature, Revolution, and Entropy, 1924), compared the necessity of the infinite development of art and literature to the infiniteness of the numerical scale. Zamyatin's argument is one of the epistemologically most logical and relevant objections against any officially preferred and condoned artistic movement, particularly socialist realism, which was put on the pedestal exactly ten years later.

8. This conventional communist definition of Nazism (the term for which is "fascism") comes from Georgi Dimitrov, who gave a major speech on this topic at the Seventh Congress of the Third International in August 1935.

9. MEW, 13:641. Trans.: Marx and Engels, *Literature and Art* (New York: International Publishers, 1947), pp. 18–19.

10. "Semaine de la pensée marxiste," 335–36.

11. See *Franz Kafka aus Prager Sicht* (Prag: Academia, 1966), p. 158.

12. See his *Werke* (Neuwied: Luchterhand, 1962–), 4: esp. pp. 483, 506, 522–23.

13. *Gesammelte Werke,* 8:360.

14. In *Proletarskaya kultura,* 15–16, 1920.

15. S. Tretyakov, "S novym godom! S 'Novym Lefom'!" *Novy Lef,* Jan. 1928, p. 1.

16. *Gesammelte Werke,* 8:361n.

17. Quoted by Olof Enckell, *Den unge Diktonius* (Stockholm: Wahlström & Widstrand, 1946), pp. 96–99.

18. A. V. Lunacharsky, *Sobranie sochineniy* (Moskva: Khudlit, 1963–67), 2:471.

19. Cf. *Marxismus und Literatur*, ed. F. J. Raddatz (Reinbek b. Hamburg: Rowohlt, 1969), 2:54–55, 58–59, 105.

20. *Ibid.*, p. 56.

21. *2000 pagine di Gramsci* (Roma: Il Saggiatore, 1964–   ), 1:552–53.

22. J. Révai, "Kölcsey Ferenc," in his *Válogatott irodalmi tanulmányok* (Budapest: Kossuth, 1968), p. 18.

23. See K. Chvatik, *Bedřich Václavek a vývoj marxistické estetiký* (Praha: Nakl. Čs. akademia ved, 1962), pp. 281–82.

24. A. Ljungdal, *Georg Lukács och marxismens estetik* (Stockholm: Bonnier, 1967), pp. 66–68.

25. *Letteratura e vita nazionale* (Torino: Einaudi, 1966), p. 23.

26. *Essays on the Materialistic Conception of History* (Chicago: Kerr & Co., 1903), p. 221.

27. B. Brecht, *Gesammelte Werke*, 8:286, 290–91, 296, 321.

28. *Ibid.*, 7:932–33.

29. A. József, *Összes művei* (Budapest: Akadémiai Kiadó, 1952–58), 3:212–13.

30. *Georg Lukács och marxismens estetik*, p. 70.

31. Cf. A. Komlós, *Gyulaitól a marxista kritikáig* (Budapest: Akadémiai Kiadó, 1960), pp. 263–77.

32. *Gesammelte Werke*, 8:339.

33. "Über James Joyce und einige ästhetische Probleme," *Internationale Literatur*, 4, no. 5 (1934):39–42.

34. *Gesammelte Werke*, 8:338.

35. Cf. Lukács, *Werke*, 4:350.

36. *Pour un réalisme socialiste* (Paris: Denoël et Steele, 1935), pp. 69–87.

37. *Bedřich Václavek a vývoj marxistické estetiký*, pp. 380–81.

38. See references in his *Art and Society* (New York: International Publishers, 1947).

39. "Digtningens problematik i vor tid," *Dagur í senn* (Reykjavik: Helgafell, 1955), pp. 219–42.

40. "A szocialista realizmus elméletének történeti és elvi problémái," *A Magyar Tudományos Akadémia Nyelv- és Irodalomtörténeti Osztályának Közleményei*, 25, nos. 1–4 (1968):50–59.

41. *Gesammelte Werke*, 8:357.

42. F. Mehring, "Kunst und Proletariat," in *Marxismus und Literatur*, 1:200–203.

43. R. Fox, *The Novel and The People* (London: Lawrence & Wishart, 1937), p. 20, 86; C. Caudwell, *Illusion and Reality* (London: Lawrence & Wishart, 1935), pp. 119, 183–85.

44. J. Révai, *Válogatott irodalmi tanulmányok*, p. 89.

45. Plekhanov, *Art and Social Life* (London: Lawrence & Wishart, 1953), pp. 169–77.

46. *Sobranie sochineniy*, 7:158–59.

47. See *Marxismus und Literatur*, 2:47.

48. See, e.g., Plekhanov, *Art and Social Life*, p. 216 (calls cubism "rubbish cubed"); Radek, *Problems of Soviet Literature*, pp. 152–55 (Joyce is a writer of the "phantasmagories of the madhouse"); Fox, *The Novel and The People*, p. 38; Abusch, *Humanismus und Realismus in der Literatur*, p. 160 (accuses Faulkner of morbidity, obscurity, and masochism); H. Koch, *Marxismus und Ästhetik*, pp. 485ff (modernism characterized by "infantilism, cretinism, nonsense, the destruction of human personality"); also, Khrushchev's various statements on "mad" modernism, in *The Great Mission of Literature and Art*.

49. Mehring, *Gesammelte Schriften und Aufsätze* (Berlin: Soziologische Verlagsanstalt, 1929-), 2:158ff; Gramsci, *Letteratura e vita nazionale*, pp. 299-300.

50. *The Novel and The People*, p. 38.

51. "Ob istoricheskom izuchenii sotsialisticheskogo realizma," *Russkaya literatura*, 2 (1965):215-30.

52. "Poznanie i otsenka i iskusstva," *Problema tsennosti v filosofii* (Moskva: Nauka, 1966), pp. 98–112.

53. Particularly significant are three volumes discussing the genesis of socialist realism in the Western European countries (*Genezis sotsialisticheskogo realizma v literaturakh stran zapada*); in the Central European ones (*Puti realizma v literaturakh stran narodney demokratsii*); and at a theoretical level, related to different national traditions (*Natsional'nye traditsii i genezis sotsialisticheskogo realizma*). All three volumes published by Nauka (Moskva), 1965.

54. Five particular sources summarizing the Kafka debate are *Khrushchev and The Arts*, ed. P. Johnson (Cambridge, Mass.: The MIT Press, 1965), pp. 83–84; D. V. Zatonsky, *Franz Kafka i problemy modernizma* (Moskva: Izd. Vysshaya shkola, 1965), pp. 3ff.; E. Fischer, *Kunst und Koexistenz*, pp. 71–74; *Franz Kafka aus Prager Sicht* (proceedings of the Kafka conference in Liblice, 1963); H. Järv, "Orgier i kafkaism," *Horisont*, 18, no. 2 (1971):30–49. The data incorporated in the text were borrowed from these sources.

55. Coutinho, *Literatura e humanismo* (Rio de Janeiro: Paz e terra, 1967), pp. 127–29, 133–34; Konder, *Os marxistas e a arte* (Rio de Janeiro: Civilização brasileira, 1967), pp. 173–81.

Conclusion

1. O. Ludwig, *Gesammelte Schriften*, ed. A. Stern (Leipzig: Grunow, 1891), 5:61.

2. *Ibid.*, pp. 61, 474.

3. *Ibid.*, p. 459.

4. *Ibid.*, pp. 458, 523; F. Spielhagen, *Beiträge zur Theme und Technik des Romans* (Leipzig: Staackmann, 1883), p. 67.

5. E. Auerbach, *Mimesis* (Bern: Francke Verlag, 1946); R. Brinkmann, *Wirklichkeit und Illusion* (Tübingen: Max Niemeyer Verlag, 1957).

Bibliography

This bibliography is fairly selective, but thoroughly international. Works containing bibliographies which serve the particular needs of the English reading public, are marked by an asterisk.

Abusch, Alexander. *Humanismus und Realismus in der Literatur*. Leipzig: Reclam, 1966.
—— *Literatur und Wirklichkeit: Beiträge zu einer neuen deutschen Literaturgeschichte*. Berlin: Aufbau, 1952.
The Age of Realism, ed. F. W. J. Hemmings. Harmondsworth, England: Penguin Books, 1974.
Akademiya nauk SSSR. Institut filosofii. *Osnovy marksistskoy filosofii*. Moskva: Gospolitizdat, 1958.
—— *Sotsialisticheskiy realizm i problemy estetiki*. Moskva: Iskusstvo, 1967.
Akademiya nauk SSSR. Institut mirovoy literatury. *Fridrikh Engels i voprosy literatury*. Moskva: Nauka, 1973.
—— *Genezis sotsialisticheskogo realizma v literaturakh stran zapada*. Moskva: Nauka, 1965.
—— *Natsional'nye traditsii i genezis sotsialisticheskogo realizma*. Moskva: Nauka, 1965.
—— *Problemy realizma*. Moskva: Goskhudizdat, 1959.
—— *Puti realizma v literaturakh stran narodnoy demokratsii*. Moskva: Nauka, 1965.
—— *Sotsialisticheskiy realizm i khudozhestvennoe razvitie chelovechestva*. Moskva: Nauka, 1966.
—— *Sovremennye problemy realizma i modernizma*. Moskva: Nauka, 1965.
Akademiya nauk SSSR. Institut russkoy literatury. *Istoriya russkoy kritiki*. 2 vols. Moskva, Leningrad: Izdatel'stvo Akademii nauk SSSR, 1958.
Alexis, Jacques-Stephen. "Où va le roman?" *Présence Africaine*, 13, 1957.

Althaus, Horst. *Georg Lukács oder Bürgerlichkeit als Vorschule einer marxistischen Ästhetik.* München: Francke, 1962.

Althusser, Louis. *Lire le Capital.* 2 vols. Paris: Maspero, 1966.

Aragon, Louis. *J'abats mon jeu.* Paris: E.F.R., 1959.

—— *Littératures soviétiques.* Paris: Denoël, 1955.

—— *Pour un réalisme socialiste.* Paris: Denoël et Steele, 1935.

—— "Réalisme socialiste et réalisme français." *Europe,* 46, no. 183 (March 1938):289–303.

Băleanu, Andrei. *Continut și forma in arta.* Bucuresti: Ed. Ştiienţifica, 1959.

*Baxandall, Lee, comp. *Marxism and Aesthetics: A Selective Annotated Bibliography. Books and Articles in the English Language.* New York: Humanities Press, 1968.

Becher, Johannes R. *Über Literatur und Kunst.* Berlin: Aufbau, 1962.

Begriffsbestimmung des literarischen Realismus, ed. Richard Brinkmann. Darmstadt: Wissenschaftliche Buchgesellschaft, 1969.

Belinsky, Vissarion Grigoryevich. *Polnoye sobranie sochineniy.* 13 vols. Moskva: Izdatel'stvo Akademii nauk SSSR, 1953–59.

—— *Selected Philosophical Essays.* Moskva: Foreign Languages Publishing House, 1948.

Bernard, Jean-Pierre. *Communisme et littérature: Le Parti Communiste Français et les problèmes littéraires 1921–1939.* Ph.D. thesis (Paris, Sorbonne), n.d.

Biró, Lajos. "Leszámolás Ibsennel." *Nyugat,* 1908, 778–86.

Bisztray, George. "Literary Sociology and Marxist Theory: The Literary Work as a Social Document." *Mosaic,* 5, no. 2 (1972): 47–56.

—— " 'With the People, Through A Thousand Dangers': East-Central European Literary Populism." *Mosaic,* 6, no. 4 (1973): 39–49.

Borev, Yury. *O tragicheskom.* Moskva: Sovetskiy pisatel', 1961.

Brecht, Bertolt. *Gesammelte Werke.* 8 vols. Frankfurt: Suhrkamp, 1967.

Brouwers, Bert. *Literatur en revolutie.* 2 vols. Meppel: Boom, 1971.

Bukova, F. M. *Sotsialisticheskiy realizm: rekommendatel'ny ukazatel'.* Leningrad, 1963.

*Caudwell, Christopher. *Illusion and Reality.* London. Lawrence & Wishart, 1935.

Chernishevsky, Nikolay Gavrilovich. *Polnoye sobranie sochineniy.* 16 vols. Moskva: Goskhudizdat, 1939–53.

—— *Selected Philosophical Essays.* Moskva: Foreign Languages Publishing House, 1953.

Chvatik, Kvetoslav. *Bedřich Václavek a vývoj marxistické estetiký.* Praha: Nakl. Čs. akademia ved, 1962.

Coutinho, Carlos Nelson. *Literatura e humanismo: ensaios de critica marxista.* Rio de Janeiro : Paz e terra, 1967.

Della Volpe, Galvano. *Critica del gusto.* Milano: Feltrinelli, 1960.

Demetz, Peter. *Marx, Engels und die Dichter: zur Grundlagenforschung des Marxismus.* Stuttgart: Deutsche Verlags-Anstalt, 1959.

*—— *Marx, Engels, and the Poets: Origins of Marxist Literary Criticism.* Rev. and enl. ed.; trans. Jeffrey L. Sammons. Chicago: The University of Chicago Press, 1967.

Dneprov, Vladimir Davidovich. *Cherty romana XX veka.* Moskva, Leningrad: Sovetskiy pisatel', 1965.

—— *Problemy realizma.* Leningrad: Sovetskiy pisatel', 1961.

Dobrolyubov, Nikolay Aleksandrovich. *Selected Philosophical Essays.* Moskva: Foreign Languages Publishing House, 1948.

—— *Sobranie sochineniy.* 9 vols. Moskva, Leningrad: Goskhudizdat, 1961–64.

Documents of Modern Literary Realism, ed. George J. Becker. Princeton: Princeton University Press, 1963.

Egbert, Donald Drew. *Social Radicalism and the Arts: Western Europe.* New York: Knopf, 1970.

Engels, Friedrich, et al. *Ibsen,* ed. Angel Flores. New York: Critics Group, 1937.

Eörsi, István. "György Lukács and the Theory of Lyric Poetry." *The New Hungarian Quarterly,* 6, no. 18 (1965): 33–46.

Ermolaev, Herman. *Soviet Literary Theories 1917–1934: The Genesis of Socialist Realism.* Berkeley: University of California Press, 1963.

Existentialism Versus Marxism: Conflicting Views on Humanism, ed. George Novack. New York: Dell, 1966.

Fadeyev, Alexandr Alexandrovich. *Sobranie sochineniy.* 5 vols. Moskva: Goskhudizdat, 1959–61.

Festschrift zum achtzigsten Geburtstag von Georg Lukács, ed. Frank Benseler. Neuwied: Luchterhand, 1965.

Finkelstein, Sidney. *Art and Society.* New York: International Publishers, 1965.

—— *Existentialism and Alienation in American Literature.* New York: International Publishers, 1965.

Fischer, Ernst. *Kunst und Koexistenz: Beitrag zu einer modernen marxistischen Ästhetik.* Hamburg: Rowohlt, (*Art Against Ideology,* trans. Anna Bostock. London: Allen Lane, Penguin, 1969).

—— *Von der Notwendigkeit der Kunst.* Dresden: Verlag der Kunst, 1959. (*The Necessity of Art: A Marxist Approach,* trans. Anna Bostock. Harmondsworth, England: Penguin Books, 1963).

Fox, Ralph. *The Novel and The People.* London: Lawrence & Wishart, 1937.

Frank, Waldo. "Values of the Revolutionary Writer." *The American Mind,* ed. Harry R. Warfel et al. 2 vols. New York: American Book Company, 1937, pp. 1327–30.

Franz Kafka aus Prager Sicht. Prag: Academia, 1966.

Friche, Vladimir Maximovich. *Problemy iskusstvovedeniya: sbornik statey po voprosam sotsiologii iskusstva i literatury.* Moskva, Leningrad: Gosizdat, 1930.

Fučik, Julius. *Literarische Kritiken, Polemiken und Studien.* Berlin: Dietz, 1958.

Fundamentos da estética marxista, ed. Nelson Werneck Sodré. Rio de Janeiro: Civilização brasileira, 1968.

Gallas, Helga. *Marxistische Literaturtheorie: Kontroversen im Bund proletarisch-revolutionärer Schriftsteller.* Neuwied: Luchterhand, 1971.

Garaudy, Roger. *Du surréalisme au monde réel: l'itinéraire d'Aragon.* Paris: Gallimard, 1961.

—— *D'un réalisme sans rivages.* Paris: Plon, 1963.

—— *Karl Marx.* Paris: Seghers, 1964.

—— *Marxisme du XXᵉ siècle.* Paris, Genève: Éd. la Palatine, 1966. (*Marxism in the Twentieth Century,* trans. René Hague. New York: Scribner, 1971.)

——. *Une littérature de fossoyeurs.* Paris: Éd. sociales, 1947.

*Georg Lukács: the Man, his Work and his Ideas, ed. G. H. R. Parkinson. London: Weidenfeld & Nicolson, 1970.

Georg Lukács und der Revisionismus. Berlin: Aufbau, 1960.

Gespräche mit Georg Lukács, ed. Theo Pinkus. Hamburg: Rowohlt, 1967.

Gibbons, Robert Ebbert. "Christopher Caudwell, Marxist Apologist and Critic." Diss. Bowling Green, 1967.

Glaser, Horst Albert et al. *Literaturwissenschaft und Sozialwissenschaften: Grundlagen und Modellanalysen.* Stuttgart: Metzler, 1971.

Goldmann, Lucien. *Pour une sociologie du roman.* Paris: Gallimard, 1964.

Gorky, Maxim. *O literature.* Moskva: Goskhudizdat, 1961.

—— *On Literature,* trans. Julius Katzer and Ivy Litvinov. Moskva: Foreign Languages Publishing House, 1960.

—— *Sobranie sochineniy.* 30 vols. Moskva: Goskhudizdat, 1949–55.

Gramsci, Antonio. *2000 pagine di Gramsci.* Vol. 1. Roma: Il Saggiatore, 1964–

—— *Gli intellettuali e l'organizzazione della cultura.* Torino: Einaudi, 1966.

—— *Il materialismo storico e la filosofia di Benedetto Croce.* Torino: Einaudi, 1948.

—— *Letteratura e vita nazionale.* Torino: Einaudi, 1966.

Gros, J-M. *Le Mouvement littéraire socialiste depuis 1830.* Paris: Michel, n.d.

Gunnarson, Gunnar. *Georg Lukács: en essay.* Staffanstorp: Cavefors, 1969.

Hansen, Arvid G. *Arbeideren i norsk diktning fra Wergeland til i dag.* Oslo: Tiden, 1960.

Hansen, Bente. *Den marxistiske litteraturkritik.* København: Reitzel, 1967.

Harper, Kenneth Eugen. "Controversy in Soviet Literary Criticism on the Doctrine of Socialist Realism." Diss. Columbia, 1950.

Hegel, George Wilhelm Friedrich. *Sämtliche Werke: Jubiläumsausgabe,* ed. Hermann Glockner. 26 vols. Stuttgart: Frommann, 1927–39.

Henrikson, Thomas. "Revolution och estetik: Otto Ville Kuusinen och Diktonius." *Ord och Bild,* 78, no. 3 (1968): 186–95.

Herzfelde, Wieland. "Über James Joyce und einige ästhetische Probleme." *Internationale Literatur,* 4, no. 5 (1934), 39–42.

Ivanov, Vasiliy Ivanovich. *O sushchnosti sotsialisticheskogo realizma.* Moskva: Khudlit, 1963.

Jameson, Fredric. *Marxism and Form: Twentieth Century Dialectical Theories of Literature.* Princeton: Princeton University Press, 1971.

Järv, Harry. "Orgier i kafkaism." *Horisont,* 23, no. 2 (1971): 30–49.

—— "Utblick: Marx försvarade konsten mot marxisterna." *Horisont,* 18, no. 5 (1971): 1–15.

John, Erhard. *Probleme der marxistisch-leninistischen Ästhetik: Ästhetik der Kunst.* Halle: Niemeyer, 1967.

József, Attila. *Összes művei.* 3 vols. Budapest: Akadémiai Kiadó, 1952–58.

Kagan, Moysey Samoilovich. *Lektsii po marksistsko-leninskoy estetike.* 3 vols. Leningrad: Gos. universitet imeni A. A. Zhdanova, 1963–66.

—— "Poznanie i otsenka v iskusstve." *Problema tsennosti v filosofii.* Moskva, Leningrad: Nauka, 1966, pp. 98–112.

Kantorovich, V. "Sotsiologiya i literatura." *Novy Mir,* 12 (1967): 148–73.

Kemp, Harry, et al. *The Left Heresy in Literature and Life.* London: Methuen, 1939.

Kenyeres, Zoltán. "Beginn der Laufbahn G. Lukács' und sein Weg zum Marxismus." *Acta Litteraria*, 7, nos. 3–4 (1965): 361–75.

—— "Lukács György és a magyar kultúra." *Kritika*, 8, no. 12 (1970): 1–10, and 9, no. 3 (1971): 4–15.

Kettle, Arnold. *An Introduction to the English Novel*. 2 vols. London: Hutchinson, 1951.

Khrushchev, Nikita Sergeyevich. *The Great Mission of Literature and Art*. Moskva: Progress Publishers, 1964.

Khrushchev and The Arts: The Politics of Soviet Culture, 1962–1964, comp., ed., and introd. Priscilla Johnson. Cambridge, Mass.: The MIT Press, 1965.

Királyfalvi, Béla. *The Aesthetics of György Lukács*. Princeton, N.J.: Princeton University Press, 1975.

Kirpotin, V. "Nakanune pervogo s'ezda." *Voprosy literatury*, 11, no. 5 (1967): 25–44.

Knipovich, Evgeniya Fyodorovna. "Franz Kafka." *Inostrannaya literatura*, 1 (1964): 195–204.

Koch, Hans. *Franz Mehrings Beitrag zur marxistischen Literaturtheorie*. Berlin: Dietz, 1959.

—— *Marxismus und Ästhetik: zur ästhetischen Theorie von Karl Marx, Friedrich Engels und Wladimir Iljitsch Lenin*. Berlin: Dietz, 1962.

Komlós, Aladár. *Gyulaitól a marxista kritikáig*. Budapest: Akadémiai Kiadó, 1966.

Konder, Leandro. *Os marxistas e a arte*. Rio de Janeiro: Civilização brasileira, 1967.

Kosing, Alfred. *Ernst Fischer—ein moderner Marxist?* Berlin: Deutscher Verlag der Wissenschaften, 1969.

Kratkaya literaturnaya entsiklopediya, ed. A. A. Surkov. Moskva, 1962–

Kritik in der Zeit: der Sozialismus, seine Literatur, ihre Entwicklung, ed. Klaus Jarmatz. Halle (Saale): Mitteldeutscher Verlag, 1970.

Küppers, Bernhard. *Die Theorie vom Typischen in der Literatur: ihre Ausprägung in der russischen Literaturkritik und in der sowjetischen Literaturwissenschaft*. München: Sagner, 1966.

The Labourer: A Monthly Magazine of Politics, Literature, Poetry, etc., eds. Ernest Jones and F. O'Connor. London: Northern Star Office, 1847.

Labriola, Antonio. *Essays on the Materialist Conception of History*, trans. Charles H. Kerr. Chicago: Kerr & Co., 1903.

—— *Socialism and Philosophy*. Chicago: Kerr & Co., 1918.

Lachs, John, comp. *Marxist Philosophy: A Bibliographical Guide.* Chapel Hill, N.C.: University of North Carolina Press, 1967.

Lafargue, Paul. " 'Das Geld' von Zola." *Die neue Zeit,* 10, nos. 1, 2, 3 (1891–92): 4–10, 41–46, 76–86.

—— "Les Origines du romantisme: Étude critique sur la période révolutionnaire." *Le Devenir social,* 2, no. 7 (1898): 577–607.

Lassalle, Ferdinand. *Nachgelassene Briefe und Schriften,* ed. Gustav Mayer. 4 vols. Stuttgart, Berlin: Deutsche Verlags-Anstalt, 1921–24.

Laxness, Halldór Kiljan. "Digtningens problematik i vor tid." *Dagur i senn: ræða og rit.* Reykjavik: Helgafell, 1955, pp. 219–42.

Lefebvre, Henri. *Contribution à l'esthétique.* Paris: Éd. sociales, 1953.

Lenin, Vladimir Ilyich. *Collected Works.* Moskva, 1960–

Lenin und Gorki: eine Freundschaft in Dokumenten, ed. Eva Kosing and Edel Mirowa-Florin. Berlin: Aufbau, 1964.

Levin, Harry. "On the Dissemination of Realism." *Proceedings of the Fifth Congress of the International Comparative Literature Association,* ed. Nikola Banasević. Belgrad, Amsterdam: University of Belgrad, Swets & Zeitlinger, n.d., pp. 231–42.

Lifshits, Mikhail. *Karl Marx und die Ästhetik.* Dresden: Verlag der Kunst, 1960.

—— *Krizis bezobraziya: ot kubizma k pop-art.* Moskva: Iskusstvo, 1968.

—— *The Philosophy of Art of Karl Marx,* ed. A. Flores. New York: Critics Group, 1938.

Literatur im Klassenkampf: zur proletarisch-revolutionären Literaturtheorie 1919–1923, eds. Walter Fähnders and Martin Rector. München: Hanser Verlag, 1971.

Literature and Marxism: a Controversy by Soviet Critics, ed. Angel Flores. New York: Critics Group, 1938.

Literaturnaya entsiklopediya, eds. V. M. Friche and A. V. Lunacharsky. Vols. 1–9 and 11. Moskva, 1929–39.

Ljungdal, Arnold. *Georg Lukács och marxismens estetik.* Stockholm: Bonnier, 1967.

Lukács, Georg (György). *Essays on Thomas Mann,* trans. Stanley Mitchell. New York: Grosset & Dunlap, 1965.

—— *Goethe and His Age,* trans. Robert Anchor. New York: Grosset & Dunlap, 1969.

—— *The Historical Novel,* trans. Hannah and Stanley Mitchell. London: Merlin Press, 1962.

—— "On Socialist Realism," *International Literature,* 4, (1939): 87–96.

—— *Schriften zur Ideologie und Politik,* comp. Peter Ludz. Neuwied: Luchterhand, 1967.

—— *Schriften zur Literatursoziologie,* comp. Peter Ludz. Neuwied: Luchterhand, 1961.

—— *Solzhenitsyn,* trans. William David Graf. Cambridge, Mass.: The MIT Press, 1971.

—— *Studies in European Realism,* ed. Alfred Kazin. New York: Grosset & Dunlap, 1964.

—— *The Theory of the Novel,* trans. Anna Bostock. Cambridge, Mass.: The MIT Press, 1971.

—— *Werke.* Neuwied: Luchterhand, 1962–

—— *Writer and Critic, and Other Essays,* ed. and trans. Arthur D. Kahn. New York: Grosset & Dunlap, 1970.

Lunacharsky, Anatoly Vasilyevich. *On Literature and Art.* Moskva: Progress Publishers, 1965.

—— *Sobranie sochineniy,* ed. Akademiya nauk SSSR, Institut mirovoy literatury. 8 vols. Moskva: Khudlit, 1963–67.

—— *V mire muziki.* Moskva: Sovetskiy kompozitor, 1958.

Luperini, Romano. *Marxismo e letteratura.* Bari: De Donato, 1971.

Maguire, Robert A. *Red Virgin Soil: Soviet Literature in the 1920's.* Princeton, N.J.: Princeton University Press, 1968.

Mao Tse-Tung. *Problems of Art and Literature.* New York: International Publishers, 1950.

Margolies, David N. *The Function of Literature: A Study in Christopher Caudwell's Aesthetics.* New York: International Publishers, 1969.

Marx, Karl, and Friedrich Engels. *Literature and Art: Selections from their Writings.* New York: International Publishers, 1947.

—— *Über Kunst und Literatur.* Berlin: Henschel Verlag, 1953.

—— *Werke.* Berlin: Dietz, 1957–

Marxism and Alienation: A Symposium, ed. Herbert Aptheker. New York: Humanities Press, 1965.

Marxism and Art: Essays Classic and Contemporary, comp. Maynard Solomon. New York: Knopf, 1973.

Marxism and Art: Writings in Aesthetics and Criticism, comp. Berel Lang and Forrest Williams. New York: McKay, 1972.

Marxism and Sociology, ed. Peter Berger. New York: Appleton-Century-Crofts, 1969.

Marxismus und Literatur, ed. Fritz J. Raddatz. 3 vols. Reinbek b. Hamburg: Rowohlt, 1969.

Marxistische Literaturkritik, ed. and introd. Viktor Žmegač. Bad Homburg: Athenäum, 1970.

Mathewson, Rufus W. *The Positive Hero in Russian Literature.* New York: Columbia University Press, 1958.

Mayer, Hans. *Deutsche Literatur und Weltliteratur: Reden und Aufsätze.* Berlin: Rütten & Loening, 1957.

—— *Von Lessing bis Thomas Mann: Wandlungen der bürgerlichen Literatur in Deutschland.* Pfullingen: Neske, 1959.

—— *Zur deutschen Literatur der Zeit: Zusammenhänge, Schriftsteller, Bücher.* Hamburg: Rowohlt, 1967.

Mehnert, Günter. *Aktuelle Probleme des sozialistischen Realismus.* Berlin: Dietz, 1968.

Mehring, Franz. *Gesammelte Schriften,* ed. Thomas Höhle et al. 15 vols. Berlin: Dietz, 1960–66.

—— *Gesammelte Schriften und Aufsätze in Einzelausgaben,* ed. Eduard Fuchs. 9 vols. Berlin: Soziologische Verlagsanstalt, 1929–

—— *Die Lessing-Legende.* Stuttgart: Dietz, 1893.

Miklós, Pál. "A marxista irodalomelmélet történetéhez." *A Magyar Tudományos Akadémia Nyelv- és Irodalomtörténeti Osztályának Közleményei,* 25, nos. 1–4 (1968): 91–98.

Munby, Lionel M., and Ernst Wangermann, comp. *Marxism and History: A Bibliography of English Language Works.* London: Lawrence & Wishart, 1967.

Musolino, Rocco. *Marxismo ed estetica in Italia.* Roma: Ed. Riuniti, 1963.

Neumann, Friedrich Wilhelm. "Sowjetrussische Literaturtheorien seit 1917." *Europa-Archiv,* 7, nos. 22–23 (1952): 5333–36.

Nyirö, Lajos. "A szocialista realizmus elméletének történeti és elvi problémái." *A Magyar Tudományos Akadémia Nyelv- és Irodalomtörténeti Osztályának Közleményei,* 25, nos. 1–4 (1968): 50–59.

Osnovy marksistsko-leninskoy estetiki. Moskva: Gospolitizdat, 1960.

Parteilichkeit der Literatur oder Parteiliteratur? ed. Hans Christoph Buch. Reinbek b. Hamburg: Rowohlt, 1972.

Parteilichkeit und Volksverbundenheit: zu theoretischen Grundfragen unserer Literaturentwicklung. Berlin: Dietz, 1972.

Philipov, Alexander. *Origin and Principles of Soviet Aesthetics Until N. Khrushchev.* New York: Pageant Press, 1964.

Pisarev, Dimitry. *Selected Philosophical, Social and Political Essays.* Moskva: Foreign Languages Publishing House, 1958.

—— *Sochineniy.* 4 vols. Moskva: Goskhudizdat, 1955–56.

Piscator, Erwin. *Das politische Theater.* Berlin: Schultz, 1929.

Plekhanov, Georgy Valentinovich. *Art and Social Life.* London: Lawrence & Wishart, 1953.

—— *Sochineniya,* ed. Institut K. Marksa i F. Engelsa. 24 vols. Moskva: Gosizdat, 1923–27.

Polska krytika literacka: 1919–1939, ed. Jan Zygmunt Jakubowski. Warsawa: Pánstw. Wydawn. Naukowe, 1966.

Popitz, Heinrich. *Der entfremdete Mensch: Zeitkritik und Geschichtsphilosophie des jungen Marx.* Basel: Verlag für Recht und Gesellschaft, 1953.

Pracht, Erwin. "Präzisierung oder Preisgabe des Realismus-Begriffs." *Sonntag,* 10–11, 1964.

Problems of Soviet Literature: Reports and Speeches at the First Soviet Writers' Congress. Moskva, Leningrad: Co-operative Publishing Society of Foreign Workers in the USSR, 1935.

Raddatz, Fritz. *Georg Lukács in Selbstzeugnissen und Dokumenten.* Reinbek b. Hamburg: Rowohlt, 1972.

Radical Perspectives in the Arts, ed. Lee Baxandall. Harmondsworth, England: Penguin Books, 1972.

Ralph Fox: A Writer in Arms, ed. John Lehmann et al. New York: International Publishers, 1937.

Révai, József. *Lukács and Socialist Realism: A Hungarian Literary Controversy.* London: Fore Publications, 1950.

—— *Válogatott Irodalmi Tanulmányok.* Budapest: Kossuth, 1968.

Rost, Gottfried, and Helmut Schulze, comp. *Der sozialistische Realismus in Kunst und Literatur: eine empfehlende Bibliographie.* Leipzig: Verlag für Buch- und Bibliothekswesen, 1960.

Sánchez Vázquez, Adolfo. *Las ideas esteticas de Marx.* Mexico City: Ediciones Era, 1965.

Sándor, András. "On Idealistic Realism." *Mosaic,* 4, no. 4 (1971): 37–49.

"Semaine de la pensée marxiste" [a symposium]. Séance du mardi 21 janvier 1964. *Europe,* 42, nos. 419–20 (1964): 330–80.

Sholokhov, Mikhail Aleksandrovich. "Acceptance [speech on the occasion of presenting him the literary Nobel prize, 1965]." *Nobel Lectures, Literature 1901–1967,* ed. Horst Frenz. Amsterdam etc.: Nobel Foundation, Elsevier Publishing Co., 1969, pp. 606–608.

Socialist Humanism: An International Symposium, ed. Erich Fromm. Garden City, N.Y.: Doubleday, 1965.

Soyuz sovetskikh pisateley. *Pervy vsesoyuzny s'ezd sovetskikh pisateley: stenograficheskiy otchot.* Moskva, 1934.

—— *Vtoroy vsesoyuzny s'ezd sovetskikh pisateley: stenograficheskiy otchot.* Moskva: Sovetskiy Pisatel', 1956.

Sprache und Stil Lenins, ed. Fritz Mierau. München: Hanser, 1970.

Stalin, Yosif Vissarionovich. *Marksizm i voprosy yazykoznaniya.* Moskva: Gospolitizdat, 1950. (*Marxism and Linguistics.* New York: International Publishers, 1951).

Steiner, George. *The Death of Tragedy.* New York: Hill & Wang, 1963.

—— *Language and Silence: Essays on Language, Literature, and the Inhuman.* New York: Athenaeum, 1967.

Stipcevic, Niksa. *Gramsci e i problemi letterari.* Milano: Mursia, 1965.

Stockhammer, Morris, ed. *Karl Marx Dictionary.* New York: Philosophical Library, 1965.

Struve, Gleb. *Russian Literature Under Lenin And Stalin, 1917–1953.* Norman: University of Oklahoma Press, 1971.

Surovtsev, Yuriy Ivanovich. *V labirinte revizionizma: Ernst Fischer, ego ideologiya, ego estetika.* Moskva: Khudlit, 1972.

Szili, Joseph. "Recent Trends of Marxist Criticism in the Countries of Eastern Europe." *Comparatists at Work: Studies in Comparative Literature,* eds. Stephen G. Nichols, Jr., and Richard B. Vowles. Waltham, Mass.: Blaisdell Publishing Co., 1968, pp. 91–107.

Tertz, Abram (pseud. A. D. Zinyavsky). *The Trial Begins. On Socialist Realism.* New York: Random House, 1965.

The Mind in Chains: Socialism and the Cultural Revolution, ed. C. Day Lewis. London: Muller, 1937.

Thomson, George. *Marxism and Poetry.* London: Lawrence & Wishart, 1945.

Tolstoy, Alexey. *Sobranie sochineniy.* 10 vols. Moskva: Goskhudizdat, 1958–61.

Träger, Claus. *Studien zur Realismustheorie und Methodologie der Literaturwissenschaft.* Leipzig: Reclam, 1972.

Trotsky, Lev (Leon). *Literature and Revolution.* New York: Russell & Russell, 1957.

—— *On Literature and Art,* ed. Paul N. Siegel. New York: Pathfinder Press, 1970.

Vandervelde, Émile. *Essais socialistes: L'alcoolisme—La religion—L'art.* Paris: Alcan, 1906.

Wellek, René. "The Concept of Realism in Literary Scholarship." *Neophilologus,* 1961, pp. 1–20.

—— "The Main Trends of Twentieth Century Criticism." *Yale Review,* 51 (1961): 102–18.

—— "What Is Reality? A Comment." *Art and Philosophy: A Symposium,* ed. Sidney Hook. New York: New York University Press, 1966, pp. 153–56.

Yezuitov, A. "Ob istoricheskom izuchenii sotsialisticheskogo realizma." *Russkaya literatura,* 2 (1965): 215–30.

Zatonsky, Dimitry Vladimirovich. *Franz Kafka i problemy modernizma.* Moskva: Vysshaya shkola, 1965.

Zhdanov, Andrey Alexandrovich. *Essays on Literature, Philosophy, and Music.* New York: International Publishers, 1950.

Žmegač, Viktor. *Kunst und Wirklichkeit: zur Literaturtheorie bei Brecht, Lukács und Broch.* Bad Homburg: Gehlen, 1969.

Zoltai, Dénes. "Elidegenedés és művészet." *A Magyar Tudományos Akadémia Nyelv- és Irodalomtörténeti Osztályának Közleményei,* 25 nos., 1–4 (1968): 60–79.

Index